Place and Placelessness Revisited

Since its publication in 1976, Edward Relph's *Place and Placelessness* has been an influential text in thinking about cities and city life across disciplines, including human geography, sociology, architecture, planning, and urban design. For four decades, ideas put forward by this seminal work have continued to spark debates, from the concept of placelessness itself, through how it plays out in our societies, to how city designers might respond to its challenge in practice.

Drawing on evidence from Australian, British, Japanese, and North and South American urban settings, *Place and Placelessness Revisited* is a collection of cutting edge empirical research and theoretical discussions of contemporary applications and interpretations of place and placelessness. It takes a multi-disciplinary approach, including contributions from the breadth of disciplines in the built environment—architecture, environmental psychology, geography, landscape architecture, planning, sociology, and urban design—in critically re-visiting placelessness in theory and its relevance for twenty-first century contexts.

Robert Freestone is Professor of Planning in the Faculty of Built Environment at UNSW Australia. He joined UNSW in 1991 after six years with Design Collaborative, a Sydney planning, research, and heritage consultancy. He has also held appointments at the University of Melbourne, University of Sydney, and the Australian National University. His books include *The Planning Imagination* (co-editor, 2014), *Urban Nation* (2012), and *Designing Australian Cities* (2004).

Edgar Liu is a Research Fellow at City Futures Research Centre in the Faculty of Built Environment at UNSW Australia. He has academic backgrounds in economic and cultural geography, and his research interests include social aspects of public estate renewals, housing as social welfare, and the conceptualization of human identities.

Routledge Research in Planning and Urban Design
Series editor: Peter Ache
Radboud University, Nijmegen, Netherlands

Routledge Research in Planning and Urban Design is a series of academic monographs for scholars working in these disciplines and the overlaps between them. Building on Routledge's history of academic rigor and cutting-edge research, the series contributes to the rapidly expanding literature in all areas of planning and urban design.

"Relph's *Place and Placelessness* is the one seminal work that gave rise to a whole literature on the subject of place. It's about time that we look back to our original source of inspiration."

—*Yi-Fu Tuan, University of Wisconsin-Madison*

"Edward Relph's classic text *Place and Placelessness* supplied a landmark in our appreciation of the threats that forces of modernity posed for the landscapes of the everyday environment. This collection of meticulously researched and thoughtful essays revisits this territory, but is no mere tribute volume. Rather, its insights into the importance of place, its fragilities and contradictions, show clearly that Relph's insights are as fresh, provocative and relevant now as they were 40 years ago."

—*Professor John R. Gold, Oxford Brookes University*

"Ted Relph's notion of placelessness opened up many new possibilities of how we understand the slippery notion of place. Many of them are realized in this multidisciplinary collection. With case studies that range from graffiti to malls and airports and with examples from Detroit to Melbourne and Seoul, it is a welcome contribution that explores how the social constructions of space create different places."

—*Professor John Rennie Short, University of Maryland, Baltimore*

"As claims to 'place-making' proliferate in these neo-liberal times, the wide-ranging essays in this 40th anniversary homage to *Place and Placelessness* update both theory and practice in a global context."

—*Professor John Punter, Cardiff University*

Place and Placelessness Revisited

Edited by
Robert Freestone
and Edgar Liu

Routledge
Taylor & Francis Group

NEW YORK AND LONDON

First published 2016
by Routledge
711 Third Avenue, New York, NY 10017

and by Routledge
2 Park Square, Milton Park, Abingdon, Oxon OX14 4RN

Routledge is an imprint of the Taylor & Francis Group, an informa business

Library of Congress Cataloging in Publication Data
Names: Freestone, Robert, editor. | Liu, Edgar, editor.
Title: Place and placelessness revisited/Edited by Robert Freestone
and Edgar Liu.
Description: New York: Routledge, 2016. | Series: Routledge research
in planning and urban design
Identifiers: LCCN 2015048756| ISBN 9781138937116 (hardcover) |
ISBN 9781315676456 (ebook)
Subjects: LCSH: Cities and towns—Psychological aspects. | Cities and
towns—Social aspects. | Spatial behavior. | Place (Philosophy) | Place
attachment. | Identity (Psychology)
Classification: LCC HT153 .P625 2016 | DDC 307.76—dc23
LC record available at http://lccn.loc.gov/2015048756

ISBN: 978-1-138-93711-6 (hbk)
ISBN: 978-1-315-67645-6 (ebk)

Typeset in Sabon
by Florence Production Ltd, Stoodleigh, Devon, UK

Contents

Figures and Tables

Figures

Tables

Contributor Biographies

Kate Bishop is a Senior Lecturer in the Faculty of Built Environment at UNSW Australia where she is also the Director of the Built Environment Interdisciplinary Learning (BEIL) program and Convenor of the People and Place research cluster. She teaches Environmental Psychology and her ongoing areas of research and professional interests include: children, youth and environments; universal design; and urban place-making.

Matthew Carmona is Professor of Planning and Urban Design in the Bartlett School of Planning at University College London. He is also a chartered architect and planner. His research has focused on processes of design governance and on the design and management of public space. He has published widely and his books include *Explorations in Urban Design* (2014), *Capital Spaces* (2012), *Public Places Urban Spaces* (2010), *Public Space: The Management Dimension* (2008), and *Urban Design Reader* (2007).

Rachel Cogger is a doctoral student and Sessional Lecturer in the Faculty of Built Environment at UNSW Australia. She completed her Bachelor of Planning also at UNSW Australia, for which she won the University Medal and the Planning Institute of Australia (NSW Chapter) award for outstanding student achievement. Her dissertation research explores the relationship between experience of place, sense of place, and soundscapes in public urban places.

Linda Corkery is Associate Professor of Landscape Architecture in the Faculty of Built Environment, UNSW Australia. A qualified landscape architect and planner with over 20 years of professional practice in Australia, the United States and Hong Kong, her teaching and research address planning and design of the public domain and shared open spaces of cities.

Laura Crommelin is a Research Associate at the City Futures Research Centre and a sessional lecturer in the Faculty of Built Environment, UNSW, Australia. Her research interests include urban branding, DIY urbanism, and place theory. She has background in Law and Literature and was a 2012 Fulbright Scholarship recipient.

Gethin Davison is a Lecturer in Planning in the Faculty of Built Environment, UNSW Australia. He is also an associate of UNSW's City Futures Research Centre. His research interests lie in how people understand and value places, and how and why they choose to defend those places from change. He has also worked as a planner in the government and private sectors.

Kim Dovey is Professor of Architecture and Urban Design at the University of Melbourne. He has published widely on social issues in architecture, urban design and planning. His books include *Becoming Places* (2010), *Framing Places* (2008), and *Fluid City* (2005). He currently leads a series of research projects on place identity, informal settlements, transit-oriented development and creative clusters.

Hazel Easthope is a Senior Research Fellow and Australian Future Fellow at the City Futures Research Centre in the Faculty of Built Environment at UNSW Australia. Since joining the Centre in 2007, her research in the areas of housing, home and urban planning has focused particularly on the implications of the implementation of compact city policies. Her other research interests include the meaning of home and the relationships between housing tenure and residential satisfaction.

Robert Freestone is Professor of Planning in the Faculty of Built Environment at UNSW Australia. He joined UNSW in 1991 after six years with Design Collaborative, a Sydney planning, research and heritage consultancy. He has also held appointments at the University of Melbourne, University of Sydney, and the Australian National University. His books include *The Planning Imagination* (co-editor, 2014), *Urban Nation* (2012), and *Designing Australian Cities* (2004).

Aseem Inam is Director of TRULAB: Laboratory for Designing Urban Transformation and the John Bousfield Distinguished Visitor at the University of Toronto, Canada. He is the author of the books *Designing Urban Transformation* (2013) and *Planning for the Unplanned: Recovering from Crises in Megacities* (2005). He has worked professionally in Brazil, Canada, France, Greece, Haiti, India, and the United States.

Jon Lang is an Emeritus Professor in the Faculty of Built Environment at UNSW Australia. He directed the joint MArch/MCP program in urban design at the University of Pennsylvania during the 1980s. He was Head of the UNSW School of Architecture between 1996 and 2000 and then taught in the Masters of Urban Development and Design program from 1995 to 2015. His books include *Functionalism Revisited* (co-authored, 2010), *Urban Design* (2005), and *Urban Design: The American Experience* (1994).

Edgar Liu is a Research Fellow at City Futures Research Centre in the Faculty of Built Environment at UNSW Australia. He has academic backgrounds in economic and cultural geography, and his research interests include social aspects of public estate renewals, housing as social welfare, and the conceptualization of human identities.

Nancy Marshall is a Senior Lecturer in the Faculty of Built Environment at UNSW Australia. Her research priorities fall under the specific categories of urban governance and place-making through planning strategies and social policy. She is currently researching the social outcomes and physical transformations of place-making activities on public, urban open spaces such as plazas, parks, and pop-ups.

Lucy Montague is a Senior Lecturer in Urban Design at the University of Huddersfield, England. Her primary research interests focus on the design aspects of the urban: in particular, the role of theory in the creative process of urban design and research by design methodologies.

Edward Relph is Emeritus Professor of Geography at the University of Toronto, Canada. He is the author of *Place and Placelessness* (1976), which was reprinted in 2010 and has been translated into several languages. His books and articles have explored humanistic geography, phenomenology, urban landscapes, and sense of place.

John Tomaney is Professor of Urban and Regional Planning in the Bartlett School of Planning at University College London and Visiting Professorial Fellow to the Faculty of Built Environment at UNSW Australia. His research focuses on local and regional development, urban and regional governance and questions of local and regional identity. He is the author and editor of several books including *Handbook of Local and Regional Development* (2010) and *Local and Regional Development* (2006).

Ilan Wiesel is a Senior Research Fellow and Australian Discovery Early Career Research Award Fellow at the City Futures Research Centre in the Faculty of Built Environment at UNSW Australia. His research is dedicated to the study of social injustice and inequality in contemporary cities, and seeks to understand the nature of social disadvantage experienced by marginalized social groups as well as the forms of privilege experienced by the wealthier and more powerful city residents.

Foreword

I first encountered Edward Relph's *Place and Placelessness* in my second year as an undergraduate at University College London on a course called Humanistic Geography in 1985. It was undoubtedly one of two or three books that made me interested in the subject I was studying, and eventually led to me becoming a geographer who focused on issues of place and mobility. It stood out from many seemingly more urgent and applied texts I had been reading in other courses, by drawing my attention to a core idea that seemed integral to what it is to be human. To my twenty-year-old brain, this seemed simultaneously more important (conceptually central) and less immediately relevant (it wasn't going to help us figure out any immediately pressing problem). It was written in such a way that it was both philosophical and accessible. Its central concepts of place, placelessness, authenticity, and existential insider and outsider made me think. The more time I spent thinking, the more I became engaged with both the discipline and the world around me.

It was immediately apparent to me at the time, as someone who was also being exposed to work on cultural politics, that the book was not without some shortcomings. The places and landscapes that seemed to most concern Relph were mass-produced ones, such as large tracts of identical houses or the post-modern simulations of theme parks. These were also the very kinds of places and landscapes that people appeared actually to want. They were popular among people who did not have the resources to invest in notions of authenticity. I could not help but wonder, for instance, if the working-class areas of British northern cities, marked by extensively replicated terraced houses all looking pretty much the same, might be condemned as placeless. There seemed to be an element of elitism in such judgments.

Forty years after it was published, it certainly seems to be the case that Relph's book was prophetic on a number of counts. *Place and Placelessness* foreshadowed the later arrival of the idea of 'non-place,' developed by the French anthropologist Marc Augé. It also prefigured the contemporary obsessions with places such as airports, theme parks, gated communities, heritage parks, McMansions, and the so-called 'clone towns' in Britain with High Streets all containing the exact same lines of chain stores. All of these, at one time or another, have become news items across the world as concerned citizens (not just geographers or academics) expressed an interest in the kinds of places we want to live in in the 21st century. At the same time we have seen cottage industries of television programs, books, agencies, and real estate companies telling us how to not be placeless—how to create individual and authentic places and lifestyles in the face of the homogenizing force of globalized consumer capitalism. Needless to say, this effort to sell us authenticity is deeply ironic. In this sense, Relph's book was prophetic and far-sighted.

There are few books, in other words, that deserve the kind of celebration that this text represents as much as *Place and Placelessness*. Reading the diverse array of essays in this volume makes it clear that Relph's foundational work still informs heterogeneous research projects conducted across the world by scholars in many disciplines and from different generations. Most monographs slip unnoticed into peaceful obscurity—but not *Place and Placelessness*. This timely and welcome revisiting is testimony to that.

Tim Cresswell
History and International Affairs
Northeastern University

Revisiting Place and Placelessness

Edgar Liu and Robert Freestone

Introduction

Since its publication in 1976, Ted Relph's *Place and Placelessness* has been an influential text in thinking about cities and city life across a number of disciplines, including human geography (Relph's own disciplinary background), sociology, architecture, planning and urban design. For four decades, ideas put forward by this seminal work have continued to inform discussion and spark many debates, from the concept of placelessness itself through how it plays out in our societies to how city designers might respond to its challenge in practice. Relph's book—the idea and its possibilities—transformed how 'place' as a subject is researched and understood. There are now broader recognitions of the complexities of place and placelessness as theoretical concepts and their importance to livability and quality of life.

The Concept of Place

The concept of place has been the focus of research within the disciplines of the built environment for many decades. Despite this centrality, it remains a restless if not contentious concept. As Cresswell (2004: 1–2) explains, "place is everywhere" and is "a word that seems to speak for itself," and therefore most people understand and perceive places in divergent ways, although a spatial connotation persists. This spatial dimension is reflected in the many definitions of the term, including in specialized reference books such as *The Dictionary of Human Geography*, which defines place as simply "a portion of geographic space" (Duncan 2000: 582). Within the social sciences, there is growing recognition of the role(s) humans play in shaping places and, as such, places are more generally defined as "spaces which people have made meaningful" (Cresswell 2004: 7) and are thus increasingly conceptualized as social constructs.

Cresswell (2004: 8) describes the spatial quality of places as their materiality (see also Agnew 1987); to him, places are bounded and non-contiguous with "space between them," although the boundaries of places are often not well defined. As such, places can come to describe spaces of differing scales and sizes, from those as big as nations to those as small as the corner of a room. Places may also be understood as pauses in time rather than an unchanging reality, an understanding highlighted in the works of Massey (1995) and Tuan (1977). There is thus a temporality of places (Cresswell 2008).

Recent conceptualizations of place have explored perceptions beyond spatiality and temporality. As Tuan (1977: 18) notes, "an object or place achieves concrete reality when our experience of it is total, that is, through all the senses as well as with the active and reflective mind." Sepe (2013a: 111) for one argues that a place may consist of five sensory stimuli—visual, audio, scent, taste and tactility—each influenced by "local, religious and political identities" as well as "other cultural motivations." Such multi-sensory approaches to the understanding of place depart from the traditionally visually orientated discussions, despite early warnings about treating places as "little more than frozen scenes of human activities" (Pred 1984: 279).

At the broader, philosophical level, approaches taken in the studies of place can be categorized into at least two perspectives: phenomenological and epistemological. A phenomenological approach to place focusses on its being (e.g. Relph 1976; Tuan 1977), while an epistemological one concentrates on the origin of the concept and the theory of place (e.g. Casey 1996; Sack 1997). Both continue to feature prominently in contemporary place research, though the epistemological approach appears to be more widely adapted within the social sciences, especially since the cultural turn of the 1990s (Kearns and Moon 2002; Cresswell 2004).

The Works of Relph

The ongoing theoretical debate on the concepts of place and placelessness finds early roots in a seminal collection of Relph's writings (1973; 1976; 1981; 1987). In his doctoral thesis, Relph (1973: 182–3) defined the concept of placelessness as "a weakening of the identity of place to the point where they not only look alike but feel alike and offer the same bland possibilities for experience." By his 1976 work, Relph had come to define placelessness as the casual eradication of distinctive places in the wake of the forces of modernization. These are many and profound, including mass communications, mass culture and technological transformations; centralized state power dictating standardized and impersonal planning, which lacked sensitivity to the particularities of locality and sought to imitate abstract a priori models of spatial organization; centralized 'big business' economic power pursuing mass production and risk minimization and, in the process, producing commodified places where economic efficiencies are privileged over lived experiences; and increased mobility, particularly of tourists, disrupting historic ties between people and place through asserting a culture of homogenization.

Relph (1976: 117) uses the term "placelessness" to describe the ubiquitous landscape resulting from these processes—"a flatscape, a meaningless pattern of buildings." Placeless spaces are variously anonymous and exchangeable, substituting direct experience with an other-directedness of artefactual representation designed for outsiders. They substitute uniformity and standardization for diversity. There is formlessness and lack of human scale, impermanence and instability. This conceptualization of place and placelessness was deeply embedded in a broader paradigm-shifting theoretical position in human geography contesting positivistic approaches to the understanding of space as undermining the real meanings derived from human experience and interaction (Ley and Samuels 1978).

In Relph's early work, authenticity is an important dimension. For Relph (1976), authenticity of place is the result of "being lived-in," where the place serves as a symbolic or functional centre of life for both individuals and communities. An authentic sense of place derives from insideness, from a sense of belonging to a place and its community, but one that is not overly self-conscious. Relph raised the concern that inauthenticity—associated with kitsch and superficiality—had become prevalent in industrialized and mass societies.

Relph's (1981) later work on humanist geographies dwelt on the paradox of modern landscapes, which are dehumanizing precisely because they are excessively humanized, as they are almost entirely conceived and planned by humans to serve functional human needs, albeit only those that can be assessed in terms of efficiency or improved material conditions. Much of this critique is focused on modern suburban landscapes subject to 'hyper-planning,' encompassing every micro-detail and leaving no space for ambiguity, spontaneity, autonomy or human emotion.

While not without its own critics as a conceptual frame of reference, Relph's contributions helped trigger an ongoing theoretical debate on place and placelessness, drawing in contributions from a range of disciplinary perspectives. Notably, the French anthropologist Marc Augé (1995) proposed the distinction between solitary and collective contractual obligations as a frame to distinguish 'place' from 'non-place.' For Augé (1995), non-places are those spaces which cannot be defined as relational, historical or concerned with identity. Augé's explanation of non-place, accentuating the lack of social relations, is set apart from Relph's concept of placelessness, which emphasizes the lack of a sense of place as experienced by individuals (Kellerman 2006). The notion of non-place arguably carries less negative moral connotations than placelessness (Cresswell 2004).

Critiques of Place and Placelessness

Early appraisals of Relph's treatment came from the discipline of human geography, not least because it was billed as a geography text discussing mainly human places. The importance of the argument being made was well appreciated. Porteous (1978: 74–5) praised Relph's adaptation of a phenomenological approach, which provided a much-neglected "emotional link between people and places" in many contemporary geographical studies. To Smith (1978: 117), the book was a greatly welcome contribution to geographical studies, and one destined to redirect the course of human geographic studies from "the detailed description of particular places and the development of spatial models for analyzing systems of places" to "writing about what places really are."

Conversely, contemporary critics also identified limitations. Smith himself (1978: 117) criticized Relph for going down a well-trodden path of criticizing suburbia—"I found the traditional condescension toward suburbia a little tedious"—rather than recognizing the existence of 'place' in the suburbs. Furthermore, he found the theoretical separation of "self-consciously and unself-consciously made places" difficult concepts to decipher, a separation that could have benefited from more unpacking (Smith 1978: 117). Despite its origins in human geography, Entrikin (1977: 423) noted that it is of "slightly less interest [. . .] to those geographers looking for an analysis of the concept of place and its role in geographic research." While he conceded "a provocative essay on the nature of place and on the increasing homogeneity of the contemporary landscape" and, through its phenomenological approach, a "counterbalance [to] the overemphasis of economic and spatial rationality in contemporary place-making," he felt it lacked a "balance between criticism and alternative courses of action" (Entrikin 1977: 424). Buttimer (1977) came to a similar conclusion. While very much a piece of human geographic study, she felt that the arguments were almost "exclusively anthropocentric" (Buttimer 1977: 623–4) and risked alienating physical geographers and believers of the value of non-humans in shaping and using places.

Regardless, since the 1970s, *Place and Placelessness* has come to be recognized as an influential, if not classic, text. It has been recognized as one of just 26 "key texts in human geography" (Hubbard et al. 2008) with its elaboration on "the continuing dissolutions of places and insideness in the world" (Seamon and Sowers 2008: 50) still relevant—and indeed influential—decades on. At the turn of the millennium, Gold (2000: 613–4) praised the book as "a text that challenged rather than supported dominant approaches to human-environment relations" and in the process became "one of a handful of texts that radically expanded the purview of geographical research on human-environmental relations." Stock (2000: 615) agrees and describes Relph's work as not just of "historical value" but opening up "many research directions that are yet to be explored."

Relph and Place Studies

The concept of placelessness has proven remarkably adaptable in different contexts. For Beatley (2004) it is the product of forces of globalization and sameness stifling sustainable modes of living; Birkeland (2008) also responds to the same challenge. Friedmann (2010) interprets it in *noir* terms as capturing the ennui and dormant violence of a lifeless suburbia. Miles (2010) seizes it to similarly convey a deadening levelling of experience denoting the pervasive impact of consumption on post-industrial cities. As a metaphor for modern urban desolation and dislocation, it has informed literary and filmic readings (Seamon 2008; Stratton 2014). Interpretations of placelessness underpin more bespoke studies of landscape representations (DeBres and Sowers 2009) and the semiotics of newsstands (Iqani 2011).

Many other place-related concepts also found their origins, or at least their way, into Relph's 1976 book (Stock 2000). In his later work, he explored these ideas in greater detail. Here we mention just three—sense of place, insideness/outsideness, and place-making—all of which have infiltrated the thinking behind the discussions featured in this book.

Sense of Place

Of the many place-related discussions included in *Place and Placelessness*, those on people's sense of place have garnered the most subsequent attention from both Relph himself, as well as from other scholars with an interest in people–place relations. To Relph, a sense of place must be developed authentically through extended association (such as the place where one is born and bred), and is often articulated as a sense of identity with a place. In 1991, he defined sense of place as "an innate faculty, possessed in some degree by everyone, that connects us to the world," a learned awareness "that is used to grasp what the world is like and how it is changing" in terms of its environment, economy and politics (Relph 1991: 208). It is also varied depending on the individual and encompasses a diversity of sensory awareness spanning "sight, hearing, movement, touch, memory, imagination and anticipation" (Relph 2007: 19). It is perhaps this multi-faceted connection to everyday life that attracts many scholars to anoint sense of place as the epicentre for place studies. Contemporary interpretations of this include Massey's (1991) discussion of a global sense of place and, more recently, Manzo's (2008) consideration of displacement and the loss of a sense of place.

Manzo's work (2008) reflects on the increasing influences of globalization and mobilities in changing people's identity with places and how the concepts of place and placelessness can (and should) be reinterpreted in shifting and evolving global contexts. This harks back to Relph's (2007) discussion of sense of place and virtual realities, where developments in technologies have muddied the lines of the real and the virtual. He concedes that, more so than in the real world, the (re)creation of authenticity in the virtual world is difficult to achieve. Indeed, Perkins and Thorns (2012: 109–110) highlight that the advent of tele-transformations may have eroded traditional "formerly very close connections to place and local community" and bring up questions of trust, integrity, safety and security in increasingly blurred worlds. Merriman (2013: 200), however, warns of an over-generalization of the impact of increased mobilities and the risk of overlooking "the diverse ways in which people inhabit these spaces and landscapes," including those in the virtual worlds.

Insideness/Outsideness

Inherently related to his discussions on sense of place is Relph's conceptualization of the qualities of insideness and outsideness. To Relph (1976: 71), a sense of insideness represents an unselfconscious connection to place:

> What appears from the outside to be homogenous and placeless, is from within closely differentiated into places the personalization of property, by association with local events and the development of local myths and by being lived in, all of which give a genuineness and authenticity to somewhere quite inauthentically created.

As such, to feel inside a place is a far more intimate association than simply having a sense of place, enabling a connection on a deeper level enriched by histories: "to be inside a place is to belong to it and to identify with it, and the more profoundly inside you are the stronger is this identity with the place" (Relph 1976: 49). This level of intimacy may also exist in places that may appear to be placeless to outsiders. For Relph, outsideness refers to the lack of identity with a place. While on paper insideness and outsideness are direct oppositions, as Relph (1976: 49) acknowledged, "the dualism of inside and outside is not quite as clear as it appears at first sight."

To this end, Relph (1976: 51–55) identified several different levels of insideness and outsideness, each of which contributes to an individual's sense of place and belonging:

- Existential outsideness: the weakest of all levels of identification with place, which Relph equates to a sense of not belonging, feelings of uninvolvement with and alienation from the place.
- Objective outsideness: a deep level of conscious disassociation to place deliberately adopted by people, for example, who may morally object to the activities that take place in these places.
- Incidental outsideness: when an unselfconscious disassociation with the place or the setting of the place is incidental to the activities that take place there, such as a transitory place.
- Vicarious insideness: in which a person may identify with the place vicariously without having visited at first hand, such as with an iconic place or a World Heritage site.
- Behavioural insideness: a level of identification involving a person having physically been in the place with a deliberate "attending to the appearance of that place" (Relph 1976: 53).

- Empathetic insideness: demanding a level of sympathy in the significance of the place, "much as a person might experience a holy place as sacred without necessarily believing in that particular religion" (Relph 1976: 54).
- Existential insideness: the highest level of identification with place, with a deep sense of belonging.

In more recent interpretations, however, these concepts are most commonly simplified into just a dualism of insideness and outsideness. Research into these two concepts has predominantly been concerned with people's attachments to their local environments in different settings (e.g. Rowles's 1980 discussion of ageing in a rural community, and Soini's 2004 discussion of rural Europe) and by different groups (e.g. Lim and Barton's 2010 discussion of children's sense of place in urban areas). Across other, non-built environment disciplines, insideness is sometimes equated to a sense of place attachment (e.g. Ponzetti's 2003 study on ageing in rural America) and more recently to the concept of belonging (e.g. Lefever's 2012 study on tertiary students' on campus life). In a similar vein, more recent explorations of outsideness are most commonly linked with discussions of social exclusion (Bonfanti 2012) or otherness (Min 2001), both of which highlight how certain socio-demographic groups are excluded from those who are identified as, or self-identify as, 'being inside.'

Place-making

In Chapter 5 of *Place and Placelessness*, Relph introduced the term place-making, by which he meant the process through which the identity of a place is derived. This process can emerge authentically and unselfconsciously through extended awareness, or be created deliberately for explicit purposes. More contemporary interpretations of place-making, however, most commonly take on the latter meaning—the conscious creation of places for diverse social ends and increasingly their fashioning for commerce and consumption. In the contest of urban regeneration, for example, place-making is often included as one critical element that drives the decision-making processes behind the visioning and implementation plans. As Palermo and Ponzini (2014: n.p.) explain:

> The regeneration of critical urban areas through the redesign of public space with the intense involvement of local communities seems to be the central focus of place-making according to some widespread practices in academic and professional circles.

The increasing popularity of place-making as an area of study has prompted such scholars as Palermo and Ponzini (2014) to call for its recognition as a field of study distinct from those of urban planning, urban design and architecture. This is perhaps rather exciting for many professional place-makers who have created their own niche market but would also aggravate others as yet another simplistic interpretation of the concept of place and how it can be 'authentically' (re)created.

Since the early 2000s, place studies have become a veritable industry with many different enterprises and directions even beyond these concepts. Lewicka's (2011) survey of the academic 'place attachment' literature records a robust and popular field befitting the importance of place in human existence, somewhat short on theoretical precepts but not lacking diverse methodological innovation. Alongside this intellectual fascination with people–place relationships comes an applied engagement with the processes of 'place-making' with its own diverse threads including community building, sustainable design, public realm planning, public art, rights to the city and place branding. The diversity and momentum of discourse is such that Relph's contributions can be entirely forgotten (Gieseking and Mangold 2014). In that setting it seems timely to revisit 'place and placelessness.'

Beyond the Binary

The focus of this expedition is the very binary at the heart of Relph's original formulation in the 1970s. He has recalled that "in the early 1970s when I was writing *Place and Placelessness*, the world seemed to present itself as a series of quite clear oppositions" (Relph 2000: 617). The result was a sense of either/or dualisms: authentic/inauthentic, insideness/outsideness, place/placeless. The hegemony of this sort of conceptual thinking in both intellectual and experiential terms was subsequently destabilized (Cloke and Johnston 2005) with postmodern thought across the social sciences and humanities mounting one critical challenge. Into the 21st century, the forces and outcomes of globalization—notably people's increased mobility, technological change and enhanced engagement within diverse communities of association at different scales and in different ways—have all broken down simplistic categorizations of attachment, identity and authenticity.

Southworth and Ruggeri (2011: 501) criticize those like Relph in *Place and Placelessness* who apparently "see the world in dualities." They argue that:

> The dichotomy of place versus placelessness does not capture the complex and multifaceted contemporary city, which presents many degrees and shades of 'placeless,' whether urban, suburban, rural or natural, old or new. Traces of placeless can be seen everywhere, and designers need to become more sophisticated at dealing with this gradient of placeness.

Their concept of a multi-faceted gradient is a more compelling, realistic and nuanced conceptualization of place identity in the modern world than a simple place/non-place dichotomy. These attributes need not be mutually exclusive and a more effective paradigm responsive to the complexities and contradictions of locality, globality, culture, experience and subjectivity recognizes the possibilities of their simultaneity. Better understandings of both place and placelessness today start not with their polarity but their hybridity.

Revisiting Place and Placelessness

Drawing on evidence from Australian urban settings and across the globe, this edited volume is a collection of cutting-edge empirical research and theoretical discussions of contemporary applications of place and placelessness. It takes a multi-disciplinary approach, including contributions from across the breadth of disciplines in the built environment—architecture, environmental psychology, geography, landscape architecture, planning, sociology, and urban design—in critically re-visiting place and placelessness in theory and in application in 21st century contexts. It also engages with other contemporary built environment discussions on people-place relations, belonging, and community. The intent is to convey the continuing relevance of notions of 'place and placelessness' when approached critically and adapted to diverse problem settings.

The project emerges from work of the People and Place Research Cluster in the Faculty of Built Environment at the University of New South Wales (UNSW Australia) in a joint initiative leveraging off an academic partnership with The Bartlett School of Planning at University College London and other international linkages. Most of the papers were presented at a symposium held in Sydney in early September 2014 on the theme 'Place and Placelessness in the 21st Century City' at which Relph was the keynote speaker.

This edited volume is split into four main parts, each with a set of essays that reflect on how the concepts of place and placelessness manifest respectively in terms of urban design theory, the personal experiences of places, urban policy and practice, and within a more critical and multicultural urbanism. These categorizations are not rigidly mutually exclusive and in reality the themes of design, experience, practice and critique surface in various ways in many chapters. The chapters are bookended by this introductory revisiting of place and placelessness, plus a short afterword by Relph himself. In his opening chapter, Relph reflects on how his earlier understandings of place and placelessness have changed since their 1970s beginnings, especially the paradox that is the similarities one finds amongst different distinctive places.

Place/lessness in Design

As discussed above, the majority of early interpretations of Relph's *Place and Placelessness* were largely limited to the field of human geography. This work's influence on other built environment disciplines, however, cannot be casually overlooked. In this first section, four chapters from urban design, landscape architecture and city planning backgrounds, highlight issues in the contemporary role of these professions in the making of place.

In Chapter 2, Jon Lang responds to the common critique (including from Relph himself) that the professions of planners and urban landscape designers are some of the main professions responsible for the spread of placelessness. This is especially through the application of visually similar urban and landscape designs across disparate regions with little apparent link to the history of particular localities. Limitations often come from competing urban design paradigms that constrain the opportunities for personalization. The two dominant paradigms of recent decades—neo-liberalism and new urbanism—also leave little room for collaborative design decisions that effectively incorporate end-user desires for shifting the use and identity of a place. While Lang concedes that if an authentic sense of place is to be achieved it is important to create a physical world that affords the 'behaviour settings' that constitute localities within specific cultures, users often find ways of adapting and personalizing their experiences of newly designed and built places even if they are look-alikes. Design alone does not make the place, but rather "the ways individuals inhabit it and make it their own" (Fay and Sellbach 2008: 247).

This discussion is continued in Chapter 3 by Lucy Montague, who argues that it is the urban designer's role to respond to various and sometimes conflicting interests in generating plans and proposals in the process of place-making. She proposes that urban design theory captures urban meaning, which is then reflected in the physical form of built environments. If form follows function, pattern mimics paradigm. While the end results may sometimes look placeless, they may in fact reflect changed (and changing) urban meanings. In the process, understandings of, and the context in which, concepts like placelessness as introduced by Relph must also have evolved over time. As such, while a newly designed 'place' may visually look place-less, it may in fact represent a paradigmatic shift within urban design theory as well as how its users identify with that place.

In his more recent works, Relph calls for new approaches to environ-mental designs that self-consciously respond to local structures of meaning, experience and physical form, with attention also paid to the variety of levels at which people experience place. These new approaches are explored by Linda Corkery and Gethin Davison respectively in Chapters 4 and 5. In Chapter 4, Corkery discusses the creating of places from a landscape archi-tect's perspective. She argues that landscape architects design contemporary public environments by responding to local history, the physical reality of the sites and social context. This is cast as positive place-making centred on valuation of the public realm, a kind of urban acupuncture with no shortage of exemplars (e.g. Place Leaders Association 2008). Through two Sydney case studies of parks wrought from dispiriting brownfields sites in prime waterfront locations where public access was previously denied, she demonstrates a contemporary interpretation of Relph's assertion on sense of place, that it cannot necessarily be designed or constructed but derived from within the human experience. The creation of urban public landscapes to enable recreation in previously inaccessible or placeless places may achieve just that, by giving meaning to them, no matter if the actual experiencing of that meaning is for just brief periods at a time or for a more permanent association.

In interpreting Relph's works, Arefi (1999: 184) argues that the main concerns with the consequences of placelessness since the publication of *Place and Placelessness* "reflect the ahistoric, aspatial aspects of the global economy on place." Such an emphasis on history places much value on "rootedness as the most natural, pristine, unmediated kind of people-place tie" (Arefi 1999: 183). While respecting and connecting to a place's history is important to the creating (or preserving) of a sense of place, an over-emphasis may lead to protectionism for the sake of preserving local histories. In Chapter 5, Davison explores the use of planning instruments in metropolitan Melbourne and how these are used to regulate the identity of places. He focuses especially on Relph's concept of insideness. Through the use of critical discourse analysis of planning texts, he reveals that, despite the protection of place 'character' now being of high priority in planning decision-making, disregard continues to be shown for the various ways in which places are known and experienced by 'insiders' in everyday life. In part, the protection of 'character' focuses predominantly on how the neighborhood, as a geographic place, should look visually when, as Relph has argued, a sense of place emerges from more than just what it looks like but how people identify with it. The current planning legislation that strongly favors the visual 'character' of a place thus overlooks other, equally if not more, important contributors of sense of place, especially in how people experience the built environment. As such, the fundamental significance of interrelating physical milieu and social space is underscored (Sepe 2013b).

Place/lessness in Experience

The four chapters in the first section establish that while design plays an important role in people's sense of place, it is how people relate to and experience place that really shape the identity of a place. This is the focus of the four chapters in this second section: people's experiences of places. In the first two contributions, John Tomaney and Hazel Easthope continue the exploration of the concept of 'insideness,' one (Chapter 6) from a more theoretical perspective, while the other (Chapter 7) is embedded in the realm of housing policy. In the other two chapters, Rachel Cogger and Kate Bishop tackle the different ways places can be experienced, one (Chapter 8) from a sensory perspective, and the other (Chapter 9) from the perspective of a specific demographic cohort—children and young people.

In Chapter 6, Tomaney provides a theoretical overview of the concept of insideness. Specifically, he counter-argues Relph's original position that, with increasing prevalence of globalization, notions of insideness are becoming gradually degraded. He argues that, despite a more global and mobile existence, local attachment—and senses of insideness and belonging—remain significant to many people. How such local attachment and insideness are experienced, however, may have been transformed and take on different forms and meanings from those described by Relph in 1976. These transformed meanings of local attachment can have wide-ranging social and political implications, such as the rise of 'small nationalism' movements where increasingly more and more intranational regions are looking to capitalize on people's sense of regional belonging.

In Chapter 7, Easthope turns the discussion of insideness to the context of the home as a special kind of space that holds considerable social, psychological and emotive meaning, reflecting residents' sense of belonging. She argues that the ways in which people can become attached and committed to a place differ as a result of the power they have to remain there and become involved. As such, she argues that the freedom (or control) that people are afforded to influence a place significantly impacts their sense of belonging and how (if at all) they relate to that place. Her argument is set in an Australian context and of recent changes in the role of private rental housing providing an opportunity to challenge social norms about the relationship between tenure and tenants' control.

In Chapter 8, Cogger argues that sensory dimensions other than solely visual are central to how people experience places. While this 'sensescape' is slowly being recognized in urban planning practices and research (Andringa et al. 2013), development and assessment have still tended to place a stronger focus on visual aesthetics rather than considering all of the senses and the impact they have on people's experiences of place. After reviewing how different senses influence how people experience and identify with places, she uses soundscapes as a demonstration of the influence of non-visual sensory stimuli, highlighting especially the role of the acoustic environment in people's engagement with—or disengagement from—place.

Discussions of how specific groups experience place—and indeed placelessness—in our urban environments are slowly emerging within the built environment disciplines. Examples include Penny and Redhead's (2009) discussion of the impact of sport on place and mobility, and Shim and Almeida Santos' (2014) discussion of tourists' experiences of 'authentic' places and cultures. In Chapter 9, Bishop extends these discussions to children and young people's experiences of urban places, a territory opened up in the 1970s (Lynch 1977). In particular, she argues that children's access to and experiences of urban places is historically conditioned by surrounding social attitudes and local environmental opportunities. The needs of children and young people, however, have never been a focus of city planning and design. Shifts in the social demographics of western societies, coupled with increased demand for urban residential intensification, threaten to further reduce children and young people's social status and environmental opportunities. Increase in social risk aversion also removes children from their neighborhoods, leading to a decline in children's presence in the public space. Bishop offers some insights into how children and young people's experiences and use of urban places can be potentially increased.

Place/lessness in Practice

While many scholars agree that place as a concept has no discernible geographic or spatial scale (e.g. Cresswell 2008), discussions regarding placelessness have tended to focus on the neighbourhood scale. In explaining his concept of placelessness, Relph (1976) predominantly used examples at the neighbourhood scale, such as newly-built housing estates, or transitory spaces such as airports. As times and technology have moved on, however, discussions regarding the prevalence of placelessness have also expanded. In this third section of the book, discussions of placelessness are set at four different scales, ordered here from the largest to the smallest.

In Chapter 10, Laura Crommelin discusses the concept of placelessness at the city scale, using the US city of Detroit as a case study. With the burgeoning of place-making as an urban design and revitalization strategy in recent years, some organizations (such as Project for Public Spaces, or PPS) are increasingly teaming up with city governments to redefine and rebrand cities as distinctive places to boost their competitiveness in the tourism and business sectors. In 2012, with municipal bankruptcy looming, PPS and a local billionaire property owner stepped in with a three-year 'Downtown Place-making Plan' to redevelop key public spaces throughout Detroit. While the stocks of place-making continue to soar, projects like that seen in Detroit highlight the challenges and contradictions associated with putting the idea of place-making into practice when government funding is constrained and the private sector assumes a key driving role. Winton (2009: 185) has tellingly cautioned that giving the market free rein can in fact result in "the creation of remarkably similar places, wherever they might be."

In Chapter 11, Robert Freestone and Ilan Wiesel revisit one of the examples that Relph (1976, 1981, 1987) time and again used to exemplify placeless places. In both popular and academic discourse, airports have been caricatured as either anodyne functional landscapes or modern institutions promoting the production of generic tourist landscapes as agents of mass travel. Since the 1970s, however, other perspectives, particularly surfacing in the 'mobilities' literature, have more empathetically acknowledged airports as complex experiential places. Moreover, over the last quarter of a century, airports themselves have undergone major makeovers through product diversification. Much like Harner and Kinder's (2011) discussion of the renewal of university campuses as self-sustaining townships that incorporate education, residential and commercial interests, airports are being transformed by new urban design strategies promoting mixed use and "spaces to stay" (Güller 2015: 119). Through case studies of three airports in Australia and New Zealand, Freestone and Wiesel question whether the modern day airport cities can still be considered placeless.

In Chapter 12, Nancy Marshall discusses the transformation of another type of public space—urban squares—to showcase how some contemporary, deliberate place-making efforts can help in evoking meaningful associations to all of their users. Drawing on examples from around the world, she demonstrates that there are rich differences in contemporary urban square designs. The more 'successful' ones invariably showcase a flourishing civil society supported by the physical environment (Woolley et al. 2004). Without strong cultural associations and acknowledgement of an inclusive "right to the city" (Mitchell 2003), public life and all of its benefits may lead these urban squares to becoming placeless.

In the final chapter of this section, Chapter 13, Edgar Liu brings the discussion of placelessness to the micro-scale, almost like the magazine stands of London discussed by Iqani (2011). Opening another window into the politics of public restrooms (Molotch and Noren 2010), Liu examines their graffiti to question the rigid perception of place identities and how this rigidity may ultimately contribute to the persistence of placelessness. He draws on one of Relph's (1976) earliest discussions on the three elements that constitute placelessness—(in)authenticity, (lack of) distinctiveness and (dis)connection—and examines these in view of Butler's (1990) theorization of human identities. In the process he asks whether the same fluidity in understanding human identities—that they may be multiplicitous and ever-changing rather than singular and static—can be equally applied to the understanding of place identities, so that a place may have more than one identity at any time depending on who is identifying with that place.

Place/lessness in Question

The fourth and final section brings into question the modern day applicability of the concepts of place and placelessness. A casual literature search would reveal that these concepts are more often discussed in a Western or Global North context; indeed, the majority of 'places' discussed throughout this volume are from Western societies. A study of shopping malls in Seoul, South Korea by Shim and Almeida Santos (2014: 108) presents familiar conclusions and evidence for the place-erosion of capitalist consumerism (highlighted in Rigg 2007) in arguing that "contemporary tourism landscapes do not reflect local characteristics but instead represent modernized and illusory environments within enclosed commercial spaces, which, in turn, offer tourists hollow experiences that serve to further decontextualize meaning and place." The first two chapters of this final section extend this discussion in more nuanced ways.

In Chapter 14, and once again picking up on Relph's concept of inside-ness, Matthew Carmona discusses an apparent contradiction in the very distinctive *habitus* of the Japanese city (Shelton 2012). To a visitor, the Japanese urban environment has a split personality stemming from legacy traditions that emphasize order, restraint and harmony side by side with a contemporary urbanism that is often ultra-modern, brash and discordant. This split personality echoes the original thesis advanced by Relph that in contemporary urbanism there is a place/placelessness divide. Writing from an 'outsider' perspective, Carmona explores the nature of five Japanese cities—Tokyo, Osaka, Sapporo, Kyoto and Yokohama—to question whether this binary offers the best lens through which to understand the divergent character in contemporary Japanese urban landscapes.

In Chapter 15, Aseem Inam more emphatically shifts gaze to the Global South (Parnell and Oldfield 2014) in critically exploring place-based informal urbanisms prevalent in Africa, Asia and Latin America. He specifically examines their interface with the public realm through comparative practice-based case studies set in São Paulo and New York City. Eschewing stereotypes and pursuing a consultative approach to unpacking the meanings, experiences and possibilities of urban space, this analysis further disrupts any simple notion of dualisms. Inam demonstrates that informality and formality do not necessarily belong to different kinds of places, but rather that their practices are fundamentally intertwined. Their constant interactions provide further proof—as famously highlighted by Cresswell (2004)—that places are constantly in flux and evolving, presenting opportunities for contests and debates that place and placelessness are increasingly hybridized rather than dichotomized.

Such a hybridized view of place and placelessness is also discussed by Kim Dovey in Chapter 16. Written in the form of a personal reflection, Dovey is critical of developers and politicians reducing place discourse to profitable slogans and slippery conceptions of place identity that are accommodated all too easily by neoliberal ideology. He argues that place and placeless-ness need to be understood as contested concepts that can be variously empowering and dangerous depending on the political context and how they interact with local practices of self-organization and resistance. Ultimately looking beyond the binary, he suggests our concerns for the creation and protection of valued places in complex settings are better captured by the notion of assemblage, requiring a critical multi-scalar deciphering of interconnected parts and processes (McFarlane 2011).

As Yi-Fu Tuan (1977: 202) tellingly observed some time ago, place and placelessness are such complex, multivalent terms asking often unanswer-able questions of the human condition that clearly "do not make the life of the social scientist and planner any easier." This book does push us further towards decoupling them as antithetical binaries. In a closing coda, Relph responds to our multi-disciplinary applications of his concepts of place and placelessness, and offers his thoughts on how this line of thinking will continue to influence place and other related studies in the future. Although the last word in this book, this reflective piece, and the book as a whole, is not an uncritical celebration of a key text published forty years ago but represent a small collective and forward-looking gesture to better understand and enhance the urban condition in a humanistic place-centred way at a time when the challenges from all directions remain daunting.

References

Agnew, J. (1987) *Place and Politics: The Geographical Mediation of State and Society*, Boston: Allen and Unwin.

Andringa, T.C., M. Weber, S.R. Payne, J.D. Krijnders, M.N. Dixon, M.N., R. van der Linden, E.G.L. de Kock and J.L.J. Lanser (2013) "Positioning soundscape research and management," *Journal of the Acoustical Society of America* 134, 2739–2747.

Arefi, M. (1999) "Non-place and Placelessness as Narratives of Loss: Rethinking the Notion of Place," *Journal of Urban Design* 4, 179–193.

Augé, M. (1995) *Non-places: An Introduction to Supermodernity*, London: Verso.

Beatley, T. (2004) *Native to Nowhere: Sustaining Home and Community in a Global Age*, Washington DC: Island Press.

Birkeland, I. (2008) "Cultural Sustainability: Industrialism, Placelessness and the Re-animation of Place," *Ethics, Place & Environment* 11, 283–297.

Bonfanti, S. (2012) "Analyzing Migrant Youth's Patterns of Social Exclusion in Sweden: What Role for Ethnicization Processes?," *Social Justice and Democratization: The Second ISA Forum of Sociology*, Buenos Aires, 1–4 August.

Butler, J. (1990) *Gender Trouble: Feminism and the Subversion of Identity*, London: Routledge.

Buttimer, A. (1977) "Book Review: Place and Placelessness," *Annals of the Association of American Geographers* 67, 622–624.

Casey, E. (1996) "Embracing Lococentrism: A Response to Thomas Brockelman's Critique," *Human Studies* 19, 459–465.

Cloke, P. and R. Johnston (2005) *Spaces of Geographical Thought: Deconstructing Human Geography's Binaries*, London: Sage.

Cresswell, T. (2004) *Place: A Short Introduction*, Oxford: Blackwell.

—— (2008) "Place: Encountering Geography as Philosophy." *Geography* 93, 132–139.

DeBres, K. and J. Sowers (2009) "The Emergence of Standardized, Idealized, and Placeless Landscapes in Midwestern Main Street Postcards," *The Professional Geographer* 61, 216–230.

Duncan, J. (2000) "Place," in R.J. Johnston, D. Gregory, G. Pratt and M. Watts (Eds.) *The Dictionary of Human Geography*, fourth edition, Oxford: Blackwell, 582–584.

Entrikin, J. (1977) "Book Review: Place and Placelessness," *The Professional Geographer* 29, 423–424.

Fay, R. and U. Sellbach (2008) "Affordable Places," in F. Vanclay, M. Higgins and A. Blackshaw (Eds.) *Making Sense of Place*, Canberra: National Museum of Australia, 247–254.

Friedmann, J. (2010) "Place and Place-making in Cities: A Global Perspective," *Planning Theory and Practice* 11, 149–165.

Gieseking, J. and W. Mangold (Eds.) (2014) *The People, Place, and Space Reader*, New York: Routledge.

Gold, J. (2000) "Commentary 1," *Progress in Human Geography* 24, 613–615.

Güller, M. (2015) "From Sprawl to City: A Vision for Sustainable Airport Regions," in S. Conventz and A. Thiersten (Eds.) *Airports, Cities and Regions*, London: Routledge, 102–127.

Harner, J. and F. Kinder (2011) 'Placelessness in a Deregulated City: University Village in Colorado Springs," *Urban Geography* 32, 730–755.

Hubbard, P., R. Kitchin and G. Valentine (Eds.) (2008) *Key Texts in Human Geography*, London: Sage.

Kearns, R. and G. Moon (2002) "From Medical to Health Geography: Novelty, Place and Theory after a Decade of Change," *Progress in Human Geography* 26, 605–625.

Iqani, M. (2011) "Reading the Newsstand: The Signifiers of Placelessness in London Magazine Retail Sites," *Space and Culture* 14, 431–447.

Lefever, R. (2012) "Exploring Student Understandings of Belonging on Campus," *Journal of Applied Research in Higher Education* 4, 126–141.

Lewicka, M. (2011) "Place Attachment: How Far Have We Come in the Last 40 Years?" *Journal of Environmental Psychology* 31, 207–230.

Ley, D. and M. Samuels (1978) *Humanistic Geography: Prospects and Problems*, Chicago: Maaroufa Press.

Lim, M. and A.C. Barton (2010) 'Exploring Insideness in Urban Children's Sense of Place," *Journal of Environmental Psychology* 30, 328–337.

Lynch, K. (1977) *Growing Up in Cities*, Cambridge, MA.: MIT Press.

McFarlane, C. (2011) "Assemblage and Critical Urbanism," *City* 15, 204–224.

Manzo, L. (2008) "The Experience of Displacement on Sense of Place and Well-being," in J. Eyles and A. Williams (Eds.) *Sense of Place, Health and Quality of Life*, Farnham: Ashgate, 87–10.

Massey, D. (1991) "A Global Sense of Place," *Marxism Today* June, 24–29.

—— (1995) "Places and Their Pasts," *History Workshop Journal* 39, 182–192.

Merriman, P. (2013) "Roads," in P. Adey, D. Bissell, K. Hannam, P. Merriman and M. Sheller (Eds.) *The Routledge Handbook of Mobilities*, London: Routledge, 196–204.

Miles, S. (2010) *Spaces for Consumption: Pleasure and Placelessness in the Post-Industrial City*, Los Angeles: Sage.

Min, E. (2001) "Bakhtinian Perspectives of the Study of Intercultural Communication," *Journal of Intercultural Studies* 22, 5–18.

Mitchell, D. (2003) *The Right to the City: Social Justice and the Fight for Public Space*, New York: Guilford Press.

Molotch, H. and L. Noren (Eds.) (2010) *Toilet: Public Restrooms and the Politics of Sharing*, New York: NYU Press.

Palermo, P.D. and D. Ponzini (2014) *Place-making and Urban Development: New Challenges for Contemporary Planning and Design*, New York: Routledge.

Parnell, S. and S. Oldfield (Eds.) (2014) *The Routledge Handbook on Cities of the Global South*, London: Routledge.

Penny, S. and S. Redhead (2009) "We're Not Really Here: Manchester City, Mobility and Placelessness," *Sport in Society: Cultures, Commerce, Media, Politics* 12, 755–764.

Perkins, H.C. and D.C. Thorns (2012) *Place, Identity and Everyday Life in a Globalizing World*, London: Palgrave Macmillan.

Place Leaders Association (2008) *Place Making for the Future: 14 Case Studies in Sustainable Urban Design*, Sydney: Place Leaders Association.

Ponzetti, J.J. (2003) "Growing Old in Rural Communities: A Visual Methodology for Studying Place attachment," *Journal of Rural Community Psychology*, E6.

Porteous, J.D. (1978) "Book Review: Place and Placelessness," *Canadian Geographer* 22, 74–76.

Pred, A. (1984) "Place as Historically Contingent Process: Structuration and the Time-Geography of Becoming Places," *Annals of the Association of American Geographers* 74, 279–297.

Relph, E. (1973) "The Phenomenon of Place: An investigation of the Experience and Identity of Places," PhD dissertation, University of Toronto.

—— (1976) *Place and Placelessness*, London: Pion.

—— (1981) *Rational Landscapes and Humanistic Geography*, London: Croom Helm.

—— (1987) *The Modern Urban Landscape*, London: Croom Helm.

—— *(1991) "Sense of Place,"* in S. Hanson (Ed.) Ten Geographic Ideas that Changed the World, New Brunswick: Rutgers University Press, 205–226.

—— (2000) "Author's Response: Place and Placelessness in a New Context," *Progress in Human Geography* 24, 617–619.

—— (2007) "Spirit of Place and Sense of Place in Virtual Realities," *Techné* 10, 17–25.

Rigg, J. (2007) *An Everyday Geography of the Global South*, New York: Routledge.

Rowles, G.D. (1980) "Growing Old 'Inside': Aging and Attachment to Place in an Appalachian Community," in N. Datan and N. Lohmann (Eds.) *Transitions of Aging*, New York: Academic Press, 153–170.

Sack, R.D. (1997) *Homo Geographicus: A Framework for Action, Awareness, and Moral Concern*, Baltimore: Johns Hopkins University Press.

Seamon, D. (2008) "Place, Placelessness, Insideness, and Outsideness in John Sayles' Sunshine State," *Aether: Journal of Media Geography* 3, 1–19.

Seamon, D. and J. Sowers (2008) "Place and Placelessness (1976): Edward Relph," in P. Hubbard, R. Kitchin and G. Valentine (Eds.) *Key Texts in Human Geography*, London: Sage, 43–51.

Sepe, M. (2013a) "Places and Perceptions in Contemporary City," *Urban Design International* 18, 111–113.

—— (2013b) *Planning and Place in the City: Mapping place identity*, London: Routledge.

Shelton, B. (2012) *Learning from the Japanese City: West Meets East in Urban Design*, second edition, London: E and FN Spon.

Shim, C. and V. Almeida Santos (2014) "Tourism, Place and Placelessness in the Phenomenological Experience of Shopping Malls in Seoul," *Tourism Management* 45, 106–114.

Smith, C. (1978) "Book Review: Place and Placelessness," *The Geographical Review* 68, 116–118.

Soini, K. (2004) " 'Between Insideness and Outsideness: Studying Locals' Perceptions of Landscape," in H. Palang, H. Soovali, M. Antrop and G. Setten (Eds.) *European Rural Landscapes: Persistence and Change in a Globalizing Environment*, Dordrecht: Kluwer Academic, 83–97.

Southworth, M. and D. Ruggeri (2011) "Beyond Placelessness: Place Identity and the Global City," in T. Banerjee and A. Loukaitou-Sideris (Eds) *Companion to Urban Design*, London: Routledge, 495–509.

Stock, M. (2000) "Commentary 2," *Progress in Human Geography* 24, 615–617.

Stratton, B.J. (2014) " 'Everything Depends on Reaching the Coast': Inscriptions of Placelessness in John Hillcoat's Adaptation of The Road." *Arizona Quarterly* 70, 85–107.

Tuan, Y.F. (1977) *Space and Place: The Perspective of Experience*, Minneapolis: University of Minnesota Press.

Winton, A. (2009) *Ground Control: Fear and Happiness in the Twenty-First Century City*, London: Penguin.

Woolley, H., S. Rose, M. Carmona and J. Freeman (2004) *The Value of Public Space: How High Quality Parks and Public Spaces Create Economic, Social and Environmental Value*, London: CABE Space.

1 The Paradox of Place and the Evolution of Placelessness

Edward Relph

Introduction

Within every place there lies a contradiction. No matter whether places are defined as containers, geographical localities, communities, territories of meaning, nodes in networks, or exceptional buildings and public spaces, their identity is always a function both of difference from, and similarities with, other equivalent places. A truly unique place would be incomprehensible, and if all places were the same the very idea of them would be nonsense. To appreciate the distinctive identity *of* somewhere requires understanding its sameness *with* elsewhere. This is the paradox of place. Distinctiveness is defined by reference to sameness. Place is a figure against a background of placelessness. The two are inseparable.

Relationships between place and placelessness are not constant. Place is a concept that spans everything from cupboards to continents, so relationships vary with spatial scale: a phenomenon such as an urban renewal involving slab apartment blocks, which at one scale can be interpreted as placeless, at a local level is a place with its own name (for example, see Figure 1.1). And the relationships vary over time. Distinctiveness usually prevailed in pre-modern eras, if only for the reason places were mostly made by those who lived in them using whatever materials were to hand because it was either impossible or very expensive to modify sites and move building materials around. It was not until the decades following World War Two when placelessness, which I defined in the 1970s (Relph 1976: 90) as "the weakening of the identity of places to the point where they not only look alike but feel alike and offer the same bland possibilities for experience," became dominant.

In this chapter I argue that what appeared in the 1970s as an opposition between place and placelessness has subsequently evolved into something that seems like a fusion in which the two are tangled together. I suggest, first of all, that placelessness in the 1950s and 1960s was a powerful force manifest in attitudes and development approaches that were clearly anti-place. But in the 1970s concerns for place distinctiveness began to be reasserted through the emergence of heritage designation and post-modernism, and shortly thereafter processes hitherto associated with placelessness, such as corporate standardization, came to be mollified through diversification and place branding. This weakening of the once clear distinction between place and placelessness has, I argue, since been hastened by increased mobility, international migrations, and electronic communications, and these together have turned places everywhere into networked hybrids of distinctiveness and sameness. Disembedding and uprooting are now as likely to be voluntary as imposed, and to be precursors to re-embedding in places of our own choosing. I conclude that increasingly transitory, transnational, and multi-centered experiences have turned places everywhere into tangled manifestations of distinctiveness and sameness. The paradox of place now lies in the fact that while these two aspects can be differentiated it has become virtually impossible to disentangle them.

The High Age of Placelessness

Placelessness involves detachment from the particularity of places. For an individual it is the experience of not belonging anywhere, of being an outsider or a refugee. For those uprooted by civil wars or environmental disasters it is a social condition. As a geographical phenomenon, which is the sense in which I usually use it, placelessness is manifest wherever human-made landscapes lack distinctiveness and have little connection with their geographical contexts.

Some ideas of placelessness have positive connotations. Yi-Fu Tuan (in Tuan and Strawn 2010) has suggested that in religion there is directional thrust from the power of sacred places to an idyllic sense of placelessness that transcends the mundane rootedness of life on earth. And in his book *The View from Nowhere* the philosopher Thomas Nagel (1986: 19) maintains that when we reason we use arguments that "are not limited by our particular location, by the places we occupy." Reason, he implies, allows us to escape parochialism, to grasp the universal problems and possibilities of humanity, and to develop tolerance for differences and compassion for others. Nagel's argument is a powerful and important one, not least because it tempers the exaggerated sense of place that can lead to exclusionary attitudes and even ethnic cleansing. On the other hand, when reason is pushed to its rationalistic limits it brings diversity to its lowest common denominators, reduces people to statistical units, and treats places as empty locations.

The deep origins of the modernist placelessness of the 1950s and 1960s lay in the development of rational, objective philosophies in the 17th century that regarded human minds as somehow outside the world they contemplated. In due course this way of thinking filtered into policies and practices, including colonialism in which the transportation of people, animals, plants, and ideologies to other continents displaced local cultures and ecologies. Rationalism was central to the development in the 19th century of utilitarian philosophies and industrial technologies that leveled hills and reduced places to exchange values. It was, however, not until the first decades of the 20th century that an appropriate aesthetic style for modernism was created, one both rational and consistent with innovative technologies facilitating speed, mass production, and electric power. Modernist designs explicitly rejected everything old, celebrated the future, used universally available materials of metal, glass, and concrete, and were intended to work equally well everywhere. In almost every respect, these designs were indeed placeless.

Before World War Two the impact of modernist design on urban landscapes was limited to a handful of buildings and planning projects. In the quarter century after the war placeless modernism came into its own. This was partly a matter of necessity. War-damaged cities in Europe and Japan had to be rebuilt, and both there and elsewhere efficient solutions were needed to provide housing, schools, shops, and workplaces for rapidly growing populations. Furthermore, the loss of life and destruction caused by two world wars had made it abundantly clear that humanity shared one world and old ways of doing things had not worked well. Modernist approaches offered new, progressive ways to plan, rebuild and expand towns and cities, and from this perspective old places were impediments to progress and evidence of outdated approaches to place-making.

For two decades politicians, architects, planners, engineers, and corporations were caught up in an enthusiasm for various forms of creative destruction that would wipe the slate clean, renew blighted areas in cities, build new towns and suburbs, and give rise to a brave new world. In one sense, it was a remarkable achievement. Many people ended up better housed and with more stuff—cars, televisions, refrigerators, opportunities to travel—than they had ever had before. From the perspective of place, however, sameness rapidly began to displace geographical diversity. In the early 1970s when I was writing *Place and Placelessness*, the contrast between remaining older places and new modernist ones was obvious. Apartment slabs in Chicago and Toronto had a striking family resemblance to those in Moscow; social housing projects replaced pleasant old streets with sterile open blocks; suburbs and new towns were laid out in pods of scarcely differentiated houses; commercial strips lined with fast food and petrol station chains extended the uniform reach of multi-national corporations around the world (Figure 1.1).

I was not aware of it at the time, but with the benefit of hindsight it is clear that even by 1970 modernist placelessness was already beginning to lose authority. In the two preceding decades dramatic and destructive changes to distinctive places and landscapes had occurred with minimal public consultation, no environmental assessments, and very little public outcry. But in the late 1960s there were dramatic changes in cultural and political attitudes—apparent in widespread public protests for civil rights, against the Vietnam War, for women's equality, against environmental degradation and, on a somewhat more modest scale, against the eradication

Figure 1.1 Placeless modernist Cabrini Green Apartments in Chicago. Slab
apartments built in the 1950s and 1960s replaced almost everything of
the former urban landscapes. The apartments have now been
demolished

Source: Author, 1985.

of distinctive places. Those protests led in various ways to changes in practices and policies now so completely taken for granted that the conditions
and ideas they challenged are difficult to imagine.

The Reassertion of Distinctiveness

In the early 1960s Jane Jacobs offered implicit criticisms of modernist
placelessness in *The Death and Life of Great American Cities* (1961: 443)
when she condemned the "desegregated sortings" of modernist planning and
praised the "organized complexity" of older unplanned parts of cities.
However, the first practical signs that placeless approaches were losing
momentum came in the last part of the decade with successful popular
protests both against the construction of expressways (Jacobs was directly
involved in New York and Toronto) and against the demolition of old
buildings to make way for new developments. The latter were precursors
to the 1972 UNESCO Convention for the Protection of the World Cultural
and Natural Heritage, which was a major turning point in the recognition of the value of place distinctiveness. It established the idea of World
Heritage Sites and called upon participating nations to pass legislation to
protect built heritage, which most of them did. Old places and buildings

that only a year or two before had been generally regarded as obsolete and worthless suddenly became attractive, essential resources. Heritage preservation, which protects a key element of place diversity, immediately became an integral part of urban planning and design almost everywhere. There has been no turning back.

The change in attitudes to place heralded by heritage protection was echoed in several different and apparently unrelated ways over the next three decades. In architecture the stylistic stranglehold that modernism had held on design was broken by the emergence of post-modern approaches that once again made it acceptable to decorate buildings. At about the same time, old inner city residential neighborhoods, many of them recently slated for clean-sweep renewal, came to be identified as desirable places to live and were gentrified. Town planning experienced its own post-modern turn in the 1980s with the introduction of 'neo-traditional' or 'new urbanist' approaches that included elements of vernacular built-forms and turned the modernist principle, that the future should reject the past, on its head (Figure 1.2).

Even multinational companies, hitherto primary agents of uniformity, began to pay attention to place distinctiveness. I was in the habit of

Figure 1.2 An instance of the reassertion of distinctiveness. This poster promoting the new urbanist development of Cornell near Toronto showed developer Larry Law shaking hands with Andrés Duany, the doyen of the neo-traditional movement

Source: Author, 1995.

photographing McDonald's fast food restaurants wherever I traveled in an attempt to document their essential sameness, but several years before 1990 it became clear to me that these were actually becoming increasingly varied, often slipped into old buildings and otherwise adapted to their urban settings. At about the same time developers began to master-plan new suburban developments around distinctive themes, often with some regional stylistic reference—Colonial in New England, brick neo-Gothic around Toronto. Corporations also began to change their locational strategies for head offices because their professional employees wanted to live and work somewhere distinctive with good restaurants, parks, golf courses, and a vibrant street life. For business consultants such as the Economist Intelligence Unit and Mercer this provided an opportunity to develop methodologies to measure and rank the attractiveness of different cities as places to live and do business. Although these rankings have a neo-liberal function that promotes competition between global cities and exacerbates inequalities between winners and losers, their introduction soon translated into the realization by municipalities that their place identity matters. Place branding and marketing, such as the I Love NY campaign, were invented as means to promote distinctiveness, encourage foreign investment and attract tourists. Place branding has been helped by creating 'destination' architecture for museums and galleries, encouraging government investments in efficient transit, hosting international festivals and sporting competitions, and providing strong support for universities and schools, all of which benefit local citizens as well as attracting foreign attention and investment.

I am well aware that these instances of the reassertion of place distinctiveness can be criticized on conceptual, aesthetic, and ideological grounds as being manipulative and arbitrary. My point is that, taken together and given their range of applications, they are compelling evidence of the growth of a broad resistance to the sort of placelessness that prevailed in the 1950s and 1960s. But not everyone is so sure. In 1994, Howard Kunstler wrote *The Geography of Nowhere* (1994) as an expression of his anger about what he saw, to paraphrase some of his phrases, as depressing, brutal, ugly, unhealthy, and spiritually degrading developments that no longer constituted a credible human habitat. From my perspective, however, there was in the 1990s considerably less nowhere in urban landscapes than there had been twenty years earlier. Of course, the processes of placelessness and their manifestations had not been entirely thwarted. They continued to be very evident in the sort of careless urban development that Kunstler criticized. However, by the end of the century they had unquestionably lost their previous, almost unquestioned dominance as the preferred way to develop cities and change landscapes.

This was not some superficial readjustment from placeless making to place-making. The reassertion of distinctiveness constituted a change far deeper than decorative cladding on post-modern buildings and neat slogans for place branding because it was contemporary with an epistemological upheaval that undermined the very foundations of the rationalism that stood behind placeless modernism. In 2001 Stephen Toulmin (2001), a well-respected philosopher of science, looked back over the previous four decades and saw evidence of a sudden and remarkable loss of confidence in ideas of rationality that had endured for over three centuries. His opinion is widely shared by other philosophers. Deep weaknesses in rationalism had been revealed in the first half of the 20th century by Heidegger, Wittgenstein and the Frankfurt school. More recently Thomas Kuhn (1996) had shown that scientific truth is not determined by objective methods alone but at any given time is an expression of a consensus of scientific views, a conclusion that subsequent philosophers have been unable to undermine. We are still too close to this loss of confidence in rationalism to grasp the range and complexity of its implications, but the upshot appears to be that objective, scientific methods for acquiring and judging knowledge, even though they are widely accepted and often effective ways to understand the nature of things, cannot be shown logically to be the only correct, or even best, methods. Rationalism has lost its privileged position as a way of understanding reality. A philosophical door that for several centuries effectively excluded heterogeneity has been opened, and difference in all its diverse social and geographical manifestations has entered.

This epistemological upheaval is, to use Thomas Kuhn's familiar term, a paradigm shift. It stands behind recent deep changes in social attitudes towards minorities, for instance aboriginals and first nations who were previously subjected to policies of displacement and assimilation and whose distinctiveness, rights, and sacred places are now acknowledged. It lies in the background to the recognition of gender and sexual equality. It is apparent in the acknowledgement of the importance of heritage and ecological diversity. It has undermined the placeless aesthetics and practices of modernism and is the basis for the reassertion of distinctiveness in places. But, and this is a substantial qualification, it involves more than a recovery of the local processes that created the diversity of pre-modern places. This was intimated in the 1972 UNESCO Convention for the protection of *world* heritage that nevertheless addressed the destruction of *particular* heritage sites; in other words, the global and the local, placelessness and place, were seen as intimately interlinked. This was an early and specific instance of what I think has happened generally with the release of heterogeneity into an interconnected world. Places everywhere, no matter how big, small, new, or old, have begun to evolve into hybrids of local distinctiveness and globally shared sameness.

Hybridity and Hybrid Places

Lucy Lippard (1997: 10), who has a particular interest is the role of artworks in creating and defining places, claims that: "We are living today on a threshold between a history of alienated displacement from and longing for home, and the possibility of a multi-centered society that understands the reciprocal relationship between the two." She is explicit about the consequence of what this means: "Each time we enter a new place, we become one of the ingredients of an existing hybridity, which is really what all 'local places' consist of" (Lippard 1997: 6).

Places have to some degree always been hybrids. Medieval walled towns were not hermetically sealed, people went on pilgrimages or were forced into armies, taking their ideas and ways of doing things with them, and bringing ideas from away back home. Local practices have always been modified by knowledge from elsewhere. The difference now is that former limitations to moving people, things, and ideas around, and which once contributed enormously to making and preserving distinctive place identities, have been transcended. Experiences associated with lifetimes rooted in just one or two places were narrow but deep. They have been widely supplanted by experiences of many places visited briefly or lived in for a few months or years, experiences that are broad and comparative yet relatively shallow. Broad experiences inevitably import practices and ideas from elsewhere, integrating them with whatever is locally distinctive. The resulting hybridity of distinctiveness and sameness has become an unavoidable aspect of contemporary everyday place experience (Figure 1.3).

Although he does not use the expression, the idea of hybridity is clear in Marc Augé's (1995) widely referenced account of what he calls "non-places," by which he means airports, health clinics, motorway service centers, and similar facilities deemed to have no history, no cultural connections, and where our role is that of client or customer. Augé stresses that place and non-place are always intertwined. They are, he suggests, like opposed polarities in which the former is never completely erased and the second never totally completed. "In one form or another, ranging from the misery of the refugee camp to the cossetted luxury of five star hotels, some experience of non-place (which is associated with the acceleration of history and the contraction of the planet) is today an essential component of all social existence" (Augé 1995: 119; see also 79, 107). The converse is equally true: the possibility of place is never absent from any non-place. Airports may be non-places designed to process passengers as efficiently as possible, yet have their own identities and place names—Heathrow, Kennedy, Schiphol—and their links to the distinctive regions where they are located is often referenced in souvenirs for sale and art installations connecting with local environments.

The multi-centeredness Lippard mentions has two aspects. One stems from the sheer popularity, ease and affordability of travel and mobility. For many in the developed and developing worlds life is not rooted. Freedom of choice about where to live, rather than the necessity of having to live somewhere because of insufficient means to move elsewhere, is now widely taken for granted and exercised. People move within cities, across nations and around the world with a frequency and in numbers that would

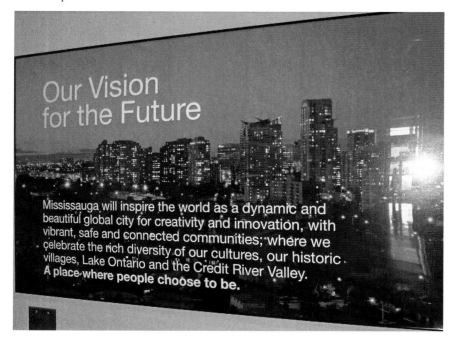

Figure 1.3 Early 21st century place hybridity. Mississauga is a peripheral city
in the Toronto metropolitan area entirely developed since 1970,
where half the population is foreign born. This poster celebrating
Mississauga's 2013 strategic plan identifies the diverse aspects of hybrid
identity—its role as a global city, its historic villages and particular
local setting, its creativity, its connected communities and diversity
of cultures, and that it is a place where people choose to be

Source: Author, 2013.

have been inconceivable a couple of generations ago. At any given moment
about 500,000 people are in the air, somewhere between places. There are
parts of the world where people's lives still have narrow horizons, but
even modest economic development soon leads to experiences of many different places. And with mobility comes the expectation that even in very
different places it is preferable for some things to be reasonably convenient
and familiar—bathrooms, airports, ATMs, types of food, signs in languages
and alphabets that can be understood, and so on. These sorts of common-
place amenities are mostly taken for granted. Unless their sameness with
other places is very prominent they are, in effect, bracketed-off from our
place experiences while the distinctiveness of geographical settings, skylines,
public squares and streets, passers-by, festivals, and the overall ambience
attract most of our multi-centered place attention.

A second, related aspect of multi-centeredness has resulted from the great
international migrations that have occurred since 1970. Unlike migrations

associated with colonization, which were mostly from Europe to new worlds, these have involved more or less simultaneous movements from South and East Asia, the Middle East, Africa, Latin America, and Eastern Europe, to large cities in all the more developed countries. Governments of receiving nations, which once encouraged assimilation to the dominant culture, now promote multiculturalism. Moreover, electronic communications and relatively inexpensive air travel allow new immigrants to keep in constant contact with family and friends in the home country. It is not unusual, for example, for the young children of transnational families to be raised by grandparents back home while their parents earn two incomes in their new nation, send frequent remittances, and travel back and forth when they can. In effect, it has become possible to live lives that are multi-centered and transnational, and to have deep obligations to several places in two or more countries all at once.

Heterogeneous transnationalism is evident in ethnic enclaves of global cities in the names of shops and restaurants and the types of foods and things they sell. The Canadian poet Dionne Brand (2001: 110–111) simply lists the signs in one neighborhood in Toronto she knows well: "Selam Restaurant, Jeonghysa Buddhist Temple, Oneda's Market, West Indian and Latin America Foods, Afro Sounds, Lalibela Ethiopian Restaurant, Longo's Fruit and Vegetables . . ." These are in the inner city where most of the commercial buildings and streets were constructed a century or more ago and named for people from another imported culture—Baldwin, Palmerston, Dundas, Shaw. Different cultures and their connectivities have been juxtaposed and superimposed onto pre-existing urban landscapes to create complex polytopias occupied simultaneously by many different geographies. Leonie Sandercock (2003) refers to this sort of urban mixture as "cosmopolis," and argues that planning practices and policies, many of which are phrased in the standardized language of modernism that was in fashion when they were introduced, are utterly inadequate for addressing the issues of diverse immigrant communities and "mongrel cities" which demand slow negotiation and constant attention to cultural differences.

Cosmopolis is a social expression of the space–time compression of economic globalization that, according to David Harvey (1989) and others, has intensified since about 1970. Global capitalism depends on measurements and manipulations of cash flows, profits, and productivity without regard for local consequences, and is therefore a bastion of placeless modernity, an attitude that is manifest in non-place landscapes of hotels, container ports, and corporate offices. Yet, while corporate skyscrapers serve similar administrative purposes, they each strive to distinguish themselves architecturally from other corporate skyscrapers and they combine to create distinctive urban skylines that have become symbols of the identity of particular cities. At a mundane level economic globalization permeates everyday life everywhere and in every culture through its services, employment, and its values: appliances from Korea, computers designed in

America and assembled in China, cars from Germany and Japan, clothes made in Bangladesh, wines from France and Australia, pasta from Italy, fair-trade coffee from Costa Rica or Ethiopia. The overt placelessness that might be expected to result is mitigated because they combine differently in different specific places and merge into the distinctive configurations of the settings to which they contribute.

"Electronic messages," Joshua Meyrowitz writes in his book *No Sense of Place* (1985: 117), "do not make social entrances; they steal into places like thieves in the night." They have no respect for heterogeneity, they pass through walls and leave almost no mark on cities, except for cell phone towers and satellite dishes, yet in the course of a few decades they have changed almost everything we do and profoundly contributed to the hybridity of places. Marshall McLuhan (1964) foresaw this long ago. He argued then, when placelessness was at its zenith and long before personal computers and the internet, that electronic media have the effect of an implosion, racing around the world at the speed of light, shrinking it, turning it in on itself and allowing everywhere to become a center (McLuhan 1964: 47). "The city becomes terrestrial in its scope," he wrote, "and the planet, in turn becomes a global village" (McLuhan 2003: 141). He anticipated that this would be arduous, filled with media gossip and nosey electronic neighbors because it allows everyone and every self-selected group to communicate and to express opinions about anything they choose. In the global village diversity proliferates, but without any clear order.

Subsequent commentaries have elaborated and reinforced McLuhan's prescient interpretations. Paul Virilio (1997) claims that teletechnologies lead to an atopia of immediacies and instants over which one has no control, in which questions of local and global are irrelevant. Meyerowitz (1985: 125) states more simply that: "Electronic media destroy the specialness of time and place." In an argument that substantiates ideas of hybridity, Rowan Wilken argues in *Teletechnologies, Place and Community* (2011) that their implication for place is that they have been superimposed or inserted to such a degree that almost everywhere is now a blend of inward-looking community and outward-looking social relations, of exclusion based on assumed geographical and social boundaries, and of connections with like-minded people elsewhere. In short, conventional notions of inside and outside, of place and placelessness, do not work well any more. Everywhere has become, to some degree, a microcosm of everywhere else. It doesn't matter if somebody has stayed in one locality and avoided a multi-centered life; the rest of the world has slipped into their place anyway.

Like most products of globalization, electronic communications have been absorbed into everyday life. The geographer Paul Adams (2005) refers to our daily encounters with electronically mediated experiences of remote places as "extensibility," a word intended to capture the way we shift back and forth between the immediacies of where we are and the imaginaries of somewhere else. It has become easy to engage comfortably with two or more

Figure 1.4 The fusion and hybridity of place. Placeness and placelessness expressed in a single graphic designed by Fatemeh Aminpour, Faculty of Built Environment, University of New South Wales and reproduced here with her permission

Source: Aminpour, 2014.

places simultaneously. Andrew Blum, whose popular book *Tubes* (2012) describes the infrastructure of the internet, once reflected about his experience in Toronto of watching a live game of the World Cup that was being hosted in Korea on a TV in a store window while being surrounded by a crowd of Korean immigrants who were talking on cell phones with friends who were actually in the crowd at the game in Seoul. "My immediate surroundings—the 'here' of my day-to-day existence—is full of elements of far away places," Blum (2002: 5) wrote. "I may be eager to understand this place, but this place is not explicitly or even primarily about here. Instead, it is a 'hybrid place,' best characterized by the presence of other places." Its genius loci does not come from the earth, but arrives on a wire, and it is neither placeless, nor a non-place, nor exactly virtual. It is, in fact, a combination of all those and the actual setting, a blend of place and placelessness (Figure 1.4).

From Disembedding to Re-Embedding

There is little question that social and technological changes of the last forty years have had profound impacts on how place can be understood. According to the sociologist Anthony Giddens (1990: 18–26) what has happened is "disembedding"—social relations have been lifted out of their local contexts and places have become "phantasmagoric" because they are "thoroughly penetrated by and shaped in terms of social influences quite distant from them." Almost everywhere is now a peculiar amalgam of place and non-place, layered, a blend, a composite, a synthesis, a gathering, a hybrid of different histories and geographies.

Disembedding is only part of the story, however. It seems to me that it has been widely accompanied by what might be called "re-embedding"— the formation of new social relationships and connections with places chosen for their distinctive attributes by like-minded groups. Retirees are attracted to mild climates and great natural environments—'snowbird' Canadians pass winter in second homes in the warm climates of Florida and Arizona, Scandinavians go to southern Spain for the same reason. Urbanites migrate to gentrified older parts of cities with a vibrant street life of cafes and bars. Gay villages have developed in cities around the world. People from diverse backgrounds have sought out locations where they can create intentional communities committed to principles of sustainability and co-housing. Transnational migrants gather in ethnoburbs and ethnic enclaves. All of these places may be phantasmagoric in so far as they are shaped by imported social influences and are networked with other similar places and communities elsewhere, and some of the designs of their built environments may be placeless, but they all possess a quality that, to use an old geographical word, might be called 'togetherness.' They are occupied by people who are deeply engaged with them, who renovate buildings and adapt them to their own needs, grow organic foods, organize festivals, learn the language, become actively involved in local politics, volunteer their skills to clean up the environment and help those less fortunate, argue about priorities, and enjoy the place where they have chosen to live even if they live there only part of the time and only for a few years before moving elsewhere.

Conclusion

There is an installation in the city of Victoria in Canada that celebrates the Songhees First Nation who occupied the land there before the British arrived and pushed them aside into reserves. It has this script: "We Songhees were moved from the place where our ancestors worked, laughed, celebrated and lived. Our daily lives are very different from that of our ancestors . . . Our ways live both with and within us and cannot be displaced." This could serve as a manifesto for many re-embedded communities in the early 21st century. In the last forty years relationships between what is local and what is shared, between place and placelessness, have been intertwined. We have, in some sense, all been displaced and disembedded, not forcibly but by the gentle attractions of mobility and communication, and then found ways to reconnect with new places because we find ways to re-embed the values and aspirations we carry with us. Place experience is now less a matter of roots, necessity, and the responsibilities of inheritance than a matter of making the most of where we happen to be. For the Songhees this was a consequence of necessity; for many others it is to do with choice. Re-embedding is about selecting a place to live, and then investing it with something of yourself.

Since 1970 the once clear opposition between place and placelessness has progressively dissipated, both as its various processes have been adapted to the diversity of places and as those places have been increasingly infused with things, ideas and people that have diverse origins. The paradox of place is now that the appreciation of the distinctive identity *of* somewhere requires understanding its sameness *with* elsewhere, yet in effect elsewhere is now part of everywhere. While the distinctiveness of particular places has always been a function, both of the changing ways in which borrowed elements are gathered together and how they intertwine with local environments and history, in the early 21st century these have become so intensely mixed up that to distinguish what has local origins from what has been copied or borrowed is both difficult and of dubious value. This does not, I think, mean that placelessness has disappeared. I continue to see evidence of it wherever careless, uninterested, or destructive practices undermine distinctiveness. Such practices diminish the quality of built environments, and they certainly warrant criticism. But what has happened is that placelessness has changed its character. It has become increasingly subtle and in various ways a positive aspect of everyday life. Paradoxically, in an interconnected world it can also arise locally as well as remotely, for instance in unthinking attempts to protect distinctiveness by copying practices that were successful in the protection of distinctiveness somewhere else. It appears that there is now very little about either placelessness or place that can be taken for granted.

References

Adams, P. (2005) *The Boundless Self: Communication in Physical and Virtual Spaces*, Syracuse: Syracuse University Press.

Augé, M. (1995) *Non-Places: Introduction to the Anthropology of Supermodernity*, London: Verso.

Blum, A. (2002) "Hybrid Place: The Experience of the Local and the Remote," MA Thesis, Department of Geography, University of Toronto.

Blum, A. (2012) *Tubes: A Journey to the Center of the Internet*, New York: Harper Collins.

Brand, D. (2001) "Ossington to Christie: Toronto," in *A Map to the Door of No Return*, Toronto: Vintage Canada.

Giddens, A. (1990) *The Consequences of Modernity*, Stanford: Stanford University Press.

Harvey D. (1989) *The Condition of Postmodernity: An Enquiry into the Origins of Cultural Change*, Oxford: Basil Blackwell.

Jacobs, J. (1961) *The Death and Life of Great American Cities*, New York: Vintage Books.

Kuhn, T. (1996) *The Structure of Scientific Revolutions*, Chicago: University of Chicago Press (first published 1962).

Kunstler, J.H. (1994) *The Geography of Nowhere: The Rise and Decline of America's Man-Made Landscape*, New York: Touchstone.

Lippard, L. (1997) *The Lure of the Local: Senses of Place in a Multi-Centered Society*, New York: W.W. Norton.

McLuhan, M. (1964) *Understanding Media: The Extensions of Man*, Toronto: Signet Press.

McLuhan, M. (2003) "Fordham University Lecture" [1981] in S. McLuhan and D. Staines (Eds.) *Understanding Me: Lectures and Interviews/Marshall McLuhan*, Toronto: McLelland and Stewart, 122–145.

Meyerowitz, J. (1985) *No Sense of Place: The Impact of Electronic Media on Social Behaviour*, London: Oxford University Press.

Nagel, T. (1986) *The View from Nowhere*, Oxford: Oxford University Press.

Relph, E. (1976) *Place and Placelessness*, London: Pion.

Sandercock, L. (2003) *Cosmopolis II: Mongrel Cities of the 21st Century*, London: Continuum.

Toulmin, S. (2001) *Return to Reason*, Cambridge: Cambridge University Press.

Tuan, Y-F. and M. Strawn (2010) *Religion: From Place to Placelessness*, Chicago: The Center for American Places at Columbia College.

Virilio, P. (1997) *Open Sky*, London: Verso.

Wilken, R. (2011) *Teletechnologies, Place, and Community*, New York: Routledge.

Part 1
Place/lessness in Design

2 An Urban Designer's Perspective
Paradigms, Places and People

Jon Lang

Introduction

Cities are constantly metamorphosing but at any moment they have a specific physical design that provides both the background for everyday life and a canvas for communicating symbolic messages about the state of a society. The design is the result of myriad piece-by-piece unselfconscious actions of individuals and large-scale self-conscious efforts of institutions, social reformers, politicians, and property owners headed by the often squabbling power elites of a city (Mills 1956).[1] In making these decisions individuals and organizations generally act in their own self-interest but sometimes altruistically on behalf of others. In doing so they operate as part of the 'capital web' of a society's investment decisions (Crane 1960) and within or outside the 'invisible web' of the laws that forms part of its evolving moral code (Lai 1988).

To some observers the whole social, economic, and political framework within which cities develop is the subject of urban design (Cuthbert 2004; Carmona 2014). In this chapter, the traditional meaning of urban design as project design is employed, not the broad definition of urban design as the political economy of cities that shapes their physical form. Urban design thus involves establishing a vision of a city, or much more likely a precinct within it or, even more likely, a few blocks within it, and creating the mechanisms to bring that vision into fruition (Lang 2005; 2014). As such, it is an intrusion into the capital web of investments and the invisible web of laws within which everyday urban development decisions are usually made. It is a highly self-conscious process shaped by economic and political necessities, urban design ideologies in the form of current design paradigms, and, often, the egos of designers.

Cities around the world compete with each other for investment capital. To succeed, they feel they have to be modern and, moreover, look modern. They need to be up-to-date. Considerable effort has been made, and is being made, by these competing cities to upgrade the quality of their public realms and to provide high quality commercial, residential, and entertainment precincts to attract what has been coined the 'creative class' of people who are seen to spur economic development (Florida 2002). As the globalization of the world's economy has gathered pace since the 1980s, so we have seen an unprecedented number of large-scale urban design schemes being implemented in cities large and small across the world. The results, whether driven by the public or private sector, are said to be 'placeless' (Relph 1976; 1987). This chapter examines that assertion.

Place is a multivalent term. This chapter begins by considering its potential meanings for designers involved in the creation of urban design projects. Those observers who regard many recent schemes as similar and thus 'placeless,' wherever in the world they may be, use the term to mean that the projects are similar in appearance. There is a certain veracity to this observation, but does it matter? Cities comprise a nested set of often overlapping behavior settings, so that each urban design, when viewed in its day-to-day existence, is clearly of its locality; people and their activities give each its unique sense of place. If one accepts this viewpoint, the affordances of our contemporary urban design paradigms in striving for a sense of place both in appearance and in status can be examined. It will be argued that whatever paradigm is applied each new scheme, large or small, is personalized piece-by-piece over time by its users to fit the peculiarities of a locality and a time. Some design paradigms make this process of transition easier than others.

Place, Competition, and Globalization

Dictionaries provide several interrelated meanings for 'place.' In the design fields it is usually defined as a *locale* associated with events or a *locality*, a geographic setting. Place can also refer to position in a hierarchy. Two closely related hierarchies are of importance in urban design: *temporal* and *status*. The physical character of a city contributes to its sense of locale and locality, and to a sense of its place in time and its status.

Cities are seen to be modern or outdated in terms of their social and physical infrastructure and to have a location in a status hierarchy from 'world class cities' at the top of the ranking down through aspiring cities to those that are considered to be backwaters, and finally those in decline. Many city leaders, the power elite of both the public and private sectors, wish their cities to be seen as modern, up-to-date, and of high status. They seek to have prestigious value-added developments that are the hallmark of a 'world city.' These precincts may be new business districts, institutional complexes of museums, art galleries, concert halls and opera houses, or residential areas. Revamped streets, squares, and parks can be added to the list. Creating urban designs to be clearly of a geographic and cultural place can be in conflict with them being seen as modern and prestigious.

Although every city is unique, many of their recently developed precincts are said to be placeless (Kunstler 1994). Cities vying to be high status and modern wherever they are located in the world end up with precincts that are visually similar. Many recently built central business districts of cities, for instance, seem to have the same qualities despite being located in very different geographic, climatic, and cultural zones. They are products of the globalization of the urban design services.

The urban design process tends to be one in which generic solutions that are developed within specific design paradigms regarded as models of good practice are applied with only minor adaptations in city after city. A few architectural firms dominate high-level international competition for urban design services (Olds 2001) and they have a major impact on the built form of new precincts and, more generally, on city planning (for an example, see Altani et al. 2012). They work globally and, as the leaders of the design professions, they set the stylistic trends for lesser firms to follow. For example, the East China Architectural Design Institute based in Shanghai has been commissioned to design the Gujarat International Finance Tech City (GIFT), a new central business district (CBD), for Ahmedabad in India. The project is based on a current global design model that many municipal authorities seek to enhance the reputation of their cities. A place in the modern, up-to-date, crystalline, high status design world is what is important to them; a concern for the livability of the product within its geographic and cultural context becomes negligible. Ahmedabad, in the economic doldrums since the decline of its textile industry, wants a precinct that will place it in the group of developments that includes La Défense in Paris, Docklands in London, Shinjuku in Tokyo, and Lujiazui in Pudong, Shanghai. They were able to buy the image.

Particular urban design types have become products, or brands, that can be plucked off the shelf by a purchaser. The power elite in cities—the municipal authorities, wealthy property developers, politicians, and the taste makers among the architectural cognoscenti—hold the power to run the development of their cities by shaping political attitudes and the right, directly or indirectly, to select designs that possess the heroic imagery they seek. The designs that they seek are those that have a place in the international firmament of star cities. When completed, these designs have no sense of being part of a geographical locale or cultural context. Does it matter?

Globalization and Urban Design Paradigms: Action and Reaction

To many observers the globalization of the world's economy is the path to eliminating poverty in the world. Henry George, for instance, over a century ago considered this universalization to be highly desirable. His libertarian ideas have been influential to this day and have had a major impact on much current urban design thinking. The urban design paradigms and generic solutions of globalization are seen as the response to the common problems faced by cities.

During the first half of the 20th century Walter Burley Griffin and Le Corbusier were among those architects who took the position that there is "no longer any difference between races, and there should be no artificial barrier erected between them" (Griffin 1946). Walter Burley Griffin and Marion Mahony Griffin's design for Canberra merged two universally applied design paradigm—the City Beautiful and the Garden City—that were developed in America and Europe during the late 19th and early 20th centuries. The most celebrated advocate for the internationalization of architecture and, particularly, urban design was Le Corbusier. In 1930 he wrote: "I propose a single building for all nations and all climates" (Le Corbusier 1990: 110). He created a set of generic models for urban design that could be applied anywhere.

The observation of Werner Hegemann on Le Corbusier's urban design proposals sums up the desire of many governments today. They seek the design products of globalization:

> not because they are desirable, healthy, reasonable . . . but because they are theatrical . . . unreasonable and generally harmful and . . . part of the money making activity of the metropolis.
>
> (cited in Oeschlin 1993: 287)

Yet Hegemann too sought a universal urbanism that would benefit humanity (Collins 2005).

Serious questions can be raised about the urban designs of the globalized economy. The need to create a more sustainable world as many non-renewable resources become depleted, the needs of the poor, the quality of a locale's natural ecology, and issues of a sense of place tend to remain largely unaddressed or at best are treated superficially.

In the urban design field, both in theory and practice, there has long been a strong reaction to the universalizing tendencies of the urban designs of globalization. While seen as a recent phenomenon, this reaction goes back, at least, to British, French, and Italian colonial architects attempting to localize their work by incorporating elements of the aesthetic traditions of specific colonies in the buildings they designed. In the 19th century there were the Indo-Saracenic buildings in India and in the 20th century the work of French architects in North Africa and Vietnam and Italian architects in Libya. These efforts at indigenization of building and urban design types were undertaken without fully understanding the nature of their localities. They focused their attention on the visual, not the social environment; they dealt with the visual, not the behavioral world. Understanding the nature of localities elucidates the problem.

The Nature of Localities

Localities consist of a nested set of what architects have traditionally called "activity spaces" (Haviland 1967) and ecological psychologists "behavior settings," the latter term coined by Roger Barker (Barker 1968; Schoggen 1989). Behavior settings consist of a *standing*, or recurrent, pattern of activities, and a particular configuration or pattern of the built environment, or *milieu*; both coexist for a time period. The same milieu may be used for very different behaviors at different times. When the activity within it changes, the milieu will become a part of a different behavior setting. The more ambiguous, or multivalent, the milieu, the greater the multiplicity of uses that can occur. At the extreme, however, the milieu affords so much that it affords most activities poorly.

What distinguishes one locality from another are the type, number, and quality of the behavior settings that exist there. In a study of comparable small towns in Kansas in the United States and Yorkshire in England, Barker and his colleague, Phil Schoggen, showed what distinguished the two and made each unique were the behavior settings that existed in them (Barker and Schoggen 1973). For developing visions of the future city or any of its precincts, what is important is that the behavior settings afforded are rich in number for all segments of the population, as well as neither too crowded nor too poorly frequented to function well. For example, Double Bay, a precinct in Sydney, is rich in behavior settings of many types that give the neighborhood much of its character. At a gross level, the settings consist of links, channels of movement between settings, and localized behavior settings. The precinct has many links, varying in width from narrow alleys to a major road. It also possesses many different places for use by adults and children. The links and places often overlap, giving a clear identity to the locality. However, what Barker and his colleagues failed to stress is that the milieu affords more than activities; it has a geometrical appearance that distinguishes one setting from another as much as the standing patterns of activities accommodated. The patterns of built form also afford meanings in the form of many to-whom-it-may-concern messages. The architecture of Double Bay makes a major contribution to its character.

Edward Relph (1976; 1987) recognized the importance of the physical realm of cities when he included physical settings in his definition of 'place' but he underestimated the importance of the standing patterns of behavior and the people involved in giving a locality its character. Visually similar localities are often inhabited by local people carrying out local activities. The combination creates different senses of place. If these activities become universalized, a loss of a sense of place can occur.

Current urban design paradigms seek to create environments where form follows function, but the definition of function is a limited one. It does not recognize the behavior settings that establish the nature of locales within cultural contexts. The focus of paradigms is on the physical layout of the environment: the morphological form of streets, the way buildings relate to them, and the nature of buildings themselves in terms of form and uses. Thinking in terms of behavior settings is simply too hard. Instead, architects rely on standard models that are held to be exemplars of good design in addressing the specific situations they face. What then are the models that address questions of locality today?

Urban Design Paradigms and a Sense of Locality

The urban designs of corporate modernism, of economic libertarianism, and of modernist housing pay little heed to locality; they are concerned with the imagery of being up to date and of high status. These generic models are developments of the rationalist concepts of a modern world developed by Le Corbusier and at the Bauhaus, not on any empirical reality. Current urban design efforts to compete with this model can be traced back at least to an exhibition held at the Museum of Modern Art in New York during 1964. The book by Bernard Rudofsky and the exhibition, *Architecture without Architects*, held at the height of the universalizing impact of modernist urban design concepts, made architects look anew at physical patterns of settlements and the buildings within them that seemed to function well in responding to local circumstances, climates, the materials available, and indigenous customs, despite being built with limited resources (Rudofsky 1964). Some architects sought to create a sense of locality by re-creating vernacular designs. They failed, however, to take into consideration the aspirations of the inhabitants of those locales who wished to break free from the 'shackles of the past.'

An exemplary illustration of the above line of thinking is New Gournia, near Luxor in Egypt. Hassan Fathy largely replicated the design of 'old' Gournia, a village due to be flooded by the Aswan Dam on the Nile. In his design for the new settlement, Fathy demonstrated the utility of local materials such as mud-brick for modern designs but his creation, both symbolically and in its utilitarian qualities, embodied a world that the villagers wanted to reject. The new village was never fully inhabited. Current efforts to create a paradigm for localizing new urban designs have sought to avoid this outcome.

Traditional patterns of built form continue to attract the attention of designers as a means of attaining a sense of place, both in the design of precincts and individual buildings. The Riverside development in Richmond, London, designed by one of Britain's best-known architects, Quinlan Terry, relies on traditional English and Palladian forms. It is a product of the late 20th century. While Riverside may be full of meaning for its inhabitants, few visitors think of the design as being of a recent vintage. Postmodernism was one alternative to traditionalism in urban design.

Postmodernism captured the imagination of a minority of architects and clients, who rejected the blandness of modernist urban designs. The postmodernists sought to inject a greater liveliness and a sense of locality into their work by incorporating traditional elements in an abstract rather than a literal form. The associations were, however, not recognizable to lay people (Groat and Canter 1979). Postmodern designs thus failed to establish a sense of locality in minds other than those of the architectural cognoscenti.

Current efforts to create urban designs with a strong sense of locality are dominated by the neo-traditionalists. They seek to create designs that are clearly placed in modern times but also relate to their geographic locales and, implicitly, cultural settings. An earlier example is the new university town of Louvain-la-Neuve (1970s+) in Belgium. It was designed to stand in strong contrast to the somewhat stark modernist universities built in the country during the 1960s, which were perceived to be placeless and soulless. The architecture is neo-modernist, that is, it is clearly of its time although richer in detail and general character than earlier modernist forms, but its urban design harkened back to the past. In this case, the model was the medieval city with the embedding of a university in a town rather than being isolated from it in a separate campus (Laconte 2009).

Seaside, Florida (1979+) with its houses based on the regional patterns of north-west Florida and adjacent states is an early example of the work of Andrés Duany and Elizabeth Platter-Zyberk, who continue to work in the same vein today. The layout places pedestrian life before the requirements of automobiles. Stringent design guidelines created a uniformity in appearance that relates Seaside to its region. It is a brand of urban design that has become known as the 'New Urbanism.' Celebration, Florida, and Poundbury in England and the Income Tax Colony in Navi Mumbai, India, all begun in the 1990s, are among hundreds of urban designs similar in attitude. A mixed-use urban design that is now under construction exemplifies the neo-traditional approach. The Mercado development in Tucson, Arizona, is a privately developed neighborhood with a main street, eight plazas, and 800 dwelling units on a limited 14 acre (5.6 hectare) site. The master plan and building design code to create a sense of locality developed by the architects, Moule and Polyzoides, is based on a modernized interpretation of the traditional character of the Tucson barrio. Many such neo-traditional designs are sought in the marketplace. They give their inhabitants a positive self-image and a feeling that they are at home.

The criticism of using neo-traditional design as a mechanism to create a sense of place is that it applies past forms too literally. Such designs exist in an historic temporal location, not in the present. Critical regionalists, like postmodernists, believe that past forms should be used figuratively, not literally. They seek to capture the spirit of a place rather than simply visual characteristics of the past, to give new designs a relationship to their geographical context. Other advocates argue for a broader approach to dealing with locality.

Recent efforts to develop generic models of modern, sustainable urban environments include: 1) the development of new models of cities recognizing their climate and cultural contexts; and 2) the somewhat fragmented ideas of landscape urbanists. The effort to create new generic models is exemplified by the similar designs for cities in the United Arab Emirates by the Foster Partnership headed by Norman Foster and the Office for Metropolitan Architecture (OMA) under the leadership of Rem Koolhaas. The former's design for Masdar City and the latter's design for Ras El Khaimah are similar. That is not surprising, as they are responding to essentially the same environmental conditions.

Landscape urbanism represents an approach to urban design that promises much but has yet to present a coherent unified model of its advocacies to the professional world. Starting with the plea of Ian McHarg to 'design with nature,' landscape urbanists take the position that the natural ecology of an area should provide the framework or basic armature for an urban design (McHarg 1969; Steiner 2011; Kuitert 2013). In doing so, a sense of locality would be established. Applying this concept to greenfield sites may be conceptually, if not politically and economically, straightforward, but applying it to existing cities is difficult. Little has been said by landscape urbanists about how to provide for the ways of life of diverse sets of people within diverse cultural environments. Certainly a partial sense of place would be attained through respecting the natural ecology of a locale.

The two major attitudes to urban design in professional practice today remain those of international modernism, in its guise as the urban design of economic libertarianism, and the neo-traditional approach. Do we need to worry about the quality of these paradigms? Any design once implemented, it can be argued, will start to be changed to meet the needs of evolving populations, and a sense of locality will evolve out of those changes. It is the people who make the city.

Personalization and the Creation of a Sense of Place

In the face of the universalizing forces that have increased since World War Two, much remains local. In China, for instance, the universal housing types developed in the 1920s and being built now in the 21st century, end up with common touches. Some have to do with specific stylistic devices, but others have more to do with the behavior of their inhabitants. Laundry is still hung out on balconies to dry, and the people themselves and their activities locate the developments in the region. The built environment is only a backdrop to life.

The new CBDs being developed across the world that appear to be very similar will over time be adapted to meet cultural and climatic necessities. New buildings, especially religious edifices, and memorials commemorating events and people will be inserted. If GIFT in Ahmedabad is built based on the model of modern Shanghai, it will soon have to deal with the sweeping monsoon rains and searing heat of a semi-arid Gujarati summer. It will also take on the patterns of street life as exemplified by the behavior settings typical of Ahmedabad. Such changes will start to differentiate newly created precincts from others around the world because each will develop a unique set of behavior settings at the ground floor level—the world inhabited by pedestrians and automobile drivers and their passengers. The streets will be changed and it is the quality of streets that gives a city its character. Even the geometric rationality of the blocks of Le Corbusier's Chandigarh is taking on the form of the meandering patterns of Indian cities, and the unused open spaces are being occupied by informal settlements (Claire 2014).

All newly designed precincts of cities take on the patina of their inhabitants over time through usage and the piecemeal, day-to-day changes they make to the establishments that exist in it, and to the physical environment. This practice of creating a sense of a place being one's own is easier to see in ethnic precincts of multicultural cities than in their CBDs. These neighborhoods have a strong identity as districts in most cognitive representations of cities. The changes that are made by the inhabitants of precincts, or on their behalf, are primarily to street signage, the public façades of buildings, the way they address the street, their entrance steps, cornice lines, and window types and what is displayed in the windows for passers-by to see. Culturally appropriate behavior settings begin to emerge, provided the design allows for the possibility. Much modernist design precludes the possibility. It is generally a hard architecture with tight spaces (Sommer 1974), although Le Corbusier's Pessac housing with its many alterations made by its residents shows that hard designs are not an inevitable characteristic of modernist architecture (Boudon 1972; Invisible Bordeaux 2013).

Many changes made to building types can be seen in Italian areas of American cities, such as Philadelphia's Bella Vista, Hispanic neighborhoods such as Little Village in Chicago, and Chinatowns everywhere. As the population of an area changes, so does its character. Bella Vista has undergone considerable gentrification in recent years and is more clearly a neighborhood inhabited by 'yuppies' and 'dinks.' The physical nature of the area becomes adapted to meet the requirements of a different taste culture and the behavior settings that exist within it soon become those favored by the new population. The people, too, are different.

Enduring Modernism

Modernist urban design with buildings set as objects in space rather than space makers—despite many premature obituaries going back to the demolition of Pruitt-Igoe in 1972—is alive and well in many places within a political environment of economic libertarianism. Architecture today tends to be more flamboyant than its mid-20th century counterparts. Such designs function well when the assumptions about people, nature, and ways of life on which they are based coincide with contemporary culture-based activity systems, economic conditions, and aesthetic values. People do adapt to them well-enough, even when the designs have shortcomings. The designs are bold and capture the imagination. They are seen as up-to-date and prestigious. They are the desired brand of many municipal authorities.

For commercial areas, the urban designs of international economic libertarianism rule supreme in many places, and particularly in rapidly modernizing countries (Marshall 2003). Their bold individual buildings set in space attract the attention of many corporate and political leaders. The designs assume that the individual motor vehicle remains the major mode of transportation and that the requirements of pedestrians are of little consequence. It is the image that counts. Two designs for a new business core for Dammam in Saudi Arabia illustrate the difference. The spatial qualities of the design of economic libertarianism could be for almost any city anywhere. The neo-traditional design is based on the spatial qualities of old Dammam that respond to climate and cultural necessities. It is at the same time modern in its massing.

In one design for the proposed new CBD for Dammam, the buildings are set as separate elements in a lush green precinct replete with ponds. Such a design stands in strong contrast to a neo-traditional design for the same site. The density of the two schemes responds to the same brief, but density is handled very differently. The neo-traditional design follows the generic qualities of Dammam's existing street pattern, mixed-use qualities, patterns of climate control, and housing patterns. It provides a much richer set of offerings for the pedestrians in a shaded world. The neo-liberal scheme has an up-to-date image. Which is the better scheme? It depends on the criteria used in the evaluation. Ultimately, it is the power elite who make decisions, but they can be persuaded by strong arguments.

Modernist residential areas of tall, individual apartment buildings set in open space are popular in countries such as China and South Korea, where they are valued for their up-to-date qualities and the privacy they afford. Such developments have, however, been largely rejected in countries such as the United States and the United Kingdom, the so-called Anglo-Saxon world, and in western Continental Europe. Many projects in those countries have been demolished to be replaced by low-rise housing with less open space for its own sake among buildings at the same overall density as their predecessors. Even where modernist design is still in vogue, there is a great sense of opportunity costs—the designs could have been better if another paradigm had been followed and/or a much more thorough programming process with community input had been instituted. In many East European countries, such as Hungary, the unused and meaningless open spaces between blocks of buildings are being filled in by new buildings to create an environment that affords a richer range of settings for engagement in a communal life and to differentiate one design from another.

Conclusion

Given the socio-economic and political climate in which the different urban design paradigms exist today, how does one move ahead? I have been an advocate for a knowledge-based neo-functional ecological urban design process but have been told that 'designers simply do not and will not work that way.' They will work from known generic design types because they follow a mimetic design process. If this is indeed the case, what is needed by urban designers is a new and broad set of generic solutions that deal with diverse cultural environments and climates and assume different levels of technological and economic constraints. This range of possibilities would present professionals working under severe time constraints with a set of models that would form the basis for asking serious questions about how best to address the situation at hand. Whose job is it to produce these models? Surely it is that of the academic community.

Note

1   The term 'power elite' was coined by sociologist C. Wright Mills (1956). Today it is estimated that of the USA's 320 million people, 250 men and women are the most influential in the three branches of the federal government and 220 control the nation's major television channels and newspapers and thus the information we receive. The internet is, however, increasingly democratizing access to knowledge about what is happening in the world.

References

Altani, B., M. Sibley and L. Munnuchin (2012) "Evaluating the impact of the internationalization on urban planning in Saudi Arabia,"in M. Pacetti, G. Passerini, C.A. Brebbia and G. Latini (Eds.) *The Sustainable City VII*, Volume 1, Southampton: WIT Press, 291–301.

Barker, R.G. (1968) *Ecological Psychology: Concepts and Methods for Studying the Environment of Human Behavior*, Stanford, CA: Stanford University Press.

Barker, R.G. and P. Schoggen (1973) *Qualities of Communal Life*, San Francisco: Jossey Bass.

Boudon, P. (1972) *Lived-In Architecture: Le Corbusier's Pessac Revisited*, G. Onn (trans), Cambridge, MA.: MIT Press.

Carmona, M. (2014) "The place-shaping continuum: A theory of urban design process," *Journal of Urban Design* 19, 2–36.

Claire, A. (2014) "Le Corbusier's modern city, reinvented," *The Guardian Weekly*, 3 October: 31.

Collins, C.C. (2005) *Werner Hegemann and the Search for a Universal Urbanism*, New York: W.W. Norton.

Crane, D. (1960) "The city symbolic," *Journal of the American Institute of Planners* 26, 285–286.

Cuthbert, A. (2006) *The Form of Cities*, Oxford: Blackwell.

Florida, R. (2002) *The Rise of the Creative Class and how it is transforming work, leisure, community and everyday life*, New York: Basic Books.

Griffin, M.M. (1946) *The Magic of America*, unpublished manuscript. New York: New York Historical Society.

Groat, L. and D. Canter (1979) "A study of meaning: does Post-Modernism, communicate?" *Progressive Architecture* 60, 84–87.

Haviland, D.S. (1967) "The activity/space; a least common denominator for architectural programming," paper presented at the *AIA Architects, architect-Researchers' Conference*, 25 October 1967.

Invisible Bordeaux (2013) "Le Corbusier's Cité Frugès: timelessly modern and back in fashion," available at www.invisiblebordeaux.blogspot.com.au/2013/08/le-corbusiers-cite-fruges-timelessly.html, accessed April 20, 2015.

Kuitert, W. (2013) "Urban landscape systems understood by geo-history map overlay," *Journal of Landscape Architecture* 8, 54–63.

Kunstler, James. (1994) *Geography of Nowhere: The Rise and Decline of America's Man-Made Landscape*, New York: Free Press.

Laconte, P. (2009) *La Recherche de la Qualité Environnementale et Urbaine. Le Cas de Louvain-la-Neuve (Belgique)*, Lyon: Éditions du Certu.

Lai, R.T. (1988) *Law in Urban Design and Planning: The Invisible Web*, New York: Van Nostrand Reinhold.

Lang, J. (2005) *Urban Design: A Typology of Procedures and Products illustrated with over 50 Case Studies.* Oxford: Architectural Press.

—— (2014) "Comments on 'The place shaping continuum: a theory of the urban design process,'" *Journal of Urban Design* 19, 41–43.

Le Corbusier (1990) *Precisions on the Present State of Architecture and City Planning*, E. Schreiber Aujane (trans), Cambridge, MA.: MIT Press.

McHarg, I. (1969) *Design with Nature*, Garden City, NY: Natural History Press.

Marshall, R. (2003) *Emerging Urbanity: Global Projects in the Asia Pacific Rim*, London: Spon.

Mills, C. Wright (1956) *The Power Elite*, New York: Oxford University Press.

Oeschlin, W. (1993) "Between Germany and America: Werner Hegemann's approach to urban planning," in J.P. Kleihues and C. Rathberger (Eds.) *Berlin/New York Like and Unlike, Essays on Architecture and Art from 1870 to the Present*, New York: Rizzoli, 282–297.

Olds, K. (2001) *Globalization and Urban Change: Capital, Culture and the Pacific Rim Mega Projects*, Oxford: Oxford University Press.

Relph, E. (1976) *Place and Placelessness.* London: Pion.

—— (1987) *The Modern Urban Landscape*, Baltimore: Johns Hopkins University Press.

Rudofsky, B. (1964) *Architecture without Architects: an Introduction to non-pedigreed Architecture*, Garden City, NY.: Doubleday for the Museum of Modern Art.

Schoggen, P. (1989) *Behavior Settings: A Revision and Extension of Roger G. Barker's Ecological Psychology*, Stanford, CA.: Stanford University Press.

Sommer, R. (1974) *Tight Spaces: Hard Architecture and how to Humanize It*, Englewood Cliffs, NJ.: Prentice Hall.

Steiner, F.R. (2011) "Landscape Ecological Urbanism: Origins and Trajectories," *Landscape and Urban Planning* 100, 333–337.

3   Theory's Role in Placelessness

Lucy Montague

Introduction

In 1976, Edward Relph invoked the term 'placelessness,' a quality he defines in phenomenological and experiential terms. He argues that three aspects contribute to a place's identity—its physical setting, its activities, and the social meaning attributed to it. This chapter focuses on the physical aspects— showing how the characteristics that are commonly deemed to be 'placeless' are the consequence of a contemporary approach to development in which ubiquitous products are introduced across wide geographic areas without responding to their context. It will be proposed that this is a reflection of urban meaning, synthesized in a particular group of urban design theories. To commence, a portfolio is presented of the types of development typically judged to be placeless.

Anywhere Places

Instances of placeless environments are plentiful. Over the length and breadth of the United Kingdom (UK), developments can be found whose qualities are symptomatic of this phenomenon. These typically include retail parks, leisure parks, business parks, in fact any kind of developed 'park,' and volume housing (which might also be called 'residential parks'). Their generic quality means that they could in fact be anywhere in the country, and determining their location from their appearance is a virtually impossible task.

To illustrate the degree of standardization and the irrelevance of context in these developments, examples are offered from different parts of the UK. These locations have been selected because they are geographically distributed across the country and representative of typical towns and sub-urbs. Figure 3.1 shows volume housing and Figure 3.2 depicts retail parks, both of which are seen en masse throughout the UK. The physical homo-geneity in these environments is apparent through even casual comparison, and either one of them could be anywhere. The degree of sameness they

Figure 3.1 Hadleigh Drive, Sutton, Greater London
Source: Author, 2015.

exhibit surpasses that which Relph (1976) suggests is necessary for a user
to read and understand her/his environment.

The activities in these developments are always singular, creating
extensive mono-use areas dedicated entirely to housing, or to retail, or to
office space, and so on. Of course, this singular function leads to limited
hours of activity in that space. They are also installed in either out-of-town
locations or peripherally attached to an existing urban center. This makes
them highly car-dependent, which contributes to their visual uniformity. The
residential developments exhibit very similar layouts: driveways and garages
to the front of the properties, pitched roofs, comparable window-to-wall
ratios, and relatively large footprints on small plots. Additionally, the
building materials used are not necessarily customary in their locations. The
retail and leisure parks are largely characterized by the swathes of car
parking that dominate them. In both cases, the structures that accommodate retail or leisure uses do not use local materials or any architectural
details that may tie them to their location. Nor do they attempt to respond
to fundamental aspects of the site, such as orientation. This could be interpreted as "the making of standardized landscapes that results from an insensitivity to the significance of place" (Relph 1976: preface). They epitomize
the category of 'non-place' reported by Augé because, like motorways, chain

Figure 3.2 Fife Leisure Park, Dunfermline, Fife
Source: Author, 2015.

hotels, and supermarkets, they appear "the same or similar regardless of where they are situated in time and space" (Rogers 2013: 347). They are global and transferable products, largely unaffected by geographic, cultural, spatial, and temporal contexts.

However, these types of development, and the placeless phenomenon, have not occurred in a vacuum. As with all urbanization, they are the consequence of forces that act to determine the way in which a place is created and changed, and ultimately the form that it takes over time. In the following section, the focus will shift from observing the symptoms of 'anywhere places' to examining the cause. To do this, urban design will first be defined, linking it intrinsically with the social, economic, and political processes within which it is embedded. It will be argued that 'anywhere places' can be seen as the result of these—the physical embodiment of contemporary urban meaning.

Expressing Urban Meaning

Urban design is contested as a term, a discipline, and an activity. While the many attempts at a definition all offer some kind of insight into the field and its function, they are heavily criticized as being either tautological or axiomatic, "radically empiricist, functional, technocratic, historicist, or practice and skill-based definitions" (Cuthbert 2007: 184), and therefore chiefly devoid of any meaning. Cuthbert argues that they fail to forge any theoretical links between urban design activity, the historical process, social development, and other professions. However, Castells' definition of urban design as "the symbolic attempt to express urban meaning in certain urban forms" (Castells 1983: 304) is preferable in this respect, as it theoretically embeds urban design activity in other urban, social, and political functions. Urban meaning is defined as "the structural performance assigned as a goal to cities in general (and to a particular city in the inter-urban division of labor) by the conflictive process between historical actors in a given society" (Castells 1983: 303). The social structure it reflects includes economic, religious, political, and technological operations. The conflictive process is that of domination and resistance to domination. An example of this is given as the city defined by merchants as a place of trade, which will then have markets, street fairs, and socializing, as well as the associated commodification of economic activity, monetarization of work, and development of transport in order to move goods. This can be seen in tangible things such as building materials, volumes, colors, and heights, as well as the uses, flows, perceptions, mental associations, and systems of representation, which change with time, cultures, and social groups.

Castells deduces that three fundamental things shape the city: conflict over definitions of urban meaning; conflict over the implementation of urban functions; and conflict over symbolic expressions of urban meaning and/or urban functions. In essence, the physical form of the city is jointly determined by urban meaning and urban functions. Redefinition of urban meaning occurs through urban social change because "from time to time social movements will arise, challenging the meaning of a spatial structure and therefore attempting new functions and forms" (Castells 1983: 311–312). At present, the capitalist mode of production and development can be seen to dominate, manifesting its prevalent values and interests in changes to the built environment. It is evident in: the concentration and centralization of the means of production (the metropolitan area); the specialization of an area; the commodification of the city itself; and the assumed need to transport people in order to maximize the profitability of the model, collectively seen to lead to a crisis in housing, services, and social control. This is supported by Cuthbert's interpretation of Castells' definition of urban design as "the actual material expression of the history of capitalist development, writ large in the built form of cities using the medium of urban design, or more succinctly, the accrued history of symbolic capital" (Cuthbert 2007: 186).

A key point emerges from Cuthbert and Castells: there are multiple groups with conflicting interests, but urban form reflects only the interests of the dominant group, except when actively challenged by new social interests.

This correlates with the observed status quo, largely defined by capitalism, in which we have predominantly profit-driven forms of construction led by private developers. Public-sector building and housing-association contributions to the market have been actively marginalized by successive governments to the point of extinction. Self-build remains a fringe activity, arguably due to a lack of top-down facilitation. Private-sector developers, who control the market, are risk averse and perceive their offer of a limited product to limit their financial risk. They are reluctant to vary this product from site to site. It has been spatially and materially refined to optimize economic efficiency in all respects. For example, layouts are calculated to minimize the amount of road infrastructure required and maximize the number of units on any given site. As a result, environments are commonly assembled from standardized products unresponsive to their context— 'anywhere places' that are the epitome of placelessness. The effects of this standardization are further augmented by large companies operating at national or international scales rather than locally or regionally.

Hence, it is proposed that we consider urban design as the symbolic attempt to represent urban meaning spatially, and that urban meaning is the societal product of conflict between politics, economics, religion, and technology—currently dominated by the capitalist mode of production. By drawing links between 'anywhere places' and a particular group of theories in urban design, the relationship between urban meaning, theory, and the phenomenon of placelessness will now be explored.

Theories in Urban Design

Theories in urban design act as tools for the urban designer. They may have considerable integrity but are "descriptions of common urban features or processes" (Cuthbert 2007: 180) and, as such, are self-evident. Some of the most established are deeply rooted in the modernist movement and the architectural perspective. More recently, urban theory has started to emerge from new areas, outside design, such as urban sociology and human geography. Consequently, abstractions explaining urban design have been developed at a distance from urban designers, and the design process has been articulated in a variety of ways, from a variety of sources (Cuthbert 2007). While it remains subservient to a range of other influences (such as site, brief, client, users, policy, and regulation) the body of theoretical knowledge influences the urban designer's decision making within the creative process, both explicitly and implicitly (Montague 2014): it contributes to the eventual form of the built environment. John Punter (1997: 264) regards the impact of design theory and practice on the built environment to have been profound. He argues that its impact can be observed from Raymond Unwin's principles underpinning 'garden suburb' council housing, onto local councils' high-rise residential towers, which loosely take inspiration from

Corbusier's ideologies and through to the modernist foundation captured in Charles Holden and William Holford's post-war planning.

Individually, theories address the dominant issues at the time they are conceived. Collectively, a key characteristic is their cyclical nature, resulting in a dominant paradigm at any given time (Stevens 1998; Carmona and Tiesdell 2007; Cuthbert 2007). In Castells' terms, these cycles can be related to the redefinition of urban meaning.

Accordingly, Carmona and Tiesdell divide theories in urban design into three paradigms: the visual–artistic tradition; the social usage tradition; and the place-making tradition (which we are currently in; Vernez Moudon 1991; Carmona and Tiesdell 2007). Stevens (1998) advises that this could be interpreted as competition for consecration, approached in one of two ways—conservation or subversion. Those who are established and dominate the field employ the first approach, conservation, defending their position in order to maintain it through a passive defence of their orthodoxy by "holding it forth as self-evident" (Stevens 1998: 99).

Newcomers, or those already competing for consecration, have two choices. They can either "affirm the values and capital of the dominant members, and thus join them, or they can adopt the far riskier strategy of creating a new aesthetic, a new form of symbolic capital, and thus challenge the establishment" (Stevens 1998: 100). Only those who already possess substantial economic and/or social capital take this gamble, as only they can therefore afford the risk.

Simmonds (1993) also categorizes urban design theories in a way that can be seen to relate to the cycles of dominant paradigms. He contrasts conservative reformers with radical reformers, defined by their position in relation to the new city. Conservative reformers are the dominant group in Europe and the USA, well subscribed by urban design theorists and practitioners. Meanwhile, radical reformers are the nascent opposition with "little coherence" but "an emerging theme of ideas and practices with a small but growing body of followers" (Simmonds 1993: 96). He predicts that they will "mount an attack on the way conservative reformers dominate urban design thinking and practice" (Simmonds 1993: 102), a notion which resonates with Stevens' perception of contending groups within the field of architecture.

The theories categorized as conservative reform seek to suppress the emerging form of the new city, aiming to direct new kinds of growth into traditional built forms. Aesthetic and social concerns contribute to these reformers' scepticism, as they contrast chaotic built form with earlier historical development patterns as well as disrupted public realm and social polarization with more traditional examples. Capitalism is believed to be the root cause of this situation and, more specifically, "the incompetent management by local and regional governments who have failed to control new development pressures along the traditional lines they have used in the past" (Simmonds 1993: 96).

Two discrete subcategories are defined within conservative reformers. The first type of conservative reformer is one who derives his/her urban design principles and inspiration from traditional cities, and whose practice most likely involves the repair of the same subject. This contextually driven theoretical approach does not appear to identify readily with placelessness or 'anywhere places.' Instead, it is deterministic, coercing new social and economic activities into traditional patterns of built form, with a view to reforming them in the process Jane Jacobs' *The Death and Life of Great American Cities* (1962) is offered as the model approach for this group, as well as the approach captured in *Responsive Environments* (Bentley et al. 1985), which formulates a general theory around principles derived from studying the traditional city. The latter really underpins the position of the first type of conservative reformers, offering an accessible resource to guide masterplanning by synthesizing, distilling, and building on earlier work, including that of Jacobs, Gordon Cullen, and Kevin Lynch. It espouses the core principles of permeability, variety, legibility, robustness, visual appropriateness, richness, and personalization. It has wide utility and application in the UK at least, where its approach is established as the norm for dealing with interventions into existing urban areas.

The second type of conservative reformer works with greenfield sites more frequently, rejecting the emergent new city on the basis of its 'unsustainability' and disregarding the potential for information technologies and the automobile to alter the built form of the city. Instead, they design settlements modeled on small towns that pre-date these phenomena and consequently have higher densities and commercial centers. This is most commonly recognized as the approach of neo-traditionalists such as Leon Krier, Andres Duany, and Elizabeth Plater-Zyberk. Typical concepts include polycentric structures, mixed use cores, civic centers, employment and socio-economic diversity, well-designed streets, intensively used public spaces, and distinctive architectural character. This approach seems to bear some relationship to the concept of non-place. Although it replicates urban forms and structures of the traditional mixed-use city, it usually occupies greenfield sites and aesthetically often applies a heavily contextual pastiche to the architecture. It is possible to argue that this pastiche creates an inauthentic 'sameness' commensurate with placelessness, as it fails physically to articulate the material, technological, or social conditions of the period in which they are constructed and thus fails to distinguish itself from other development.

In contrast to both types of conservative reformer, theories belonging to the category of radical reformers seek to embrace the emerging new city, its form, and products. They believe that "through intelligent and caring interpretation by designers, it can become the basis for a new and better kind of city in the future" (Simmonds 1993: 96). *Learning From Las Vegas* (Venturi, Scott Brown, and Izenour 1972) is an early example of this body of theory, encouraging urban designers to study the nexus between built form and function of the contemporary city (rather than the type of form) in order to understand and design it. More recent contributions have been made by Rem Koolhaas. In contrast to their conservative counterparts, the radicals expect that changes in social and economic practices will result from cultural and physical changes in the built environment. Their view is that the impact of new technology and rapid mass transit will result in the shift of the public realm from streets and squares to out-of-town shopping centers, airports, stations, and theme parks. This is reflected in the specialization of functions and zoning (business-, science-, and innovation-parks, and other 'park-like' settings). The sympathy for these types of environments immediately suggests a relationship between this body of theory and the 'anywhere places' discussed earlier in this chapter. This will be explored in more depth in the following section.

Placelessness and the Radical Reformers

There are many factors that may contribute to the perceived phenomenon of placelessness in built environments in the modern age. Access to a wide range of construction materials has removed the restriction of utilizing locally sourced materials—something that previously maintained a certain degree of uniformity and distinctiveness within a region, thus reinforcing a sense of place. Also, it has become common for urban design and architectural services to be internationally portable, with many practitioners working on projects across the globe. One of the implications of this might be that, despite very different cultural, physical, social, and economic contexts, similar processes, principles, and understandings are applied.

However, an emerging shift in urban meaning—conflict in social, political, economic, religious, and technological forces—may be the more fundamental root of placelessness. Doreen Massey describes the current era as one "when things are speeding up, and spreading out. Capital is going through a new phase of internationalization, especially in its financial parts. More people travel more frequently and for longer distances" (Massey 1994: 167). So, as proposed earlier in this chapter, observations of contemporary society should be evident spatially as well as socially. Urban meaning should be reflected both physically in built form and intellectually in urban design theory. It should be identifiable in an emerging body of theoretical work. In this respect, consideration of Simmonds' category of radical reformers seems to point to an inherent link.

While theory (and practice) falling into the conservative category is largely contextually driven, aiming to maintain the traditional form of the city, those in the radical category reject it in favor of the form of the new city. This is linked to an optimism for technological advances and acceptance of modern patterns of development represented by spaces such as corporate retail malls and iconic, globalized architecture. In this way the theoretical position and associated spatial phenomena of the radical reformers seems to resonate strongly with types of 'anywhere place' and the qualities of 'placelessness' commonly associated with them.

While conservative approaches following the principles of Bentley, Jacobs, Cullen, and the like remain dominant, movement and information technology increasingly enables satellite and peripheral greenfield developments embracing the form of the 'new city.' Consciously or unconsciously, notions of historical commercial centres are rejected as a result of increasing car ownership and online retail activity, demonstrating how "supermodernity produces non-places, meaning spaces which are not themselves anthropological places and which, unlike Baudelairean modernity, do not integrate the earlier places" (Augé 1995: 77–78). It is possible to interpret these changes to societal patterns as signs of a change in urban meaning and evidence of spatial implications.

On these grounds it could be argued that radical reformers are direct proponents of supermodernity and therefore manufacturers of, or at least collaborators in, placelessness. The examples of 'anywhere places' offered in the first section of this chapter included retail parks and leisure parks—agglomerations of consumerism located outside historic commercial centers (Figure 3.2) and volume housing, which tends to emerge on greenfield sites that also are either peripheral to existing settlements or constitute entirely new, predominantly mono-functional, satellite settlements (Figure 3.1). These appear to align strongly with the sympathies of radical reformers, being market driven and following non-historical patterns of development. Even the utilitarian focus of the terminology associated with them points to the radical reformers' preoccupation with defined, singular functions; labels such as 'leisure spaces,' 'sports spaces,' and 'rendezvous points' are useful precisely because of their lack of characterization (Augé 1995). Further examples are readily available in the form of financial centers within global cities spatially demonstrating the value ascribed by contemporary society to capital and enterprise, physically asserted through powerful but generic urban forms symbolic of a capitalist system. Highways and business parks further exemplify the types of place associated with both placelessness and in turn the radical reformers' theoretical position.

It is proposed, then, that examples of perceived placelessness are a manifestation of the latest redefinition of urban meaning: demonstrations of urban design as the "symbolic attempt to represent urban meaning in certain urban forms" (Castells 1983: 304) and thus reflections of the radical reformers' challenge to the established paradigms of urban design theories. As Massey (1994) has observed, we are in a new age in which capital is increasingly internationalized, and more people are travelling more frequently and across greater distances. Of course, this redefinition of urban meaning is neither a sudden nor a decisive change, because the speed at which the built environment evolves is relative. As David Seamon (2008) acknowledges, Relph first

Figure 3.3 The abrupt arrival of redefined urban meaning, Kunming,
             Yunnan Province, China

Source: Temple, 2014.

pointed to this concept several decades ago, yet it remains relevant and worth
revisiting. China may present a contemporary exception to this, where
current rates of urbanization are so rapid that new urban meaning arising
from social, cultural, economic, religious, and technological change is visibly
evident in the collision of old and new (Figure 3.3). Instances such as this
illustrate in a particularly dramatic fashion not only a temporal, architectural, or material clash, but an abrupt collision between a new, redefined
urban meaning and its eschewed predecessor.

Conclusion

Placelessness can be defined as a phenomenon observed through a proliferation of environments that are "the same or similar regardless of
where they are situated in time and space" (Rogers 2013: 347). Its qualities
are exemplified in the ubiquitous urban forms of volume housing, retail
parks, leisure parks, business parks, and motorways. These are products
often developed remotely, mass-produced in factories, and transported to
sites. Declining the opportunity to respond to context, they instead
assume generic, universal forms, layouts and materiality for the primary

purpose of minimizing perceived risk and maximizing profit. Determining their location from their appearance is an impossible task. They are what we could call 'anywhere places.'

But no urban form is a random creation. If we accept Castells' (1983: 304) earlier definition of urban design as "the symbolic attempt to express urban meaning in certain urban forms," it becomes embedded within the social, economic, technological, and political functions that fundamentally influence it. Urban form therefore reflects inherited spatial form as well as supporting new interests, functions, and conflicts. Societal changes occasionally redefine urban meaning, which is then spatially manifested in new urban forms and functions. At present, this meaning is largely captured by the capitalist mode of production, its values, and interests. This is manifested in the profit-driven environments created by private developers.

Urban meaning, and changes to it, can be seen reflected in the discipline's cycles of theory, with a dominant paradigm at any given time. Its cyclical nature can be interpreted as competition for consecration within the field. While those established in the field hold a position of conservation, newcomers can either subscribe to this in order to gain acceptance or adopt a riskier subversive position, attempting to affect a paradigm shift and gain the dominant position.

Simmonds' definition of two theoretical positions for urban designers can be seen to relate directly to this interpretation. He identifies the conservative reformers as dominant in Europe and the US, and their challengers as the radical reformers. These two groups are defined by their position in relation to the new city. While the conservatives draw on traditional urban form and attempt to negotiate new urban functions into that spatial structure, the radicals embrace the emergent form of the new city, accepting that economic and cultural forces such as mass transit and a market economy will result in physical changes to the built environment.

Studying the position of the radical reformers and their acceptance of new urban forms such as out-of-town retail parks, theme parks, and transit corridors, it seems there is very close ideological alignment with the types of 'anywhere place' symptomatic of placelessness: "a space which cannot be defined as relational, or historical, or concerned with identity" (Augé 1995: 77–78). Their theoretical position, and the associated spatial structures, can also be seen as a consequence of a redefinition of urban meaning. New urban meaning and functions are exhibited in new patterns of development, such as volume housing and retail parks. The homogeneous nature of these spaces is virtually self-evident, unaffected by geographic, cultural, spatial, and temporal contexts. It is arguably the placeless effect of modernity—"commercialism, mass consumption, standard planning regulations, alienation, and obsession with speed and movement" (Rogers 2013: 375).

Consequently, one could conclude that the phenomenon of placelessness is potentially a paradigm shift within urban design theory—the latest iteration in a cyclic process. As the conservative reformers passively defend their nostalgic and contextual approach, the radical reformers enact active subversion through supermodernity: "the presence of the past in a present that supersedes it but still lays claim to it" (Augé 1995: 75).

Fundamentally, what has been demonstrated in this chapter is that 'anywhere places' can be seen as the result of conflictive change to urban meaning through social, economic, political, and technological forces. This redefined meaning is reflected spatially in urban form as well as intellectually in urban design theories. It remains to be seen whether, over time, this challenge will achieve dominance for the radical reformers but even its recessive presence in urban design theories is evidence of a new paradigm within the discipline that embraces placelessness.

References

Augé, M. (1995) *Non-places: introduction to an anthropology of supermodernity,* London: Verso.

Bentley, I., A. Alcock, P. Murran, S. McGlynn and G. Smith (1985) *Responsive environments: a manual for designers,* London, Architectural Press.

Carmona, M. and S. Tiesdell (2007) *Urban Design Reader,* Oxford: Architectural Press.

Castells, M. (1983) *The City and the Grassroots: A Cross-Cultural Theory of Urban Social Movements,* London: Edward Arnold.

Cuthbert, A.R. (2007) "Urban Design: requiem for an era—review and critique of the last 50 years," *Urban Design International* 12, 177–223.

Jacobs, J. (1962) *The death and life of great American cities,* London: Jonathan Cape.

Massey, D. (1994) *Space, Place and Gender,* Minneapolis: University of Minnesota Press.

Montague, L. (2014) Designing the urban: Reflections on the role of theory in the individual design process, PhD thesis, The University of Edinburgh.

Punter, J. (1997) "Urban Design Theory in Planning Practice: The British Perspective," *Built Environment* 22, 263–277.

Relph, E. (1976) *Place and Placelessness,* London: Pion.

Rogers, A. (2013) *A dictionary of human geography,* Oxford: Oxford University Press.

Seamon, D. and J. Sowers (2008) "Place and placelessness, Edward Relph," in P. Hubbard, R. Kitchen and G. Valentine (Eds.) *Key Texts in Human Geography,* London: Sage, 43–51.

Simmonds, R. (1993) "The built form of the new regional city: A 'radical' view," in R. Hayward and S. McGlynn (Eds.) *Making better places: urban design now,* Oxford: Butterworth Architecture, 95–102.

Stevens, G. (1998) *The favored circle: the social foundations of architectural distinction,* Cambridge, MA: MIT Press.

Venturi, R., D. Scott Brown and S. Izenour (1972) *Learning from Las Vegas.* Cambridge, MA: MIT Press.

Vernez Moudon, A. (1991) *Public streets for public use,* New York: Columbia University Press.

4 Reclaiming and Making Places of Distinction through Landscape Architecture

Linda Corkery

Introduction

Landscape architects work in the public domain to create shared outdoor settings that support and enhance human activities. Landscape architecture has been described as "the art . . . of arranging land, together with the spaces and objects upon it" and "a social art, serving human values" (Newton 1971: xxi-xxii). In contemporary discussions of the discipline and the profession, there is an increased emphasis given to a broad understanding of social and cultural contexts for projects, along with the fundamental concern for the natural systems that underpin design decision making and ongoing site functionality (Swaffield 2002; Waterman 2009). At the outset of a project, landscape architects engage directly with the *tangible*, material qualities of a site—its topography, soils, vegetation, hydrology—along with the *intangible* qualities of place—its history, cultural meaning, and the demographics of the likely user groups. Strategies for initiating site design emerge from this convergence of ideas and understandings, to inform the creation of settings that support a variety of activities and, potentially, engender memorable and meaningful human experiences.

Works of landscape architectural design are deemed to be successful when they capture and enhance the essence of the physical site on which they are built, while incorporating a distinctive quality that gives them significance in the everyday experience of city residents or the occasional experience of visitors. Achieving this relies on presenting a legible spatial structure using a variety of devices including planting, ground plane manipulation, structures, and sometimes water, along with paving finishes, furnishings, artwork, and so on to present a coherent ensemble. Strong, clear spatial design remains the primary goal, as this is what draws visitors into the site, directs their views, and invites their participation and habitation of the site. Positive interaction with the space(s) is what can lead to the site having a 'sense of place' for individuals who come there to use it (Dee 2012).

Landscape design practice draws on an understanding of manipulating the physical qualities of space and materials to stimulate a positive psychological response, such as 'sense of place.' Indeed, this approach is integral to the creation of meaningful and engaging built environments. Often cited principles of landscape architecture encourage designers to achieve 'sense of place' in their projects, meaning they explicitly endeavor to design and build settings that will evoke a perception of belonging, or an inclination to 'inhabit' and make a place one's own, even albeit temporarily in the case of public places (Waterman 2009).

Edward Relph's writings on place and placelessness (1976; 1993) have been influential in the development of people-place theory as it relates to landscape architecture. The notion of the *physical* place, as it responds to a *perceived* 'sense of place,' is a key idea that pervades landscape architects' thinking about site design, particularly in the public domain where multiple factors impact the resulting construction of shared spaces. For example, on some projects, the *process* of engaging with the community through planned participatory design activities or in response to community dissatisfaction with open-space development proposals becomes the galvanizing factor that encourages people to declare their sense of 'ownership' or attachment to place.

This chapter addresses Relph's (1993: 38) broad assertion that built environment professionals have "an important role . . . to play in reclaiming and making places." The discussion reviews some of the theory and research that influence professional intentions, including a reflection on how the concept of 'place' influences design thinking. It also considers ideas of 'publicness' and how 'sense of place'—ultimately, an individually derived perception—has relevance to design of the public urban landscape. The current interest in 'place-making' is also discussed, briefly tracking its emergence and popularity as an alternative approach to urban landscape design. Two recent landscape redevelopments in Sydney will be examined in the final section, each exemplifying how contemporary urban landscape design practice has dealt with the complexities of urban sites and their social contexts to create places of distinction.

Influence of Theory in Landscape Architecture

Three themes that have emerged in the "theoretical terrain of landscape architecture" since the mid-20th century, as interpreted by Swaffield (2002: 3) are: "first, what form should theoretical knowledge in our discipline take; second, what is the process of design in landscape architecture; and third, what are the qualities of space and form, meaning and experience, that the discipline seeks to create." It is within the third of these themes that theories of space and place, and placelessness, are positioned. The key theorists whose writings have informed and enlightened this focus on space, place, and meaning in everyday and designed landscapes include geographers, Edward Relph (1976), Yi-Fu Tuan (1977), and J.B. Jackson (1994), as well as landscape architecture academics, Marc Treib (1995) and Elizabeth Meyer (1997) in particular.

Swaffield (2002: 73) contends there is a "dominant view in the discipline that its role is to create meaningful landscapes. That is to say, the designer orders landscape in a way that expresses particular ideas or concepts that will be meaningful to those who experience it."

The interest in understanding how people experience space and place, how meaning evolves, and what people value about outdoor settings has accelerated formal research in environmental psychology. Initially, research on the experiential qualities of landscape focused on nature and wilderness (Kaplan and Kaplan 1989). Eventually, this expanded to nature in cities and urban landscapes (Kaplan 1995). Individual perceptions of the experience of the city and urban environments (Lynch 1960), and variable user needs and preferences in specific outdoor settings (Cooper Marcus and Barnes 1999) followed, resulting in a body of evidence that gave credibility to planning and design decision making and urban design policy.

An example of the latter was urban sociologist William Whyte's *Social Life of Small Urban Spaces* (1980). Whyte's study, undertaken in the 1970s in New York City, observed people's behavior on city streets and plazas, recording the qualities and elements that contribute to lively urban spaces. The study was prompted by a number of concerns, including the proliferation of placeless and often empty plazas throughout the city, resulting from floor-area ratio trade-offs between high-rise office tower developers and the NYC Planning Commission. People's behavior and preferences for how, where, and when they used public space eventually became the basis for revising the city's urban design codes. The study's methodology—close and astute observations, documented with time-lapse photography, and analysis of people's activities in public spaces—revealed the frequently observed, repetitive patterns of what Seamon (1980: 159) called the daily "place-ballet" of urban life. Whyte's findings exerted significant influence on planners and designers over the following years. The axioms generated for respecting people's preferences and patterns continue to resonate and have informed contemporary studies of public urban life, such as Jan Gehl's and others (Gehl 2010; Thwaites 2011; Gehl and Svarre 2013).

The Concept of 'Place' in Landscape Architecture Practice

The influence of research on the human experience of public spaces reinforced a focus on the spaces that people use and interact with in their daily lives. As the principles identified in Whyte's and Gehl's investigations gained widespread recognition and acceptance, local officials and policy makers began to appreciate that good design could reinvigorate the public domain, improve its identity and generate places people wanted to be in— all of which could encourage people back into the city to work and live. The elements that they discovered contribute to high-quality public space— such as seating, trees, water, orientation to street life, safe pedestrian access, and access to sun and/or shade—are fundamental issues typically addressed in the professional scope of landscape architecture. As lead professionals on urban redevelopment projects, landscape architects champion 'creating place' as central to their professional mode of operating; always working with the complexity of the context, that is, its physical reality and the social milieu in which it is situated.

To ascertain a site's complexity, many interdependent factors must be understood. This composite understanding can be appreciated progressively: at the macro-scale of a city, the meso-scale of a precinct or neighborhood, and the micro/site-specific scale (Waterman 2009). The biological/ecological features, such as vegetation, soils, geology, biodiversity, hydrology, and so forth, are the living components, most readily connected to works of landscape architecture. Context also encompasses social and cultural factors, shifting demographics and community aspirations. Landscape architecture intersects with the social sciences, aligning with cultural geography and city planning to comprehend the increasing diversity of urban populations and their interactions in the public domain. In layering the two systems—natural and constructed systems with social and cultural factors— a site's original 'distinctiveness' is revealed. Landscape architects also draw on the traditions of history and theory about people and place to progress site-design concepts beyond the strictly physical characteristics of the site, with a view to creating projects that arouse a 'sense of place.'

Perhaps the most recognized works of landscape architects are those projects situated in the public domain. But what is a *public* place? Expressed most simply, public places are areas and sites that are planned and designed for public access and use (Madanipour 2010). Relph (1976: 35) notes that these places have physical and/or symbolic attributes that impart a quality he calls "insideness," or "of being inside." City squares and plazas, walled villages, districts, or neighborhoods within a city tend to "draw attention to themselves but also to declare themselves as places that in some way stand out from the surrounding area" (Relph 1976: 35). In Lynch's (1960) terminology, these places would be said to have "high imageability." Madanipour (2010: 242) would add that they should be inclusive and representative of a public process:

> If a place is equally accessible to everyone, irrespective of their physical abilities, age, gender, ethnicity, income level and social status, it can be called a public space ... (P)ublic spaces should be designed and developed as places that embody the principles of equality, by being accessible places made through inclusive and democratic processes.

'Sense of Place' in the Urban Landscape

Relph (1976: 48) also suggests that a site has an intangible attribute that lends it a distinctive quality. He writes:

(p)hysical appearance, activities and meanings are the raw materials of the identity of places ... There is another important attribute that is more difficult to pin down, namely 'spirit of place,' 'sense of place,' or 'genius of place' ... all terms which refer to character or personality.

This comment evokes the words of 18th century English poet Alexander Pope, who urged garden designers of the day to "consult the genius of the place in all," that is, to consider the lay of the land, the existing vegetation, views, and other physical qualities of the setting. In doing so, the *genius loci*, the 'genius of the place' or the 'spirit of the place,' would reveal its essential elements and the makings of a contemporary practice. Clearly, the profession has moved on since Pope's poem, written in 1731. Although Treib contends the writings of Norberg-Schulz (1980) reinvigorated the 'genius' as a 'cult figure,' and while his writings on *genius loci* and place were aligned with the discourse on phenomenology, in practice designers "adopted a more superficial approach to connect human inhabitants to their landscape setting" (Treib 1995: 50).

Hunt (2000: 224) offers the view that Pope's concept retains some relevance, stating:

> Even if *genius loci* does not objectively exist or lend itself to scientific quantification, being in part a project of the human subject upon a site, we may still understand the phrase as pointing to the phenomenal and cultural singularity of place. It is this that landscape architecture tries to address and bring out for others to appreciate.

In response to the question: "Can a 'sense of place' be designed and con-structed?" Relph (1976: 38) is unequivocal: "*Genius loci* cannot be designed to order. It has to evolve, to be allowed to happen, to grow and change from the direct efforts of those who live and work in places and care about them." Treib (1995: 60) concurs on the related quality of 'significance':

> Significance, I believe, is not a designer's construct that benignly accompanies the completion of construction. It is not the product of the maker, but is, instead, created by those who follow: those who occupy, confront, and ultimately interpret. Like a patina, significance is acquired only with time. And like a patina, it emerges only if the conditions are right.

What About 'Place-making'?

Accepting that concepts of 'place' and 'sense of place' are influential in landscape architecture, what about the idea of 'place-making'? Relph uses the term in his early writing, but it doesn't appear to have been widely adopted in professional practice for another 10 to 15 years. In their

1995 book, *Place-making: The Art and Practice of Building Communities*, Schneekloth and Shibley's commitment to what they termed 'place-making,' re-introduced the term but within the scope of social activism, that is, working with communities to articulate their attachment to a particular neighborhood or place within a city. This approach has been carried on and extended in the practice and writings of landscape academics Ann Spirn (1998), Randolph Hester (2006), and Jeffrey Hou (2010). Their involvement with communities may or may not result in built projects; the process of engagement itself is seen to be foundational for place-making, and responds to Relph's (1993) insistence that the people who live and work in a locale must be part of the process in creating successful places.

In contemporary parlance, the professional activity of 'place-making' has become largely process-orientated rather than tied narrowly to production of a built project. For example, in the local government level context, it might be overseen by a 'place manager,' often situated in a community services department whose primary activity is engaging with the community at public meetings or in workshops—or coordinating consultants—to produce visions, strategy reports, and guidelines, but not always generating designs for construction. The design brief that evolves out of this list of desires may include ambitions such as 'creating a sense of place.' However, if the designers commissioned to design and document a local project are not directly involved in these initial interactions with the community, they are left effectively disconnected from the real 'client' for their work. Thus, 'place-making,' delivered in this mode, may result in a perfunctory or superficial translation of 'place' for a given site and its community.

Reclaiming and Making Place on Two Sydney Sites

Relph (1976: 47) identifies three fundamental components of place: "the static physical setting, the activities, and the meanings . . . The first two of these elements can probably be easily appreciated, but the component of significance and meaning is much more difficult to grasp." Stedman (2003: 671) describes a similar three-part framework in a weaving together of "the physical environment, human behaviors, and social and/or psychological processes." Environment-behavior research focuses on the second and third of these components, seeking to understand how people ascribe meaning to places and what they consider to be the significance of places. Research techniques such as surveys, interviews, and focus groups are used in these investigations, along with informal but structured techniques such as observation and behavior mapping. Studying 'traces' of people's use of a site can also provide indicators of the meaning and/or attachment that people ascribe to a public place (Zeisel 2006). Stedman's (2003: 671) concern is that environment-behavior research has "neglected the role of the physical environment" and, he contends, landscape attributes contribute to the development of place meaning and place attachment, separate from socially constructed meaning.

On-site observation and tracking of traces have been used to analyze two recently re-developed Sydney public open spaces to understand how and if they have secured distinctive identities, along with research on the background to the community opposition to the originally proposed developments that eventually led to the designs for the parks' developments. Relph's and Stedman's three-part frameworks are combined here to describe and discuss the resulting public facilities. The three key components are context/physical setting, behaviors/activities, and social/meanings.

By way of context, these two projects have been selected because each reveals, in its before/after transformations, a relationship to Relph's place/placelessness dichotomy. The first is Ballast Point, located in an inner western Sydney suburb; the second, Pirrama Park, is also west of the central business district, in Pyrmont, and located within the jurisdiction of the City of Sydney. Both parks were created on reclaimed post-industrial sites located on Sydney Harbor. Pirrama Park is located in a rapidly developing, high-density urban neighborhood, while Ballast Point is situated in a more remote physical position at Birchgrove a little further west.

Both sites had accommodated multiple land uses over the decades, primarily for industrial purposes linking them to the economic development of Sydney. The industrial pre-history meant that extensive remediation was required before public access could be implemented. On both sites the initial redevelopment proposals were for multi-family residential construction—proposals that sparked intense and extended community activism. Local citizen groups demanded reconsideration of the plans and mobilized to express their concern for preservation of the character of the places, displaying a strong sense of place attachment. The resulting spaces can be said to exhibit the outcome of combined political forces with determined community groups. The struggle achieved improved design solutions for the public domain in these two established neighborhoods.

Assessing them for their physical design quality, each project reveals distinctive urban ecologies and has employed current 'best practice' approaches to site engineering, with sensitive attention to historic origins and evolution. Design, discussion, and implementation delivered two quite different sorts of public open space, with unique expressions of materiality, but both ultimately responsive to local needs and aspirations to create something of relevance to their locales. Without the political will driving and supporting the process and championing the communities' causes—at the state level in the case of Ballast Point and at the city government level in the case of Pirrama Park—it is questionable whether there would have been successful outcomes.

Ballast Point Park

Context/physical setting: Ballast Point Park, a 2.6 ha (6.4 acres) site, sits prominently at the tip of the Birchgrove peninsula in the western reach of

Sydney Harbor, about 7 km (4.3 miles) west of Sydney's CBD. The main upper entrance to the park is located at the end of a quiet residential street, reached after travelling through the now gentrified neighborhood of Birchgrove along narrow, old streets lined with small, former workers' cottages. This gives the place the feeling of being somewhat 'tucked away.' However, from the opposite direction it is more extroverted, jutting out into the water along the Harbor's indented shoreline. The immense reconstructed headland comprises a series of terraces constructed of sandstone-filled gabion walls, affording panoramic views of the Harbor. Immediately following completion, it presented a raw, somewhat forbidding appearance, but with use and weathering, and as the plantings have gained height and filled-out canopies, the site projects a more welcoming, park-like presence. Traditional park facilities—playground, barbecue and picnic areas, site interpretation—are also included on the site.

Behaviors/Activities: Before European colonization at the end of the 18th century, this location was used by indigenous people for fishing and feasting, like many other sites of occupation along Sydney Harbor. In the 1800s, sandstone was quarried for ballast to weight ships returning to England, hence the name Ballast Point. An industrialist's villa called 'Menevia' was built on the site in the 1860s, its foundations revealed during excavations for the new park. From the 1920s until 2002, the site was occupied by Caltex, covered with fuel storage tanks and a place for production and storage of industrial lubricants and leaving the site highly contaminated (JMD, Context & CAB Consulting 2005).

Like many parks that resulted from the remaking of former industrial sites, Ballast Point challenges traditional ideas about what a park is, what it should look like, and the elements that need to be provided for park visitors. Many daily park users walk or run through it, as the site is well connected to the adjoining neighborhoods. Other visitors travelling from afar bring their gear to occupy the spaces temporarily—setting up for a bocce game, having a barbecue or picnic, or simply relaxing on the lawn overlooking the Harbor (Figure 4.1).

Meaning: Local residents fully expected that once industrial operations ceased and vacated the site, it would be converted into public open space. The proposal for multi-family residential development was vigorously opposed, and a quickly formed Balmain Community Committee lobbied the local council for their preferred outcome—a public park. To the committee, the site was a much-needed open space resource for the growing population of Balmain, and presented the possibility of something unique that would be highly valued. Visitors use the park's spaces for family celebrations and have left behind padlocks on the gabion wall cages, declaring various kinds of attachments. Expression of the site's history in the interpretive material and the remnant industrial structures ensures that the site carries multiple meanings of 'place' into the future (Figure 4.2).

Figure 4.1 Bocce at Ballast Point Park, Birchgrove. Ballast Point Park's design
includes some traditional park offerings such as play areas and
barbecues, as well as unspecified spaces, such as this one amid remaining
heritage industrial structures that accommodates a game of bocce

Source: Corkery Consulting, 2014.

Figure 4.2 A throwback to its industrial past. Ballast Point Park: Remnant
industrial structures, objects and materials from the site's layered
history give meaning to the current experience of the place, such
as the objects and footings from 'Menevia,' the maritime villa
that once stood here

Source: Corkery Consulting, 2014.

Pirrama Park

Context/physical setting: Pirrama Park is also located on the Harbor, on a site formerly occupied by the Commonwealth Sugar Refining Company, later the headquarters of the State Water Police. Bounded on the east by a sandstone cliff, the park sits at a pivotal location of Pyrmont, in a precinct that has transformed from industrial use into a prestigious, high-density, mixed commercial–residential neighborhood (Figure 4.3). Within walking distance of the Darling Harbor entertainment district and the Sydney Casino, the Pyrmont neighborhood also includes social housing from the 1920s. The park is built on largely reclaimed land, and wraps around the end of the peninsula, opening up to an expansive view of the Sydney Harbor Bridge and views to the Sydney CBD.

Behaviors/Activities: Pirrama Park provides an expected range of recreation facilities—play area, barbecue and picnic facilities, walking paths, landscaping—in a unique setting and with unusually unrestricted access to the waterfront. Runners, walkers, and cyclists have good connections from adjoining areas of the city. Children enjoy playing with natural materials—water, sand, and native plantings—and clambering over sandstone building remnants and unique play equipment. A large timber kiosk and belvedere rooftop serves coffee and food. The site's history is interpreted throughout

Figure 4.3 Green among the high-rises. Pirrama Park: Westerly views from the site take in the new high-density, mixed-use towers of Jackson's Landing and the Anzac Bridge beyond

Source: Corkery Consulting, 2014.

Figure 4.4 Laying claim to the place. The opening of Pirrama Park attracted local
    residents from the adjoining neighborhoods, demonstrating a strong
    'claim' on the park from the beginning, speaking to the success of the
    consultation process and the distinctiveness of the park's design

Source: Corkery Consulting, 2009.

the site in paving details, and the reconstruction of a sheltered bay allows
direct contact with the water. Pirrama Park is used throughout the week by
local residents and office workers, individually and in groups, and it also
attracts playgroups who travel there from all around Sydney. On sunny
weekends, the park is fully occupied with children and adults, barbecues
and picnic areas are claimed early in the day, and dozens more people sitting,
chatting, exercising, strolling and fishing at the waterfront.

Social/Meaning: This site has been the focus of speculation since the
Colonial Sugar Refinery ceased operations in 1995 and sold the site to a
private developer. The site was also the base for the State Water Police until
the City of Sydney was finally able to purchase it for parkland. The planning
and design process involved extensive community consultation and went
through several development application reviews before final approval, which
may account for the way the site has been enthusiastically embraced by its
local community (Figure 4.4). In 2010, the project's multidisciplinary team
of designers received an urban design award in the Australian National
Architecture Awards. The jury's citation acknowledged the response to the
social issues that assisted in shaping the park's design: "The consultation
process is somehow ever present in the completed project—it feels as if the
park caters for just about any activity for which the community could imagine
it might be used" (Architecture AU 2010).

Discussion

Both Ballast Point and Pirrama Park have been widely published, nationally and internationally, and awarded numerous professional accolades. Along with the evidence of high visitation rates, these are good indicators of successful transformations into places of distinction, valued by residents and visitors alike. The processes of planning, designing, and constructing these two landscapes did not in themselves confer a 'sense of place.' However, two distinctive *places* have indeed been created. Their transformations from inaccessible, post-industrial 'no-go' zones into memorable and unique urban parks give the sites contemporary 'meanings' while subtly embedding memories of their former uses. Each site has acquired a new purpose, allowing people to use it, enjoy it, learn about its past, and value it for how it enhances their everyday lives. So, it could be said that it is possible to *make place*, but that a 'sense of place' arises within the experience of the place. With the varied spaces and elements present in these two parks, the sense of place experienced will vary for every individual visitor.

Key processes or design features that delivered these two well-used and valued places include a number of commonalities. For both projects, the initial planning phase included in-depth investigations into the sites' histories, extending back to the likely uses by indigenous inhabitants. A contemporary understanding of past social/cultural characteristics and industrial uses was also documented, and this in turn suggested spatial and material choices for the subsequent design decisions. The spatial design of both sites considered the multiple directions from which people would arrive at the sites. Both parks display intentional 'choreography' of movement, experience, and gradual revelation of the site and the views beyond. This heightened sense of visual and spatial drama reinforces both parks' distinctive qualities. Remnants of the previous uses of the sites connect 21st century visitors to those who lived or worked on these sites before, with traces of previous occupation.

Both sites are clearly human-made settings, but each has dramatic exposure to nature—the Harbor, with borrowed landscapes of distant waterfronts, views to the changing spectacle of the sun and sky, along with the animation of the Harbor's activities. The designers have selected distinctive elements and features, materials, finishes, and furnishings that are at once familiar but used in novel ways. As a result, the experience of each park leaves a lasting impression of being someplace unique—unlike any other, but not 'out of place.'

Finally, the stories of how both parks originated out of hard-fought community campaigns give these public spaces great significance and local value. They are symbols of the public interest winning out in opposition to the privatization of public lands. The narratives of these events have now become part of the ongoing story of each site. While these stories may or may not be apparent to most of the people who use them now and in the future, they add a foundation for the place narratives in future iterations of the sites.

Conclusion

In the long run, does the idea of 'place' really matter? Aren't there greater societal concerns on which we should be focused, such as the increasing urgency of climate change, environmental sustainability, or spatial justice? In a 2006 essay, Relph (2006: 323) writes that how strongly people identify with a place may, in fact, be a precursor to their giving credence and/or concern to the issues of climate change impacts, and related prospects of those valued places being degraded in other ways. Relph (1976: 38) has referred to these locations as "fields of care, settings in which we have had a multiplicity of experiences and which call forth an entire complex of affections and responses."

In designing and constructing urban landscapes, as demonstrated at Ballast Point and Pirrama Park, landscape architects have reclaimed and remade two previously inaccessible sites, to create local places where people enact everyday recreation activities. If these parks make a positive impression and meet the physical and psychological needs of the visitors, they will be considered distinctive and meaningful places in people's minds, worthy of care and ongoing concern. As Relph asserted, sense of place cannot be designed or constructed—it can only be generated in the minds and hearts of the people who come to a site to use it and inhabit it, even for just brief periods at a time, a key aim in the creation of shared urban open space.

References

Architecture AU (2010) "Jury Statement: National Architecture Awards 2010," available at www.architectureau.com/articles/pirrama-park-pyrmont-national/, accessed August 31, 2015.

Cooper Marcus, C. and M. Barnes. (1999) *Healing Gardens: Therapeutic Benefits and Design Recommendations*, New York: John Wiley & Sons

Dee, C. (2012) *To Design Landscape: Art, nature & utility*, London: Routledge.

Gehl, J. (2010) *Cities for People*, Washington, DC: Island Press.

Gehl, J. and B. Svarre. (2013) *How to Study Public Life*, Washington, DC: Island Press.

Hester, R. (2006) *Design for Ecological Democracy*, Cambridge, Massachusetts: The MIT Press.

Hou, J. (Ed.) (2010) *Insurgent Public Space*, New York: Taylor and Francis.

Hunt, J.D. (2000) *Greater Perfections: The Practice of Garden Theory*, London: Thames & Hudson.

Jackson, J.B. (1994) *A Sense of Place, A Sense of Time*, New Haven, Connecticut: Yale University Press.

JMD Design, Context and CAB Consulting. (2005) *Ballast Point Masterplan Report*, Sydney: NSW Planning Department.

Kaplan, S. (1995) "The restorative benefits of nature: Toward an integrative framework," *Journal of Environmental Psychology* 15, 169–182.

Kaplan, R. and S. Kaplan. (1989) *The Experience of Nature: A Psychological Perspective*, New York: Cambridge University Press.

Lynch, K. (1960) *The Image of the City*, Cambridge, Massachusetts: MIT Press.

Mandanipour, A. (Ed.) (2010) *Whose Public Space? International Case Studies in Urban Design and Development*, London: Routledge.

Meijering, J.V., H. Tobi, A. van den Brink, F. Morris, and D. Bruns (2015) "Exploring research priorities in landscape architecture: An international Delphi study," *Landscape and Urban Planning* 137, 85–94.

Meyer, E. (1997) "The Expanded Field of Landscape Architecture," in G. Thompson and F. Steiner (Eds.) *Ecological Design and Planning*, New York: John Wiley and Sons, 45–79.

Newton, N. (1971) *Design on the Land: The Development of Landscape Architecture*, Cambridge, Massachusetts: Belknap Press of Harvard University Press.

Norberg-Schulz, C. (1980) *Genius Loci, Towards a Phenomenology of Architecture*, New York: Rizzoli.

Relph, E. (1976) *Place and Placelessness*, London: Pion.

—— (1993) "Modernity and the Reclamation of Place," in D. Seamon (Ed.), *Dwelling, Seeing and Designing: Toward a Phenomenological Ecology*, Albany: State University of New York Press, 25–40.

—— (2006) "A Pragmatic Sense of Place," in F. Vanclay, F.M. Higgins and A. Blackshaw (Eds.) *Making Sense of Place: Exploring Concepts and Expressions of Place through Different Senses and Lenses*, Canberra: National Museum of Australia Press, 311–323.

Seamon, D. (1980) "Body-Subject, Time-Space Routines, and Place-Ballets," in A. Buttimer and D. Seamon (Eds.) *The Human Experience of Space and Place*, London: Croom Helm, 148–165.

Seamon, D. and R. Mugerauer (Eds.) (2000) *Dwelling, Place and Environment: Towards a Phenomenology of Person and World*, Malabar, Florida: Krieger Publishing Company.

Schneekloth, L. and R. Shibley (1995) *Place-making: The Art and Practice of Building Communities*, New York: John Wiley and Sons.

Spirn, A. (1998) *The Language of Landscape*, New Haven, Connecticut: Yale University Press.

Stedman, R. (2003) "Is it Really Just a Social Construction?: The Contribution of the physical environment to sense of place," *Society and Natural Resources* 16, 671–685.

Swaffield, S. (Ed.) (2002) *Theory in Landscape Architecture: A Reader*, Philadelphia: University of Pennsylvania Press.

Thompson, G. and F. Steiner (Eds.) (1997) *Ecological Design and Planning*, New York: John Wiley and Sons.

Treib, M. (1995) "Must Landscapes Mean? Approaches to significance in recent landscape architecture," *Landscape Journal* 14, 47–62.

Tuan, Y. (1977) *Space and Place: The Perspective of Experience*, Minneapolis: University of Minnesota Press.

Vanclay, F., M. Higgins and A. Blackshaw (Eds.) (2008) *Making Sense of Place: Exploring Concepts and Expressions of Place through Different Senses and Lenses*, Canberra: National Museum of Australia Press.

Waterman, T. (2009) *The Fundamentals of Landscape Architecture*, Lausanne, Switzerland: AVA Publishing SA.

Whyte, W. (1980) *The Social Life of Small Urban Spaces*, Washington, DC: The Conservation Foundation.

Zeisel, J. (2006) *Inquiry by Design: tools for environment-behavior research*, New York: W.W. Norton and Company.

5 Regulating Place Distinctiveness

A Critique of Approaches to the Protection of 'Neighborhood Character' in Melbourne

Gethin Davison

Introduction

The final chapter of *Place and Placelessness* contains a manifesto of sorts for city planners and designers. Distilling the key learnings from earlier sections of the book, Relph begins by reiterating his concerns about the scale of the eradication of distinctive places and the spread of placelessness. He then turns to the question of how the management and creation of significant places should be approached. Here city planners and designers are criticized for a general insensitivity to place and their treatment of space as abstract and uniform. They are urged to treat places not merely as physical locations or clusters of land uses, but as profound centers of human existence. Places, Relph argues, are directly experienced phenomena replete with meanings and activities—and our approach to their management and design needs to reflect this richness. Not only should the planning and design of places involve a self-conscious response to local structures of meaning, experience, and physical form, they must also attend to the variety of levels at which people experience place.

Forty years on, and the concept of place has gained significant currency in city planning and design practice. One of the most obvious manifestations of this is the wealth of planning regulations that exist today expressly to protect the 'character' of established places. In early 2015, character is a consideration in planning decision-making across the major cities of the UK, USA, Canada, Australia, and New Zealand.[1] Applied in this context, the term is most often used by planning authorities in an effort to preserve or protect the distinctive features of a place; it is made a condition of planning approval that planned land-use changes and property modifications 'respect' or 'complement' the existing character of the place, or are at least 'compatible' with it.

My aim in this chapter is to show that some of the key criticisms levelled at city planners and designers by Relph in the 1970s apply equally to approaches to the regulation of place character today. I focus on the city of Melbourne, Australia, where neighborhood 'character' is a key consideration in the assessment of residential planning applications. Critical discourse analysis of planning texts is used to highlight two critiques of the way that character is regulated in Melbourne. First, there is an over-emphasis on the physical aspects of place and disregard for the ways in which places are known and experienced in everyday life. Second, planners have failed adequately to engage place 'insiders' in discussions about place. I conclude that forty years on from Relph's influential treatise on place, a need still remains for much greater acknowledgment by city planners that places are more than physical locations, and that the experts on those places are the people who live and work there, not planners themselves.

Place Distinctiveness and the Regulation of Character

Forty years ago Relph (1976) observed that contemporary trends in business, consumption, travel, city planning, and design were fast eradicating distinctive places and replacing them with a 'placeless' geography of standardized localities that looked and felt alike. Relph laid much of the blame for the spread of placelessness on the attitudes and practices of city planners and designers, many of whom were seen as viewing places merely as physical locations and placing greatest priority in their work on objectivity, efficiency, and rationality. As he pointed out, such emphases fostered an approach to city planning and design that was divorced from the way in which places are experienced, and from their meanings and significances to the people who live and work in them; the approach was placeless in its treatment of space. He called for the development of new approaches to planning and design that were self-consciously responsive to the particularities of place, and especially to the lived-world experience of them.

The dualistic qualities of distinctiveness and sameness are central themes running throughout Relph's work on place (1976; 1997; 2008). For Relph, place distinctiveness and sameness are something formed through the combinations and interrelations of three key elements—physical setting, activities, and meanings. No matter how distinctive a place appears to us, it is always the case that it shares at least some of its features with other places; everywhere, for Relph, contains aspects of both distinctiveness and sameness in a sort of continuum of place and placelessness. At one extreme of this continuum, distinctiveness is ascendant and sameness diminished; at the other end, sameness dominates and distinctiveness is suppressed. Within such thinking, the 'character' of a given place refers to the aggregate of that place's physical setting, activities, and meanings; it is the quality that enables a person to distinguish that place from another place.

The contemporary concern for character in city planning has its origins in negative reactions to the destructive and standardizing effects of modernist architecture and planning from the 1950s (Kropf 1996). References to character can be found in many of the key planning and urban design texts emerging from the early 1960s; the concept is variously discussed in the *Death and Life of Great American Cities* (Jacobs 1961) and in relation to 'townscape' (Cullen 1961), 'place identity' (Relph 1976), 'pattern language' (Alexander et al. 1977), 'the quality without a name' (Alexander 1979), '*genius loci*' (Norberg-Schulz 1980), and 'sense of place' (Steele 1981). The concept of character also became a feature of development-control processes in the UK in this period (Larkham 1996), later spreading to the USA, Canada, Australia, and New Zealand. Although originally applied mainly to preserve buildings and areas of historical significance, character has over recent years increasingly been used by planning authorities in a much broader sense to protect the range of features that are seen to distinguish one place from another.

In scholarly literature, the character of place is viewed as an aggregate quality formed through the combinations and interrelations of built and unbuilt features including, but not limited to, aspects of formal physical form, demographics, culture, geography, economics, activities, and meanings (Kropf 1996; Paulsen 2004; Dovey et al. 2009; Dovey 2010; Kendig 2010; 2012). What several of these key studies stress, however, is that character is something that people attribute to objects and that views about the character of a given place therefore differ between subjects. This recalls Relph's argument (1976) that people's experiences of a place, particularly whether they are experiencing it as an 'insider' or 'outsider,' will influence their perceptions of that place. On this point, recent empirical studies have shown divergences in the way that residents and planners perceive place character. Whereas residents typically describe character experientially as a 'feel' or 'atmosphere' (Dovey et al., 2009; Dovey 2010; Davison 2011), planners view it more through formal features of built form and land use (Davison and Rowden 2012; Davison et al. 2012). Despite the increasingly widespread use of character as a consideration in planning decision making and its subjectivity as a construct, what has not yet been examined in nearly enough detail is how the regulation of place character is actually approached by planning authorities.

Methodology

Addressing the gap in knowledge identified above, this chapter draws from a critical examination of approaches to the regulation of character by planning authorities in the Australian city of Melbourne. Melbourne was selected as a case study because in that city character is unusually central to planning decision making; Melbourne, in the context of this research, is an 'extreme' case study (Flyvbjerg 2006). The research involved analysis of planning texts used to regulate character across metropolitan Melbourne drawing directly upon the Critical Discourse Analysis (CDA) approach developed by Fairclough (1995).

Discourse analysis can be defined simply as the study of language in use; the discourse analyst is concerned with who uses language, how, why, and when (van Dijk 1997). The aim of CDA, specifically, is to examine texts with a view to revealing the hidden norms, assumptions, and values that underlie them, and to explain what their social implications might be. Critical discourse scholars especially seek insights into the role of discourse in the (re)production of dominance and inequality (van Dijk 1993; Wodak 2004). Within CDA, discourse is viewed as a social practice that is at once socially constitutive and socially conditioned; that is, discourse is seen at once to construct and reflect the social world (Fairclough and Wodak 1997). Perhaps nowhere is this more literally the case than with regulatory planning texts, which explicitly reflect societal values and aspirations while simultaneously imposing controls on what forms of development can occur.

Fairclough's (1995) approach to CDA is based on a three-dimensional framework for discourse analysis. The first dimension is *text analysis*, which involves linguistic description of texts in terms of their semantic, grammatical, vocabulary, and phonological relations (see Fairclough 2003). The second is *discourse practice*, involving analysis of the ways in which texts are produced, distributed, and interpreted. The third dimension is *socio-cultural practice*, which entails the study of discourse events in relation to wider socio-cultural practices. On the face of it, the protection of character might appear to be a wholly worthwhile activity for planning authorities and an effective counter to the forces of placelessness. What Fairclough's analytical framework provides is a means of considering the regulation of character in a more critical light and identifying potential problems associated with it. The research involved analysis of all available texts relating to the regulation of character in Melbourne. Three sets of texts were analyzed: character-based planning legislation; Victorian Government guidance on the use of character as a planning assessment criterion; and 'character studies' produced by local planning authorities.

The Victorian planning system is two-tiered but highly centralized. Most planning assessment takes place at the level of local-council planning authorities but with strong direction from the Victorian State Government. Each local planning authority has its own planning scheme, containing policy directions and statutory development controls. All planning schemes consist of a set of standard state-wide provisions produced by the Victorian Government and local provisions devised by local planning authorities.[2] There are two Victorian Government provisions concerned with character. In addition, 20 of the 31 planning authorities in metropolitan Melbourne have local planning provisions that provide further guidance or controls relating to character. Two Victorian Government documents exist to support this legislation and guide its interpretation and implementation (Victorian Government 2001a; 2004). Finally, 'character studies' are documents produced by local planning authorities to assist with the everyday implementation of character-based planning regulations. They provide detailed accounts of how character is conceived, classified, and regulated at the local level. Of the 31 metropolitan Melbourne council planning authorities, 21 had character studies in early 2015.

Texts were analyzed systematically. The Victorian Government planning provisions relating to character and the two guidance documents were analyzed first and in their entirety. Because of the length of many local planning provisions and character studies, however, it was necessary to select only certain sections for analysis. With local planning provisions, content was coded according to: the planning mechanism(s) used to regulate character; definitions of character; approaches to the classification of character; development controls used to regulate character; and the geographical extent to which the provisions applied. The sections specifying the development controls applying to individual localities were analyzed mainly for their approach rather than their specific provisions. With the character studies, most documents shared a common structure and format, and some sections were less important to the research aims than others. The sections on authorship, methodology, definitions of character, and classifications of character were analyzed in detail—with other sections analyzed more cursorily. Because of word constraints, only short passages of text have been extracted for linguistic analysis in this paper. These extracts have been selected because they either apply state-wide, or are reflective of the character studies as a whole.

The Context for the Regulation of Character in Melbourne

In 2001, regulations were introduced by the Victorian Government that made 'neighborhood character' a key criterion for the assessment of residential planning applications. It was mandated that:

> The proposed design [of residential developments] must respect the existing or preferred neighborhood character and respond to the features of the site.
>
> (Victoria Planning Provisions Clauses 54.02 and 55.02)

This followed a period in which local planning had been deregulated in Victoria by a market-led Liberal Government, elected in 1992. That deregulation, in turn, had prompted high-profile public opposition to densification and the loss of older buildings in Melbourne throughout the 1990s (Lewis 1999). The new character-based regulations were introduced by a Labor Government, elected in 1999. In announcing their introduction, the Minister for Planning (2001b: 1) stated that the regulations would "protect the character of our suburban streets" and replace the regulatory framework of the former government that had "ignited a planning war during the 1990s between developers and residents." Two guidance documents (Victorian Government 2001a; 2004) were produced to assist with the interpretation of the new character-based regulations. In the earlier of these the following definition of character is provided:

> Neighbourhood Character is essentially the combination of the public and private realms. Every property, public place or piece of infrastructure makes a contribution, whether great or small. It is the cumulative impact of all these contributions that establishes neighbourhood character.
>
> (Victorian Government 2001a: 1)

No references are provided nor any explanation of how this definition was arrived at, or by whom. The statement is subsequently made that "all areas have a character in the same way that all people have a personality" and the above definition is operationalized for planning purposes through a list of 21 features that can combine to "determine" the character of an area (Victorian Government 2001a: 3). With the exception of "patterns of use and occupation," these are solely concerned with physical aspects of character (Table 5.1). They cover such things as building massing and height, setbacks, street layout, parking, fencing, architectural style, roof form, topography, and landscaping. This physical emphasis would seem to contradict the earlier likening of character to a "personality"; personalities are about a person's internal qualities, traits, and behaviors rather than their physical characteristics such as height, build or coloring.

The new regulations meant that in order for a residential planning application to be granted approval, assessment officers must be satisfied that the proposed development respected the existing or preferred character of a place. To assist with decision-making, the Victorian Government explains in the second guidance document that:

> Respecting character does not mean preventing change. In simple terms, respect for the character of a neighbourhood means that the development should try to 'fit in.' Depending on the neighbourhood, there are two broad approaches to respecting character: respecting the bulk and form of surrounding development; respecting the architectural style of surrounding development.
>
> (Victorian Government 2004: 2

Note the language here; development 'should' only 'try' to 'fit in,' and 'respect' itself is open to wide definition and interpretation (Cooper 2005). The document subsequently explains that "preferred character" refers either to the "existing character of an area," or to "an identified future neighbourhood character different to the existing character of an area" (Victorian Government 2004: 3). No mention is made, however, of whose responsibility it is to identify the preferred character of a place or how they might do that. The section on preferred character says only that the preferred

Table 5.1 Identifying and describing key neighborhood characteristics. Extract from a table produced by the Victorian Government to assist with the identification and description of 'key features and characteristics' of neighborhood character

Matters to be Considered	Terms/features that Might help to Describe this Aspect of Neighborhood Character
The pattern of development of the neighborhood (only required where more than one dwelling on a lot is proposed)	Topography Street block length Street alignment, type, and proportions Extent of rear gardens and private open space Landscaping and vegetation in the neighborhood Patterns of use and occupation Diversity of housing
The built form, scale, and character of surrounding development including front fencing	Building mass and height Setbacks Space around properties and site coverage Car parking Fences (style and height)
Architectural and roof styles	Architectural rhythm of street Porches and verandahs Architectural consistency Roof form
Any other notable features or characteristics of the neighborhood	Waterways Street trees Details of the footpath and street Landscaping and vegetation on private lots Nearby historic buildings or features

Source: Victorian Government, 2001a: 3.

character of a neighborhood is to be "identified" with reference to factors such as the characteristics of an area, and the views of planning authorities and "the local community."

The Victorian Government's guidance (Victorian Government 2004) also suggests that local planning authorities consider commissioning a 'character study' of their jurisdiction to assist with the planning assessment process:

> The purpose of a neighbourhood character study is to identify and then support [planning] actions to achieve good development outcomes in both the public and private realms. An objective and independent assess-

ment of the character of areas will establish existing character attributes. Actions can then be identified to ensure that existing character is respected or a preferred new character is achieved.

(Victorian Government 2004: 3)

The document explains that character studies should describe and classify the existing character of an area and set out recommendations on how character should be regulated. With the approval of the Victorian Government, local planning authorities can make amendments to their planning scheme based on the recommendations of a character study. Where this happens, the character study can become part of the statutory planning assessment process: a residential planning application may then be refused approval by the planning authority on the grounds that it does not respect the existing or preferred character of a place, as outlined in the character study.

An Over-Emphasis on Formal Physical Form and Neglect of the Lived World

I now move to my first critique on the physicality of regulation. The character studies produced since the above legislation was introduced provide accounts of how character is classified and regulated by local planning authorities. Typically running over 100 pages, the common outputs of the studies are 'precinct guidelines' designed to assist officers in the assessment of residential planning applications. These are brief sections (usually four pages or less) providing place-specific descriptions of the existing character of individual precincts and of their preferred character, along with specified development guidelines for achieving that preferred character.

The Victorian Government's guidance indicates that character studies must be "objective and independent" and should classify character and establish recommendations for its regulation (Victorian Government 2004: 3). The purpose of the character studies, thus conceived, is to ensure that local planning decisions regarding character are based on objectively and independently established facts about the character of a place, not personal feelings or opinions. Not only does this emphasis on objectivity both render the feelings and opinions of place insiders about place character inconsequential and disregard the variety of levels at which places are experienced variously as either insider or outsider, it also ignores decades of research that has shown that planners, like everyone else, have values that influence their opinions, actions, and decision-making processes (Davidoff 1965; Sandercock 2003).

The character studies are presented as official documents owned by the relevant local planning authorities, but most include mention of the private planning consultancy that prepared them. When it comes to defining character and operationalizing it as a tool for planning assessment, the studies are nevertheless written from a singular standpoint and from a position of authority, as captured in this representative statement:

> People have widely differing meanings to the term 'neighbourhood character.' For many, character is about the people who live in the area; for others it is the features of the area, such as closeness to shops or transport, how much open space or traffic there is and car parking. For others it also includes the smells, sounds and colours they experience in their neighbourhood. As this Strategy will primarily set out actions to change the planning scheme, the definition of neighbourhood character will focus on the physical aspects of character that are capable of being directly described by the Planning Scheme. . . . Neighbourhood character means the way in which buildings, vegetation and the topography, in both the private and public ownership [sic], relate to each other. It's what makes one place different from another. The way these characteristics relate to each other produces a visual sense of place. Some characteristics are more important than others in creating this distinctive character. The wider aspects of neighbourhood character may be subject of other Council projects and policies [sic].
>
> (Banyule City Council 2012: 6)

In this paragraph the "differing meanings" of character that the authors believe cannot be "described by the Planning Scheme" are dismissed for the purposes of the study, with a focus on physical characteristics established. Universally across the character studies, this same position was taken— that while non-physical elements are important parts of the character of a place, they are beyond the scope of character studies. This exclusive emphasis on formal physical form surely flows from the Victorian Government's guidance documents, in which character is operationalized as a planning-assessment criterion through a list of physical characteristics (Victorian Government 2001: 3) and "respecting" character is said to involve developments responding to their context in terms of bulk, form, or architectural style (Victorian Government 2004: 2).

There is an assumption from planning authorities and consultants here that the sorts of social, experiential, and perceptual aspects of character referred to at the beginning of the extract above cannot be incorporated into planning regulations. Yet we know that the design of the physical environment influences the way that we experience and perceive that environment in the most fundamental ways (Barker 1968; Whyte 1980; Rapoport 1982; Gibson 1986; Lang 1994; Gehl 2011) and that it is frequently the intangible aspects of character—the experiences and meanings of place—that are valued the most by place insiders (Relph 1976; Dovey et al. 2009; Dovey 2010; Davison 2011; Davison and Rowden 2012). Reflecting on the various academic works identified above, it is not difficult to think of simple ways in which planning regulations could support an intangible aspect of character, such as knowing one's neighbors. Rather than simply requiring a front setback, for example, a setback with a veranda or a vegetated front garden might afford impromptu social interaction between neighbors and passers-by, as might a permeable street network, low fences, the presence of local services and public transport, and a scattering of small open spaces rather than a single larger space.

The result of the emphasis on physicality is that, while the character studies frequently involve meticulous descriptions of, and specifications for, physical form, no explicit attempt is made anywhere in them to maintain or create any aspects of place to do with the lived world. Instead, they seek only to ensure that new development "fits in" physically with its surroundings. I see three explanations for such an emphasis. First, it serves the Victorian Government's desire to make character an "objective and independent" assessment criterion. Character, as the aggregate of the distinctive features of something, cannot be objective because identifying and classifying it involves the act of human perception (Kropf 1996). Through this focus on regulating only the physical character of a place, however, the more subjective experiential and perceptual aspects of character are excluded, at least making character a *more* objective planning assessment criterion. Second, the physical emphasis makes planners the experts and arbiters of character. An acceptance of the non-physical aspects of character as legitimate planning concerns would give members of the public greater and far more uncertain agency in the formulation of development controls. Third, the physical emphasis has probably been influenced by earlier approaches to the regulation of character, in which historical and architectural aspects were the exclusive focus. This is despite the Victorian Government's current definition of character covering a much broader range of concerns.

A Failure to Engage with Insider Perspectives on Place

My second critique relates to the neglect or treatment of community input. Although most character studies refer to the importance of involving members of the public in discussions about the classification and regulation of character, actual community involvement in the preparation of character studies was limited and, moreover, appeared to have had little or no direct effect on study outcomes. In the City of Greater Dandenong, for example, the center-piece of community engagement was a workshop with members of the public. The workshop outcomes were reported on as follows:

> The audience of Workshop 2 incorporated residents, selected stakeholders (local designers/developers) and selected Dandenong Council planning staff/councillors. In order to select the general audience 100 invitations were sent out seeking an expression of interest to attend the workshop. The intention was to select a maximum of 40 participants

for the workshop. The list of 100 invitees was generated from a consulta-tion database held by the City of Greater Dandenong, which included a cross section of people from across the municipality. Although the general interest in attending the workshop was lower than expected, of the dozen people who did attend there was a robust, informed and lengthy discussion of the matters at hand. The workshop was run as an open discussion to establish what the audience valued about the exist-ing neighbourhood character of the City of Greater Dandenong and what planning issues they felt existed . . . The following highlights the key issues raised during the workshop: Poor maintenance; lack of land-scaping; some areas have too many units; issue of poor maintenance of existing housing stock.

(City of Greater Dandenong 2007: 53)

Note the use of 'audience' for attendees, implying that the attendees at the workshop were there to listen rather than to contribute. Also, if the audience of a dozen included designers and developers, planning staff, and councilors, only a handful could have been members of the public. Further-more, those members of the public attending had been identified from a council consultation database and were therefore already actively engaged in civic life. The "key issues" identified by attendees are then reported by authors in general terms, with no mention made of who said what and in what context, nor of what made these issues key and others not. There is also no indication of how these key issues influenced the remainder of the study and its recommendations.

Here and across the other 20 character studies analyzed, voices other than the authors' almost never appear. When they do, they are reported selectively and in general terms, with little or no sense of whose views they were or how they had been identified and selected for inclusion by the authors. Yet the views expressed by the community members participating in engagement exercises are nevertheless presented as if they represent a united voice for 'the community' at large; no qualifications or differences of opinion are apparent. Consider this statement about the outcomes of public consultation in Greater Dandenong:

The results from all public consultation exercises thus far suggest the community and the Council welcome and embrace appropriate change, rather than necessarily wanting to hold onto existing neighbourhood character for its own sake.

(City of Greater Dandenong, 2007: 85)

The authors thereby legitimize a pro-development approach to the regulation of character in Greater Dandenong by reporting that "the community and the Council" welcome change. Yet we know that the number of community members participating in the engagement exercises here was minuscule. In only one character study had there been a serious effort made to engage with a broad cross-section of the local population. Even in this case, however, the parameters for the discussion of character were established in advance by planning consultants and were limited to the physical features of place. Any comments from community members about aspects of place character not to do with these physical features were categorized in the consultation report as being "outside the scope" of the character study and grouped in a section entitled "Other themes" (City of Boroondara 2011: 23–24).

Although the communicative turn in planning since the 1970s has seen public participation established as an increasingly central feature of decision-making processes (Forester 1999; Healey 2006; Legacy 2010), such a degree of tokenism in approaches to public participation in planning decision making is not unusual. What makes it remarkable in the case of the Melbourne character studies, however, is the effective exclusion from the process of classifying character of the very people who help shape it, experience it daily and know it best. Places are complex centers of meaning constructed out of human intentions and experiences; it is personal or communal engagement with abstract space that gives it meaning as a place (Relph 1976). Because of this, the character of a given place can be perceived in quite different ways by groups with differing intentions for that place and experiences of it. Relph (1976) uses the concepts of insideness and outsideness to explain the effect that the intensity of a person's relationship with a place will have on their perceptions of it; a lifelong resident, as a place insider, will assign quite a different character to that place than would a place outsider such as a planning consultant or tourist. This is why perceptions of a place's character for residents and for planners may be divergent (Davison et al. 2012; Davison and Rowden 2012) and why no objectively minded planner can ever fully appreciate the range of meanings that a place can have. As Relph (1993: 34) puts it in his later work, community involvement in place-making is crucial because "places have to be made from the inside out."

Conclusion

In *Place and Placelessness*, Relph is highly critical of the treatment of place by city planners and designers, and a central aim of the book is to provide the conceptual tools that can contribute to improved practices in the management and creation of places. This is also a theme of his later writing (Relph 1993). Relph called for approaches to place-making that were more responsive to local structures of meaning, experience and physical form, and urged planners to be more attentive to the variety of levels at which people experience place. There can be little doubt that planners today are indeed more sensitive to place than the earlier generation when *Place and*

Placelessness was written. Nowhere is this increased sensitivity more clearly apparent than in the widespread use of the concept of 'character' by planning authorities in an effort to preserve and protect the distinctive features of established places.

However, what I have attempted to show here is that even where protection of the character of a place is raised to the highest priority by planning authorities, approaches to its regulation continue to be limited in their treatment of just what place means. CDA of planning texts in Melbourne was used to highlight the narrow focus of regulators on only those formal physical aspects of place readily discernible to outsiders, with the lived-world experience knowingly disregarded and the influence of local community perspectives constrained. While such an approach may produce development outcomes that are superficially sensitive to the existing place, in that new physical forms 'fit in' with their surroundings in terms of bulk and architectural style, it fails to engage with the ways in which places are experienced and known by the people who live and work in them. As Relph (1993) reminds us, the opportunities for successful place-making through physical design alone are limited.

Despite the major and lasting impact of Relph's work in *Place and Placelessness* (Seamon and Sowers 2008), three of his key messages appear not to have influenced the practice of managing and creating places, at least in Melbourne. The first is that places are not merely physical settings, but are the product of the combinations and interrelations of a physical setting, activities, and meanings (Relph 1976). All three of these components of place can and must be considered in the regulation of character. However, an appreciation of the ways in which a place's physical setting does or could "afford" (Gibson 1986) particular activities and meanings can only be acquired by planners through extensive engagement with place insiders. The second message is that planners should not strive for objectivity when it comes to matters concerning place; places are centers of meaning constructed out of human intentions and experiences, and they cannot be understood in the abstract. The third, largely unheeded, message is that places are experienced at varying levels of intensity, with an insider perspective on the character of a place likely to be quite different from the perspective of an outsider such as a planning consultant.

No one perspective on the character of a place is right or wrong, and it is therefore incumbent on city planning regulators to both consider and respond to the range of differing perspectives on place in their work. Put simply, the successful management and creation of distinctive places cannot be achieved without an acceptance from city planners that the experts on places are as much the people who live and work in them as the planners themselves.

Notes

1 A desktop survey revealed that 'character' is in early 2015 a consideration in planning decision-making in the ten most populous metropolitan areas in the USA and the five most populous in Canada, all eight Australian capital cities, the two largest cities in New Zealand, and in cities across the UK.
2 These local provisions can only become part of a planning scheme with the approval of the Victorian Government.

References

Alexander, C. (1979) *The Timeless Way of Building*, New York: Oxford University Press.

Alexander, C., S. Ishikawa and M. Silverstein (1977) *A Pattern Language: Towns, Buildings, Construction*, New York: Oxford University Press.

Banyule City Council (2012) *Neighbourhood Character Strategy*, available at www.banyule.vic.gov.au/Services/Planning/Housing/Neighbourhood-Character, accessed August 20, 2015.

Barker, R. (1968) *Ecological Psychology: Concepts and Methods for Studying the Environment of Human Behavior*, Stanford: Stanford University Press.

City of Boroondara (2011) *Boroondara Neighborhood Character Study: Stage 1 Consultation Report*, available at www.boroondara.vic.gov.au/your_council/building-planning/strategic-planning/plans/ncs, accessed August 20, 2015.

City of Greater Dandenong (2007) *Neighbourhood Character Study*, available at www.greaterdandenong.com/document/25295/dandenong-neighbourhood-character-study, accessed August 20, 2015.

Cooper, J. (2005) "Assessing Urban Character: The Use of Fractal Analysis of Street Edges," *Urban Morphology*, 9, 95–107.

Cullen, G. (1961) *Townscape*, London: Architectural Press.

Davidoff, P. (1965) "Advocacy and Pluralism in Planning," *Journal of the American Institute of Planners* 31, 331–33.

Davison, G. (2011) "An Unlikely Urban Symbiosis: Urban Intensification and Neighborhood Character in Collingwood, Vancouver," *Urban Policy and Research* 29, 105–24.

Davison, G. and Rowden, E. (2012) "There's Something about Subi: Defending and Creating Neighborhood Character in Perth, Australia," *Journal of Urban Design* 17, 189–212.

Davison, G., Dovey, K., and Woodcock, I. (2012) "Keeping Dalston Different: Defending Place-Identity in East London," *Planning Theory & Practice* 13, pp.47–69.

Dovey, K. (2010) *Becoming Places: Urbanism/Architecture/Identity/Power*, London: Routledge.

Dovey, K., Woodcock, I. and Wood, S. (2009) "A Test of Character: Regulating place-Identity in Inner-City Melbourne," *Urban Studies* 46, 2595–2615.

Fairclough, N. (2003) *Analysing Discourse: Textual Analysis for Social Research*, London: Routledge.

—— (1995) *Critical discourse analysis: the critical study of language*, New York: Longman.

Fairclough N and Wodak R (1997) "Critical Discourse Analysis: an Overview," in T. van Dijk (Ed.) *Discourse as Social Interaction*, London: Sage, 258–84.

Flyvbjerg, B. (2006) "Five misunderstandings about case-study research," *Qualitative inquiry* 12, 219–45.

Forester, J. (1999) *The deliberative practitioner: Encouraging participatory planning processes*, Cambridge: MIT Press.

Gehl, J. (2011) *Life between Buildings: Using Public Space*, Washington, DC: Island Press.

Gibson, J. (1986) *The Ecological Approach to Visual Perception*, New York: Psychology Press.

Healey, P. (1997) *Collaborative planning: shaping places in fragmented societies*, Basingstoke: Palgrave Macmillan.

—— (2006) *Collaborative Planning: Shaping Places in Fragmented Societies* (2nd edition), Basingstoke: Palgrave Macmillan.

Jacobs, J. (1961) *The Death and Life of Great American Cities*, New York: Vintage Books.

Kendig, L. (2010) *Community Character: Principles for Design and Planning*, Washington DC: Island Press.

—— (2012) *A Guide to Planning for Community Character*, Washington DC: Island Press.

Kropf, K. (1996) "Urban tissue and the character of towns," *Urban Design International* 1, 247–63.

Lang, J. (1994) *Urban Design: the American Experience*, New York: Wiley and Sons.

Larkham, P. (1996) *Conservation and the city*, London: Routledge.

Legacy, C. (2010) "Investigating the Knowledge Interface between Stakeholder Engagement and Plan-making," *Environment and Planning A* 42, 2705–2720.

Lewis, M. (1999) *Suburban Backlash: the Battle for the World's Most Livable City*, Hawthorn: Bloomings Books.

Norberg-Schulz, C. (1980) *Genius loci: Towards a Phenomenology of Architecture*, New York: Rizzoli.

Paulsen, K. (2004) "Making character concrete: empirical strategies for studying place distinction," *City & Community* 3, 243–262.

Rapoport, A. (1982) *The Meaning of the Built Environment*, Tuscon: University of Arizona Press.

Relph, E. (1976) *Place and Placelessness*, London: Pion.

—— (1993) "Modernity and the Reclamation of Place," in D. Seamon (Ed.) *Dwelling, Seeing and Designing: Toward a Phenomenological Ecology*, Albany: State University of New York, 25–40.

—— (1997) "Sense of Place," in S. Hanson (Ed.) *Ten Geographic Ideas that changed the world*, New Brunswick: Rutgers University Press, 205–226.

—— (2008) "A pragmatic sense of place," in F. Vanclay, M. Higgins and A. Blackshaw (Eds.) *Making Sense of Place: Exploring Concepts and Expressions of Place through Different Senses and Lenses*, Canberra: National Museum of Australia Press, 311–324.

Sandercock, L. (2003) *Cosmopolis II: Mongrel Cities in the 21st Century*, London: Continuum.

Seamon, D. and J. Sowers (2008) "Place and Placelessness," in P. Hubburd, R. Kitchin and G. Valentine (Eds.) *Key texts in human geography*, Los Angeles: Sage, 43–51

Steele, F. (1981) *The Sense of Place*, Boston: CBI.

van Dijk, T. (1993) "Principles of critical discourse analysis," *Discourse & Society* 4, 249–283.

—— (1997) "The study of discourse," in T. van Dijk (ed.), *Discourse as Structure and Process*, London: Sage, 1–34.

Victorian Government (2001a) *Understanding Neighborhood Character*, available at www.dtpli.vic.gov.au/__data/assets/pdf_file/0006/231648/Understanding_Neighbourhood_Character.pdf, accessed April 8, 2015.

—— (2001b) *New Housing Code to Protect Our Neighborhoods*, available at www.archive.today/34Lg#selection-8.0–103.46, accessed May 14, 2015.

—— (2002) *Melbourne 2032: Planning for Sustainable Growth*, available at www.dtpli.vic.gov.au/planning/plans-and-policies/planning-for-melbourne/melbournes-strategic-planning-history/melbourne-2030-planning-for-sustainable-growth, accessed August 20, 2015.

—— (2004) Using the Neighbourhood Character Provisions in Planning Schemes, available at www.dtpli.vic.gov.au/__data/assets/pdf_file/0018/231660/PPN28-Using-the-neighbourhood-character-provisions.pdf, accessed April 8, 2015.

Victorian Planning Provisions (no date) Planning Schemes Online, available at www.planningschemes.dpcd.vic.gov.au/schemes/vpps, accessed April 8, 2015.

Whyte, W. (1980) *The Social Life of Small Urban Spaces*, Washington DC: Conservation Foundation.

Wodak, R. (2004) "Critical Discourse Analysis," in C. Seale, G. Gobo, J. Gubrium and D. Silverman (Eds.) *Qualitative Research Practice*, London: Sage, 186–202.

Part 2
Place/lessness in Experience

6 Insideness in an Age of Mobilities

John Tomaney

Introduction

'Insideness' is a key concept in the analytical repertoire, developed by Edward Relph to understand place and placelessness: "To be inside a place is to belong to it and to identify with it, and the more profoundly inside you are the stronger is this identity with the place" (Relph 2008: 49). Place is formed as a result of the spatial concentration of human intentions, experiences, and actions. The various forms of insideness defined by Relph speak of a deepening sense of belonging to place: "Those aspects of space that we distinguish as places are differentiated because they have attracted and concentrated our intentions, and because of this focusing they are set apart from the surrounding space while remaining part of it" (Relph 2008: 28). The deepest forms of place attachment are expressed through *behavioral* insideness, which reflects a profound appreciation of the significance of a particular place and its identity, and *existential* insideness, which expresses an implicit knowledge that this is the place to which you belong. The communal dimensions of place identities are produced inter-subjectively. These forms of insideness provide a basis for engagement with the world: "To have roots in place is to have a secure point from which to look out on the world, a firm grasp of one's own position in the order of things, and a significant spiritual and psychological attachment to somewhere in particular" (Relph 2008: 38). A person who is alienated or separated from place experiences 'outsideness.'

In this chapter I review some of these contributions with the aim of challenging the suggestion that insideness is necessarily problematic and has disappeared. The chapter highlights a body of work that evidences the persistence of local attachments in the global era, although its nature may be being transformed. I pay particular attention to the historical and political dimensions of belonging, before concluding that insideness persists as part of the human condition even alongside the growth of cosmopolitan values.

The erosion of insideness is critical to the emergence of placelessness, as defined by Relph. Writing in the preface to the 2008 reprint of *Place and Placelessness*, he states that "rootedness in one place which was still common in the 1960s, has almost everywhere been substituted by a celebration of mobility" (Relph 2008: np). This is a challenge for such disciplines as human geography and planning, for which place is such a central concept and for human life itself, because belonging to place is central to personal identity. Relph recalls the relatively closed Welsh villages of his youth, now opened up by motorways extending and multiplying the places available for people to live: "place is now for many people a matter of choice rather than necessity" (Relph 2008: np). Moreover, modes of mass communication and big business transmit "generalized and standardized fashions and tastes" (Relph 2008: 92) that accelerate the trend to placelessness. Presented here is a pessimistic view of the prospects for place, which is being replaced by 'flatscapes,' lacking depth and significance in terms of intentions and experience.

Relph's notion of insideness has been subject to criticism insofar as it has been interpreted as a defense of the cultural and psychological value of local identity. Like Relph, contemporary cosmopolitan critics see social, cultural, and economic trends as leading to the eradication of the local, but this development is presented as a welcome one. In the cosmopolitan account, places are understood as open and discontinuous spaces, consti- tuted by material, discursive, and symbolic forms stretched across local- ities and regions. A topological understanding replaces a topographical approach to space. Places are defined by their momentary place in global networks and by their relationship within and beyond predefined territorial boundaries. Regions are "unbound" (Amin 2004), characterized by "thrown- togetherness" (Massey 2005), "regional assemblages" or "multi-actor topo- logical geometry" (Allen and Cochrane 2007) in which places are produced by relational processes, and "rhizomatic networks" (Painter 2008), "an im- broglio of heterogeneous and more or less expansive hybrids" (Thrift 1999: 317), or even superseded by "site-based ontologies" (Marston et al. 2005). The notion of stable places is viewed as a kind of modernist fetish reflecting the influence of Cartesian notions of bounded totalities that are essential to Western social science and find their expression in the 'cartographic anxiety' and reflecting a need to essentialize local culture.

The assumption here is that local attachments—insideness—are inherently exclusionary. Massey (2006: 35) claims to have "problematized the notion of local belonging," preferring to understand places in terms of their inherent openness and lack of identity. In the face of such processes, Amin advocates a "heterotopic sense of place" that "assumes no local cultural or economic coherence" (Amin 2004: 40). In this view, local cultural attachments under- pin "a politics of local regard and local defense" and "a conservationist regional identity that can be profoundly closed and exclusionary" (Amin 2004: 37, 35). In this perspective, the death of the local is welcomed.

Both Relph and the new cosmopolitans identify the diminishing im- portance of place attachment and identity, although they draw different political and existential conclusions from this development. Yet there is cause to qualify this interpretation of place. Recent work across a range of disciplines, including philosophy, human geography, history, political science, psychology, sociology, and planning, draws our attention to the persistence of insideness even in the context of growing mobility.

Belonging

More recent empirical research suggests local attachments remain crucial in human life as people seek a way of 'being at home' in an unstable world, although the way we belong may have changed (Savage et al. 2005). This viewpoint avers "the reification of uprootedness" (Fortier 1999: 42). Belonging arises from the practical matter of physical involvement in our environment and of "being-in-the-world" (Easthope 2009: 73), and the embodied nature of our dispositions and the necessity of their territorial location (Savage et al. 2005). Belonging connotes simultaneously feeling 'at home' and 'feeling safe.' A sense of local belonging can be expressed individually or collectively. Belonging can be attached to narratives of identity, but it may reflect also practical commitments, investments and yearnings. Moreover, the construction of place identities and terrains of belonging are juxtaposed; expressions of local belonging may embody a performative dimension that links individual and collective behavior and contributes to the formation of narratives of identity and the realization of attachments. However, belonging is formed in an intersectional context, along multiple, mutually constitutive axes of difference, of which geography is only one (Crenshaw 1989; Bourdieu 1992; Yuval-Davis 2006). Place, nevertheless, remains implicated in the formation of belonging in both its affective and political dimensions (Antonsich 2010).

The emotional dimensions of belonging are linked to the politics of belonging, but in complex and uneven ways, and concern questions about definitions of who belongs. For Pollini (2007), socio-territorial belonging arises from mutually constitutive relationships of attachment, loyalty, solidarity, and sense of affinity, which frame the processes by which a person becomes included in a socio-territorial collective and identified with it. Questions of political and social citizenship are the most prominent manifestations of the politics of belonging in the era of the nation state, especially in the face of transformations wrought by mass migration, insurgent territorial identities, and destabilizing material and cultural flows (Guibernau 2013). Geographers have shown interest in how questions of territorial belonging connect with (national) citizenship (e.g. Staehli 2011; Bauder 2014), but explorations of *local* attachment and belonging remain comparatively rare.

Mee and Wright (2009: 772) contend that belonging is an "inherently geographical concept" that connects to matters of place through modes of boundary making, while Stratford (2009) suggests that notions of belonging are intimately interwoven with symbolic and material spatialities. Yet it might be argued that contemporary geographers have shown a paradoxical lack of concern with the phenomenon of local belonging. Marco Antonsich

(2010: 645), reflecting on the absence of a discussion of the topic in a major review of the subject, contends that "belonging has no place in geography." A discussion of place attachment, as part of a recent major review of the future of identity by the UK government, drew on the work of sociologists and psychologists but paid no attention to the work of geographers (Government Office for Science 2013). More recently though, a concern with the nature, contradictions, problems, and possibilities of local belonging can be discerned in a range of geographical research and geographically inspired work in sociology, psychology, anthropology, and linguistics.

Savage et al. (2005: 53) introduce the notion of "elective belonging," referring to how people select places to live before putting down roots in order to "be at home" in a fluid world—a development that Relph saw as incipient in the 1970s. This approach rescues local belonging from the exaggerated claims of its demise in an age of mobility but, at the same time, contrasts with the tradition of 'community studies' that emerged in the UK in the 1950s and 1960s, where the emphasis was on the presence of kith and kin and length of residence as the main determinants of local belonging. For Savage et al. (2005: 29), places become "sites for performing identities" where people "attach their own biographies to their 'chosen' residential location." This choice is devoid of nostalgia and determined mainly by aesthetic and ethical criteria. It is detached from a sense of communal roots, makes no historical claims, and is mainly open to the mobile middle class.

Easthope's (2009) study of young people who left and then returned to Tasmania, Australia shows how her informants drew simultaneously upon notions of fluid, mobile identities *and* identities informed by place attachment. Wessendorf's (2010) study of place attachment among second generation Italian immigrants to Switzerland shows, typically, they are socialized into a co-ethnic diaspora but also express strong attachment to the city in which they grow up, despite—or perhaps because of—their parents' dreams of return. Christensen and Jensen (2011) provide somewhat similar evidence from their study of Aalborg, where new migrants were more likely to state a sense of belonging to the city rather than to Denmark. Inglis and Donnelly (2011) analyze data from the International Social Survey Project and other evidence to shed light on the fate of local and national belonging during the rise and fall of the Celtic Tiger in Ireland, a period of rapid economic growth, social change, increased mobility and urban and regional transformation. They find that place attachments to both county and nation remain strong and in some cases may have been strengthened, especially among the middle class. Indeed, it was those most likely to express cosmopolitan values who also expressed the strongest local attachments.

Drawing on a survey of socio-territorial belonging in Lombardy, Trentino-Alto Adige, Veneto, Friuli-Venezia Giulia, Emilia Romagna and Sardinia, Pollini (2007) finds belonging and attachment expressed at various spatial scales. Strong local attachments exist alongside expressions of cosmopolitan values and increased mobility, giving birth to multiple local attachments rather than a single cosmopolitan outlook (see also Gustafson 2014). The expression of cosmopolitan values, however, may have limited impacts on local practices. Davison et al.'s (2012) study of middle class defenders of 'authentic' place-identity in the Dalston district of Hackney leads them to question whether those who espouse the cosmopolitan character of their locality have much familiarity with their neighbors. These findings echo somewhat Savage et al.'s (2005) claim that middle class people expressing elective belonging, while voicing a theoretical commitment to cosmopolitan values, rarely act upon these in a deep way. Insideness and outsideness operate here less as a binary, or even as a continuum, but rather as mutually constitutive.

Fortier (1999) studied the evolution of the London Italian migrant community centered on St Peter's Catholic Church in Clerkenwell, once the heart of London's Little Italy, which, by the end of the 20th century, acted as a place of "re-membering" for a more dispersed community, notably through its annual festival of Our Lady of Mount Carmel. Settlements and rootings in Clerkenwell are "articulated with *multi-local terrains of belonging*" (Fortier 1999: 41; emphasis added). Suzanne Hall (2013: 50) understands belonging in a more mobile age as a "composition with gravity, with a loose collection of proliferated pods attached to and deeply affected by particular contexts." Individuals are not detached from *a* local world, but may instead belong—and even commit—in several local worlds (Gallent 2007). In short, we might comprehend "a plurality of forms of belonging, differently imbricated in space and variously constituted in relation to the permeability of their boundaries" (Antonsich 2010: 653). Yarker (2014: 166) conceives of contemporary belonging in Byker, a disadvantaged inner-city district of Newcastle upon Tyne, by adapting David Harvey's notion of "conditional permanances," which unfold within the materiality of every-day life in place. Commitments to place are real and important but always retain a provisional character: place attachments are deeply felt but fragile (Savage 2010; Yarker 2014).

Heightened rates of mobility, however, may alter the scale at which we express belonging (Gustafson 2014). Pollini (2007) observes a gradual increase in the territorial scale at which attachments are expressed. This finding is echoed in the work of Savage et al. (2005), which reports evidence of local belonging among mainly middle-class respondents in Greater Manchester who sought a distinctive location in the north of England to which to belong. It was a broadly defined regional—rather than local or national—scale to which they expressed belonging, reflecting kinship and emotional ties. This may amount to a more realistic assessment of the way increased mobility impacts on a sense of local belonging rather than seeing it being dissolved by increased migration and intensified material and sym-bolic flows. A further reflection on the paradoxical contribution of mobility to local belonging is offered by Johnstone (2010) from the perspective of linguistics. She explores the construction of the "Pittsburghese" dialect, noting that "a great deal of the work of locality production is done online, in email, through websites and blogs. This is because *many of the people who do the locality producing work about Pittsburgh and Pittsburghers do not live in Pittsburgh*" (Johnstone 2010: 400; emphasis added).

The multi-cultural (global) city is typically seen as the most likely location for the emergence of placeless forms of belonging, as in Massey's (1991: 321) account of Kilburn (in inner north-west London) with its outward looking "chaotic mix" of coexisting cultures, which is contrasted to the "stable and homogenous" archetypical mining village. Recent work has investigated in more detail how belonging works in 'super-diverse' communities. Wessendorf's (2014) ethnographic study of the London Borough of Hackney examines how relationships work in the public realm, in parochial (semi-public) settings and in private. In the public realm, a type of careful civility operates, whereby people are treated universally and (ethnic) differences ignored, while in the parochial context differences may be acknowledged and addressed. Significantly, though, the private realm remains largely closed to processes of mixing. Far from being a simple picture of fluidity and mix, conviviality in the public realm can be a means of avoiding deeper contact and engagement and reflect a lack of real interest in other lives. In this respect, "a global sense of place" does not necessarily signify the wide acceptance of cosmopolitan values (Davadson 2010). Bonnett (2010: 120) identifies the possibility of "multiple reactionary essentialisms," along with problems of loss and isolation, in places like Kilburn, but in Wessendorf's account relationships in Hackney work reasonably well and are not inherently problematic.

Noble's (2011: 167) observations of everyday practices in the context of the Sydney federal electorate of Bennelong, which comprises multi-cultural inner suburbs, reveal a playful sense of belonging that is "ironic and self-aware of its own limitations" and rarely founded on reductive and exclusionary binaries. Here, migrants invest deeply in local space and "connect their biographies with wider narratives of belonging and place, making themselves 'at home' in the process." They achieve this state by embedding their own 'ethnic' practices in existing rituals of place-making, which are themselves transformed in the process. This insight finds an echo in Lobo's (2010) account of belonging in Dandenong, an outer Melbourne suburb, where quotidian acts of care are the means by which new immigrants form and maintain strong emotional attachments to the place. Noble (2011: 167) concludes: "cosmopolitanism is often seen to entail an abandonment of a strong claim to local and national belonging. This, however, does not do justice to the complex forms of attachment found in contemporary Australia."

It was noted earlier that Savage et al. (2005) emphasize how their respondents expressed sense of belonging to the English 'north,' although the nature of its emotional pull and the sense in which it is distinguished from London (the 'cosmopolitan' proximate) remains largely unexplored. Questions of local and regional belonging assume a collective dimension when they are linked to narratives of regional identity. Vainikka's (2012: 591) research among Finnish social movements leads him to conclude that regional identities are discursive constructs that express "as an awareness of and attachments to everyday surroundings." Moreover, "symbolic land-scapes that root people in distinct space are important mediators of collective regional identities" (Vainikka 2012: 595). Unquestionably, such narratives are mutable and selective. In her study of the Finnish–Swedish border region, Prokkola (2009) maintains that, in the context of shifting geopolitics, each generation forms its own collective narratives through which individual identities are negotiated. One form in which regional narratives are given expression—and which, in turn, may contribute to a local sense of belonging—are literary and artistic activities. Prokkola and Ridanpää (2011) show how the novels of Bengt Pohjanen have contributed to the emergence of the region of Meänmaa that straddles the Finnish–Swedish border and which has become the focus for a sense of belonging. Literary forms can be the means for expressing an ironic sense of belonging that play with ideas of otherness and roots, such as Mikael Niemi's novels set in the Swedish region of Tornedalen (Ridanpää 2014). Literary and artistic expression of belonging can play a key role in the assertion of regional identities, but not necessarily in essentialist forms (see Tomaney 2010a).

Vall's (2011) history of the construction of North-East England as a 'cultural region,' among many other things, shows how the resurgence of 'regional' poetry—focused on the iconic Morden Tower venue and engendered by the publication of Basil Bunting's epic *Briggflatts*—placed the region at the heart of global cultural networks (see also Tomaney 2007). A similar trajectory is identified by Neate (2012) in her study of the Midland Group of artists in 1960s Nottingham, while Rycroft and Jenness (2012: 959) show how J.B Priestley's roots in Edwardian Bradford informed his project of "provincializing" the (London) metropole, most obviously in his book *English Journey* (1934).

In sum, recent research on local belonging emphasizes that, far from being effaced, it continues to matter to most people; that it can have individual and collective dimensions; that the notion of binary oppositions of cosmo-politan outlook versus local attachments is unhelpful, but that scales at which we belong may be multiple and changing. Savage (2010) identifies two dominant narratives of belonging, one founded on 'nostalgia' and another having an 'elective' character, which are imbricated with class relations and can be conceived as opposites, but are more likely to be in tension in particular localities.

History

Insideness, as a quality with depth, highlights the importance of historical awareness in the making of place. The role and use of history in local belonging are subject to competing claims in academic debates. It was noted above that some discussions of belonging offer an understanding that repudiates the importance of communal roots in that place and the claims of history in shaping local attachment (e.g. Savage et al. 2005). However, it is unclear whether this is always and everywhere the case. Lewicka (2014), drawing on psychological understandings of memory and on survey evidence from Poland and Ukraine, suggests a conscious engagement with the past is one means by which mobile people achieve a sense of local belonging. Personal knowledge of one's genealogical and autobiographical past is a component of personal integrity. Lewicka found a strong correlation between a declared interest in place history and a sense of place. Fortier (1999: 59, emphasis added) contends that St Peter's, Clerkenwell, is *"a place of collective memory, in which elements of the past are cobbled together to mould a communal sense of belonging."* Histories and traditions contribute to the gravitational pull of place, but vernacular practices may connect rather than inhibit relationships between the local and the global (Hall 2013).

Massey (1995) approaches the question from another perspective. She objects to arguments that assign a historical identity to local communities, which are then drawn upon in narratives of belonging. Such claims, in Massey's (1995: 183) view, presuppose an assumed identity of a place and its history; because such claims rest on "a deeply essentialist and internalist way of thinking about a place and its character." For Massey, this is exemplified in the defensive politics of white working-class communities in such places as London Docklands, where the use of history "leads to the invention of the coherence of a place" (Massey 1995: 184).

Drawing on a detailed study of census reports and naturalization records, Tabili (2011) shows how the growth of South Shields, an industrial town in the north-east of England, involved far higher rates of migration, including out and return migration, belying the categorization of such places as parochial and culturally homogenous. South Shields attracted migrants from all over northern Europe, and was home to the UK's first settled 'Arab' community. South Shields has a cosmopolitan history. While scholarship in cities such as Cardiff and Liverpool has highlighted the emergence of ethnic enclaves there, Tabili's research shows how widely and quickly migrant communities were integrated into the wider population in South Shields through work, marriage, and civic participation. Migrants encountered not simply tolerance or coexistence, but experienced mutual cultural accommodation and were afforded status in the local community. Fluid, open, and internationalized local social relations existed alongside the formation of a strong civic identity.

Of course, this is not to deny the existence of discrimination and exclusion. Tabili (2011) pays particular attention, for instance, to the attacks on long-established German butcher shops during the First World War following the sinking of the steamship Lusitania in 1915. Such attacks, however, occurred in many cities in the UK, notably London. For Tabili, such episodes cannot be explained by factors endogenous to local relations, but must be understood in the context of a wider geopolitics in which state and media vilification of "enemy aliens" played an important part.

Massey's stereotyping of "stable and homogenous" mining communities is also worth further examination. Consider the pit villages of County Durham in north-east England. The early histories of such communities demonstrate neither stability nor homogeneity. The rapid growth of the coalfield in the second half of the 19th century generated massive in-migration. A significant proportion of these migrants were Irish Catholics. Early waves of such migrants included large numbers of strike-breakers, and their arrival was on occasion accompanied by rioting. They suffered discrimination in labor and housing markets and, in some cases, lived in ethnic enclaves, even in small villages. The Catholic Church asserted its authority over these nascent communities through the building of churches and schools, and enforced social separation through canonical restrictions on exogamy. Yet within a couple of generations, Catholics had begun to rise in civic and political life, making advances in the workplace, trade unions and local government (Lavery 1917; Moore 1974; Duffy 1997; Lee 2007). Here, the 'coherence' of the community is not so much an 'invention' in Massey's terms, but instead a (fragile and imperfect) social achievement, subsequently undermined by programs of political dispossession as well as by structural economic changes The Welsh villages recalled by Relph (2008: np), where "outsiders were few" and looked upon with suspicion, in all likelihood contained a history of movement as well as stability.

Politics

For Massey, the claims of local history lend themselves to a political narrative of nostalgia "where the only real form of change resides in the tragedy of loss" (1995: 190). But Bonnett (2010) warns against the conflation of nostalgia with conservatism and the associated hostility to signs of yearning and loss. While the 'dark side' of belonging is a frequently evoked trope, there are ways in which a sense of belonging provides vital resources for living. McKenzie's (2012) ethnographic study of the disadvantaged and stigmatized multi-ethnic inner-city community of St Anne's in inner Nottingham shows a place rich with networks and a strong sense of belonging that provides highly localized use-values to residents, but with little external exchange value. Mah's (2010) ethnography of the former industrial community of Walker, a white working-class community in Newcastle upon Tyne, identifies a complex collective memory linked to a now vanished 'industrial atmosphere' that continues to shape the character of the community and contributes a valuable sense of social solidarity (see also Mah 2009). Stratford (2009) explores the mobilization of belonging as a political 'resource' in the conflicts surrounding proposed developments in Ralphs Bay, Tasmania. For Stratford, claims to belong are made in order to secure participatory space in debates about the future of the place in the face of corporate strategies founded on "the aggressive assumption that whatever belonged before has little value" (2009: 801). Devine-Wright's (2014) work draws attention to the way that concerns with procedural and distributional justice, expressed through local attachments and identities, underlie the objections raised by residents to large-scale energy projects such as wind farms, casting new light on NIMBY politics.

I have argued elsewhere in defense of 'parochialism' (Tomaney 2013). A concern with parish (the local) and its cultures and its solidarities provides a moral starting point and a locus of ecological concern for people. This is evidenced in art, literature, and poetry, which is frequently concerned with delving into the particular as a means of exploring universal human questions. The local is an aperture onto the global. Politically and culturally, it can have both progressive and regressive implications. Local identities, therefore, should be understood contextually; there is no necessary relation between local forms of identity and practices of exclusion. The denigration of the local contains its own political dangers.

Wills (2013: 137) observes the lack of attention paid to the connections between place and politics and the ways in which "local politics is generally viewed with suspicion as a product of sentimental nostalgic identification, exclusionary communitarianism and/or hostility to outsiders." But her work on the growth of the London Citizens movement shows that this is a partial interpretation at best. Here, locally organized faith, educational, and trade union organizations have built, from the bottom up, regional and national networks and in the process have "created a super-ordinate identity category that links them together" (Wills 2013: 144). Territory—including the local—remains critical to shaping geographical imaginations and political practice. This point carries much weight in contemporary European politics.

The rise of 'small nationalisms' in such places as Flanders, Catalonia, and Scotland attest to the continuing power of the claims of place, albeit at a scale beyond the village. According to Guibernau (2013), regionalist and small nationalist claims are contemporary manifestations of age-old human yearning to share things in common in order to overcome individual isolation and feelings of ontological insecurity. We can see this as a dimension of the refashioning of insideness for a more mobile age. The mass media—seen as a threat to the integrity of place in Relph's earlier work—play a critical role in the promotion of 'imagined communities' at the urban and regional scale: "I ♥ NY."

Conclusion

Recent research suggests that insideness remains a feature of the human condition in an age of mobilities. Indeed, its importance may well be increasing as individuals are confronted with intensifying and destabilizing material and cultural flows. Place remains an important field for the production of culture and materiality and the construction of discursive boundaries, while forms of territorial attachment remain an important part of the human experience with a wide range of cultural and political implications.

References

Allen, J. and A. Cochrane (2007) "Beyond the Territorial Fix: Regional Assemblages, Politics and Power," *Regional Studies* 41: 1161–1151.

Amin, A. (2004) "Regions Unbound: Towards a New Politics of Place," *Geografiska Annaler* 86B: 33–44.

Antonsich, M. (2010) "Searching for Belonging," *Geography Compass* 4/5: 644–59.

Bauder, H. (2014) "Domicile Citizenship, Human Mobility and Territoriality," *Progress in Human Geography* 38: 91–106.

Bonnett, A. (2010) *Left in the Past*, London: Continuum.

Bourdieu, P. (1992) *Language and Symbolic Power*, G Raymond and M Adamson (trans.), Cambridge, MA: Harvard University Press.

Christensen, A-D. and S.Q. Jensen (2011) "Roots and Routes: Migration, Belonging and Everyday Life," *Nordic Journal of Migration Research* 1: 146–155.

Crenshaw, K. (1989) *Demarginalizing the Intersection of Race and Sex*, Chicago: Chicago University Press.

Davadson, R. (2010) "Cosmopolitanism, Geographical Imaginaries and Belonging in North London," *Urban Studies* 47: 2945–2953.

Davison, G., K. Dovey and I. Woodcock (2012) " 'Keeping Dalston Different': Defending Place-Identity in East London," *Planning Theory and Practice* 31: 47–69.

Devine-Wright, P. (2014) "Dynamics of Place Attachment in Acclimate Changed World," in L.C. Manzo and P. Devine-Wright (Eds.) *Place Attachment: Advances in Theory, Methods and Applications*, London: Routledge, 165–177.

Duffy, G. (1997) "County Monaghan Immigrants in the Consett Area of County Durham, England, 1842–1885,' *Clogher Record* 16, 37–45.

Easthope, H. (2009) "Fixed Identities in a Mobile World? The Relationship Between Mobility, Place and Identity," *Identities: Global Studies in Culture and Power* 16, 61–82.

Fortier, A-M. (1999) "Re-Membering Places and the Performance of Belonging(s)," *Theory, Culture and Society* 16, 41–64.

Gallent, N. (2007) "Second homes, community and hierarchy of dwelling," *Area* 39, 97–106.

Government Office for Science (2013) *Foresight Future Identities. Final Project Report*, London: Government Office for Science.

Guibernau, M. (2013) *Belonging*. Cambridge: Polity.

Gustafson, P. (2014) "Place Attachment in the Age of Mobility," in L.C. Manzo and P. Devine-Wright (Eds.) *Place Attachment: Advances in Theory, Methods and Applications*, London: Routledge, 37–48.

Hall, S. (2013) "The Politics of Belonging," *Identities: Global Studies in Culture and Power* 20, 46–53.

Inglis, T. and S. Donnelly (2011) "Local and National Belonging in a Globalized World," *Irish Journal of Sociology* 19, 126–42.

Johnstone, B. (2010) "Indexing the Local," in N. Coupland (Ed.) *The Handbook of Language and Globalization*, Chichester: Wiley-Blackwell, 386–405.

Lavery, F. (1917) (Ed.) *Irish Heroes in the War*, London: Everett & Co.

Lee, R. (2007) *The Church of England and the Durham Coalfield, 1810–1926: Clergymen, Capitalists and Colliers*, Woodbridge: Boydell Press.

Lewicka, M. (2014) "In Search of Roots: Memory as an Enable of Place Attachment," in L.C. Manzo and P Devine-Wright (Eds.) *Place Attachment: Advances in Theory, Methods and Applications*, London: Routledge, 49–60.

Lobo, M. (2010) "Interethnic Understanding and Belonging in Suburban Melbourne," *Urban Policy and Research* 28, 85–99.

Mah, A. (2009) "Devastation but also Home: Place Attachment in Areas of Industrial Decline," *Home Cultures* 6, 287–310.

Mah, A. (2010) "Memory, uncertainty and industrial ruination: Walker Riverside, Newcastle upon Tyne," International Journal of Urban and Regional Research, 34(2), 398-413

Manzo, L.C. and P. Devine-Wright (Eds.) *Place Attachment. Advances in Theory, Methods and Applications*. London: Routledge.

Marston S.A., J.P. Jones III and K. Woodward (2005) "Human Geography Without Scale," *Transactions of the Institute of British Geographers* 30, 416–432.

Massey, D. (1991) "A Global Sense of Place," *Marxism Today*, June, 24–29.

—— (1995) "Places and Their Pasts," *History Workshop Journal* 39, 182–193

—— (2005) *For Space*, London: SAGE.

—— (2006) "Landscape as a Provocation: Reflections on Moving Mountains," *Journal of Material Culture* 11, 33–48.

McKenzie, L. (2012) "A Narrative from the Inside, Studying St Anns in Nottingham: Belonging, Continuity and Change," *The Sociological Review* 60, 457–475.

Mee, K. and S. Wright (2009) "Geographies of Belonging," *Environment and Planning A* 41, 772–779.

Moore, R. (1974) *Pit-men, Preachers and Politics: The Effects of Methodism in a Durham Mining Community*, Cambridge: University Press.

Neate, N. (2012) "Provinciality and the Art World: the Midland Group 1961–1977," *Social and Cultural Geography* 13, 275–294.

Noble, G. (2011) "Belonging in Bennelong: Ironic Inclusion and Cosmopolitan Joy in John Howard's (former) Electorate," in K. Jacobs and J. Malpas (Eds.) *Ocean to Outlook. Cosmopolitanism in Contemporary Australia*, Perth: University of Western Australia Press, 150–175.

Painter, J. (2008) "Cartographic Anxiety and the Search for Regionality," *Environment and Planning A* 40, 342–361.

Pollini, G. (2007) "Elements of Theory of Place Attachment and Socio-Territorial Belonging," *International Review of Sociology* 15, 497–515.

Prokkola, E-K. (2009) "Unfixing Borderland Identity: Border Performances and Narratives in the Construction of Self," *Journal of Borderlands Studies* 24, 21–38.

Prokkola, E-K. and R. Ridanpää (2011) "Following the Plot of Bengt Pohjanen's Meänmaa: Narrativization as a Process of Creating Regional Identity," *Social and Cultural Geography* 12, 775–791.

Relph, E. (2008) *Place and Placelessness*, (Reprinted Edition) London: Pion.

Ridanpää, J. (2014) "Politics of Literary Humor and Contested Narrative Identity (of a Region with no Identity)," *Cultural Geographies* online first publication, 3 March 2014.

Rycroft, S. and S. Jenness (2012) "J.B. Priestley: Bradford and a Provincial Narrative of England, 1913–1933," *Social and Cultural Geography* 13, 957–976.

Savage, M. (2010) *Identities and Social Change in Britain since 1940: The Politics of Method*, Oxford: Oxford University Press.

Savage, M., G. Bagnall and B. Longhurst (2005) *Globalization and Belonging*, London: Sage.

Staeheli, L. (2011) "Political Geography: Where's Citizenship?," *Political Geography* 35 (3), 393–400.

Stratford, E. (2009) "Belonging as a Resource: the Case of Ralphs Bay, Tasmania and the Politics of Place," *Environment and Planning A* 41, 796–810.

Tabili, L. (2011) *Global Migrants, Local Culture. Natives and Newcomers in Provincial England, 1841–1939*, Basingstoke: Macmillan.

Thrift, N. (1999) "Steps Toward an Ecology of Place," in D. Massey, J. Allen and P. Sarre (Eds.) *Human Geography Today*, Cambridge: Polity Press, 295–322.

Tomaney, J. (2007) "Keeping a Beat in the Dark: Narratives of Regional Identity in Basil Bunting's Briggflatts," *Environment and Planning D: Society and Space* 25, 355–375.

—— (2010a) "Parish and Universe: the Local Poetics of Patrick Kavanagh," *Environment and Planning D: Society and Space* 28, 311–325.

—— (2010b) "Eurocentric Social Science and the Chinese Region," *Asian Journal of Political Science* 18, 3–19.

—— (2013) "Parochialism: a Defense," *Progress in Human Geography* 37, 658–672.

Vainikka, J. (2012) "Narrative Claims on Regions: Prospecting for Spatial Identities among Social Movements in Finland," *Social and Cultural Geography* 13, 587–605.

Vall, N. (2011) *Cultural Region North East England, 1945–2000*, Manchester: Manchester University Press.

Wessendorf, S. (2010) "Local Attachments and Transnational Everyday Lives: Second-Generation Italians in Switzerland," *Global Networks* 10, 365–82.

Wessendorf, S. (2014) " 'Being Open, but Sometimes Closed': Conviviality in a Super-Diverse London Neighborhood," *European Journal of Cultural Studies* 17, 392–405.

Wills, J. (2013) "Place and Politics," in D. Featherstone and J. Painter (Eds.) *Spatial politics: Essays for Doreen Massey*, Oxford: Wiley-Blackwell, 135–145.

Yarker, S. (2014) Belonging in Byker: The Nature of Local Belonging and Attachment in Contemporary Cities. PhD Thesis, University of Newcastle upon Tyne, Newcastle upon Tyne.

Yuval-Davis, N. (2006) "Belonging and the Politics of Belonging," *Patterns of Prejudice* 40, 197–214.

7   Losing Control at Home?

Hazel Easthope

Introduction

There has been much academic discussion over the past 20 years about the extent to which people are able to feel attachment to place in an increasingly globalized and mobile world. Rapid globalization, technological advances, and the resulting hybrid nature of place experiences have been identified as factors leading to "disembedding" (Giddens 1991); described by Stones (2012: 449) as "the way in which contemporary social practices can no longer be primarily defined by the grounding, or embeddedness, in the local context of a restricted place and time." However, as Relph notes in his introductory chapter to this book, such disembedding has been accompanied by a "re-embedding," or "selecting a place to live, and then investing something of yourself in it."

These arguments build upon earlier discussions on the impact of globalization on place attachment. In the mid-1990s Harvey (1996: 246) observed that notions of places as bound, settled, and coherent communities are threatened by globalization and that this "has provoked both an increasing sense of exclusionary nationalism and localism, and an exhilarating sense of heterogeneity and porosity of cultures," while Massey (1995: 48) argued that precisely because people live in "an increasingly unstable and uncertain world" they have a desire to hold on to notions of place as secure and stable.

Thus, even in the face of massive social change the human desire to belong, and to feel a sense of attachment to place, remains strong. In this chapter, I focus on a topic that is fundamental to the everyday wellbeing of people—their relationships with the dwellings in which they live. My focus is on the extent to which people are able to feel attached to their dwellings and consider them to be home.

The extent to which a person identifies with their dwelling as a home is influenced not only by the relationship between person and dwelling, but also by the culture to which they belong. As Relph (1976: 57) notes, "individual images of a place are constantly socialized through common language, symbols and experiences." Cultural shifts in the way in which particular places and groups of places are understood therefore have the potential to influence the relationships that people have with the important places in their lives.

In this chapter I argue that two significant changes in housing patterns have impacted on the ability of people to become attached to, and identify with, their dwelling because of tensions between these ways of living and dominant cultural representations of the dwelling as home. Exemplified in Australian urban housing markets, these changes are an increase in multi-unit property ownership and an increase in long-term private renting[1]. At the same time I show how these phenomena need not *necessarily* result in people feeling less attached to their dwellings if dominant social norms and constructs of the dwelling as home, and home ownership in particular, are challenged.

This chapter begins with a brief introduction to academic literature on the dwelling as home, and relates this to Relph's discussion of what it means to be an insider in a place. An argument is made that the degree to which people can feel like an insider is influenced by the power they have to remain in a place and become involved with it. This is followed by an exploration of the connection between control over one's dwelling and feeling 'at home.' The link between control and property ownership in Anglophone countries is discussed, as is the influence of social norms and accompanying laws and regulations on the right to control property. The next section introduces the Australian case as a means to further explore these issues. Dominant social norms regarding the home in Australia, based on both physical (the detached house) and legal (owner-occupation) ideals are discussed before significant challenges to these assumptions are introduced. These challenges are the rise in long-term private renters and increasing numbers of people living in apartments. The final section discusses the potential for social change in regards to people's relationships with their dwellings.

Home

Some places hold considerable social, psychological, and emotive meanings for people. The places of greatest personal significance are often referred to as 'home.' In many cases, people consider the place in which they live to be home. As Relph (1976: 43, emphasis added) notes:

> There is for virtually everyone a deep association with and conscious-ness of the places where we were born and grew up, *where we live now*, or where we have had particularly moving experiences. This association seems to constitute a vital source of both individual and cultural identity and security, a point of departure from which we orient ourselves in the world.

The link between one's dwelling place and one's wellbeing and identity has long been recognized by housing researchers, architects, and planners (e.g. Saunders and Williams 1988; Giuliani 1991; Somerville 1997; Mallett 2004; Clapham 2010). This link finds theoretical explanation through the concept of place, and an understanding of home as a special type of place:

> Home in its most profound form is an attachment to a particular setting, a particular environment, in comparison with which all other associations with places have only limited significance. It is the point of departure from which we orient ourselves and take possession of the world
>
> (Relph 1976: 40)

However, all properties in which people live are not necessarily experienced as homes, and it is important here to distinguish between home and house. It is the way in which we inhabit a space (a dwelling) that makes it a home:

> Home . . . is a collection of milieus, and as such is the organization of markers (objects) and the formation of space. But home, more than this, is a territory, an expression. Home can be a collection of objects, furniture, and so on that one carries with one from move to move . . . The markers of home, however, are not simply inanimate objects (a place with stuff), but the presence, habits and effects of spouses, children, parents, and companions. One can be at home simply in the presence of a significant other. What makes home-territories different from other territories is on the one hand the living of the territory (a temporalization of the space) and on the other their connection with identity, or rather a process of identification, of articulation or affect. Homes, we feel, are ours.
>
> (Wise 2000: 177–178)

In these terms "the relation between home and the home is always being negotiated" (Wise 2000: 178). Relph (1976: 45) explains that the identity which a person or group has with a place is largely influenced by "whether they are experiencing it as an insider or as an outsider." He goes on to say "to be inside a place is to belong to it and identify with it, and the more profoundly inside you are the stronger is this identity with the place" (Relph 1976: 49).

Relph (1976: 50) explains that there are different ways in which a person can experience being an insider in a place. These include (but are not limited to) behavioral insideness ("physical presence in a place"), empathetic insideness ("emotional participation and involvement with a place"), and existential insideness ("complete and unselfconscious commitment to a place"). Thus, to be an insider in a place suggests that a person be attached, involved, and committed to that place. Yet the ease with which people feel like an insider in the places where they live can differ as a result of the power they have to remain in a place and to become involved with it.

Home and Control

Many researchers have noted that an important relationship exists between control over one's dwelling and whether one feels at home. As Parsell (2012: 160) notes:

> Control over a space is important to people's understandings of what it means to be at home, because this control over a space also means the ability to exercise a degree of autonomy over their lives.

Central to these discussions is the recognition that a person's dwelling can be a place from which they derive "ontological security" (Saunders 1990; Dupuis and Thorns 1998), defined by Giddens (1991: 92) as:

> the confidence that most human beings have in the continuity of their self-identity and the constancy of their social and material environments. Basic to a feeling of ontological security is a sense of the reliability of persons and things.

In English-speaking countries, literature on the relationship between home and the dwelling has largely focused on the benefits of home ownership for ontological security and control over one's dwelling, with positive outcomes for health and wellbeing (reviewed in Bridge et al. 2003; Hulse and Saugres 2008; Dockery et al. 2010; Easthope 2014). This relationship was perhaps most famously articulated in Saunders' (1989) English study, in which he argued that home ownership provides for a stronger sense of ontological security than rental housing. In part he argues that this is because owners have more autonomy over their dwellings (Saunders 1989). This claim has been debated in the housing literature (e.g. Hiscock et al. 2001). Indeed, as noted by Yip and Forrest (2002: 703–704), while "the idea of home ownership is closely associated with notions of privacy, freedom, independence and autonomy," especially in Western contexts, "many home owners are in circumstances which require collective agreement and collective action in relation to repairs, maintenance and management." Put another way, many property owners are not unilaterally able to control what happens in, and in regards to, their dwellings. Forms of collective property ownership (such as condominiums and strata schemes) provide good examples of where many decisions about the management and maintenance of the property, and the appropriate behavior of its residents, must be made collectively. Thus, the right of control of property is not absolute or 'natural,' but rather reflects social norms, which are often reflected in laws and regulations. As Singer (2000: 215–216) states, "property is not just something we protect or invade, recognize or reject; it is something we collectively construct."

This cultural dimension is important because it means that changing perceptions about dwelling ownership—and hence also dwelling rental—

have the potential to lead to significant changes in the ways in which people identify of and with their dwellings. As Ruonavaara (2012: 186, original emphasis) explains in regards to the practice of 'homemaking':

> Residents actively *make* dwellings homes by redesigning, decorating, and changing them according to their values and wishes. As different housing tenures invest residents with different degrees of power over their living space, tenure may also be relevant for homemaking. If one's housing tenure gives little say over the living space, it may not be easy to feel at home in it.

Ruonavaara's point about homemaking in the sense of redesigning dwellings could equally apply to all of the ways in which a person interacts with, and understands their relationship to, their dwelling.

I have argued elsewhere (Easthope 2014: 584) "that the right of a property owner . . . to maintain control over what happens in a property is not intrinsic to property ownership *per se*, but rather reflects the laws, customs and mores of society." These laws, customs, and mores shape the policies and legislation that determine the rights of property owners on the one hand and rental tenants on the other. Some people are afforded more opportunities to become involved with their dwellings than others. This means that cultural ideas about tenure and ownership—and the ways in which these are reflected in laws and regulations, social norms, and accepted patterns of behavior— can play a major role in influencing the extent to which people can feel at home in their dwellings.

In the following section I discuss these issues in a particular national context. I choose to speak about notions of property ownership in Australia to develop my argument. However, many of the issues addressed in the Australian case will be of relevance to many other Western countries where home ownership is valued and promoted.

A Nation of Home Owners? The Australian Case

> The material home represents the concrete expression of the habits of frugality and saving 'for a home of our own' . . . one of the best instincts in us is that which induces us to have one little piece of earth with a house and garden which is ours: to which we can withdraw, in which we can be among friends, into which no stranger may come against our will.
>
> (Menzies 1942)

This extract from a speech made by Australia's longest serving prime minister provides a succinct example of the importance of home ownership in Australian society. In particular, it voices the importance of control over the dwelling in which one lives. "into which no stranger may come against our will." Over 70 years after this speech was made, home ownership maintains an important meaning in Australian society. Saunders and Williams (1988: 88) made a similar observation in their British study:

> The home in Anglo-Saxon culture is represented by a physical ideal (the detached house) and a legal ideal (owner occupation) both of which emphasize household autonomy and both of which represent a stout defiance of collectivism.

The sense of control and autonomy that is assumed to come with the ownership of property, and in comparison, the assumption in many parts of society that rental *housing* is a short-term stop gap before purchasing 'a home of one's own,' has been largely unquestioned in mainstream Australian society. However, two significant changes are beginning to shake the foundations upon which these assumptions have rested. The first is that, as a result of sustained, and relatively rapid, increases in property prices, growing numbers of people are now long-term private renters. Private rental is not only the domain of young singles and couples as they save for a deposit for their first house. The second change is that increasing numbers of people are living in apartments. In Australia, the vast majority of these apartments are strata titled. This means that, in common with other dualistic forms of ownership overseas (such as the US condominium) people who buy into strata schemes purchase individual ownership of their unit, as well as a share in the collective ownership of the apartment building and grounds. Apartment owners therefore do not have the same individual control over their properties as people who own detached properties.

The combined result of these two significant changes is that the so-called 'Australian Dream' of owning a detached house on a quarter-acre block in the suburbs is no longer a possibility for a large, and growing, proportion of the Australian population.

The Rise of Private Rental

Currently, a quarter of Australian households (25%) rent their housing privately (ABS 2012[2]). While in Australia private rental has often been considered as a stepping stone for young people as they save a deposit to purchase a property, this is not the case for many Australian households today. In 2011, a third (33%) of private renters were long-term renters who had been living in rental properties for ten or more years. This has increased from 27 percent over the past two decades (Stone et al. 2013). Nor is private rental the domain only of young singles and couples. An increasing proportion of long-term private renter households now include children (30% in 2007–08) and there is evidence of people aging in long-term private rental (Stone et al. 2013). Rates of housing stress are also high among long-term private renters, with 63% being in the lowest 40% of the income distribution and paying more than 30% of their income on regular rental repayments (Stone et al. 2013).

Despite the importance of private rental housing as a long-term housing option for increasing numbers of people, policies and legislation relating to the management of private rental housing still appear to rest on an assumption that such housing is a short-term option in housing careers inevitably progressing towards ownership. Private rental tenants are afforded little control over how they use their dwellings and their abilities to remain in, or make changes to, their dwellings are limited. For example, private tenants are unable to make many changes or improvements to their dwellings without the permission of their landlord, evictions are allowed without a reason given by the landlord ('no-grounds' evictions), and unrestricted rental increases are also allowed.[3] Some tenant advocates have raised concerns that this has enabled retaliatory evictions and rental increases in situations where tenants have requested repairs or improvements to their properties (Hulse et al. 2011: 67).

These conditions are often taken for granted by both investor owners and tenants in Australia. Yet they are not intrinsic to private rental. Different countries offer much greater control to private rental tenants over their dwellings. A good example is Germany, where the majority of rental housing is owned by private landlords, a large proportion of whom are small-scale 'mum and dad' investors. Yet in Germany, no-grounds evictions are not allowed, rents are regulated, and tenants have rights to make some improvements to their properties (Hulse et al. 2011).

The Rise of High Density Living

Governments around the world are promoting compact city policies (OECD 2012) and all of Australia's five major cities have metropolitan strategies that promote such urban consolidation. These policies promote the building of new residential dwellings to renew existing urban areas. The majority of these new dwellings are being delivered as apartments. In Australia, the vast majority of privately owned apartments are owned under strata title. Strata title is a dualistic form of property ownership in which people purchase private ownership of a lot (usually the inside of a single apartment and any associated parking or storage spaces) in a strata scheme, as well as a joint share in the common property (usually the building, grounds, and land on which the apartment building sits). Already, one in eight Australians (3 million people) live in strata-titled property (Easthope et al. 2012).

The increase in strata ownership in Australia has meant that the change in the physical features and appearance of dwellings (apartments as opposed to houses) and the associated change in the activities and functions of those dwelling places (including the requirement that they be collectively owned and managed) have influenced people's experiences of their dwellings. In particular, many find that they are not able to exercise the control over their dwelling that they expected to accompany their ownership of the property. This is exacerbated by the fact that existing owners have no say as to who buys (or moves) into their strata scheme and, as a result, people with very different priorities can find themselves owning property in common and sharing responsibility for its management. Australian and international studies have reported on conflicting priorities in strata schemes between resident and investor owners (Guilding et al. 2005), owners in different economic positions (Yip and Forrest 2002: 715), and tenants and owner-occupiers (Bugden 2005: 12). In addition, not all strata residents have an equal say in decisions affecting their strata scheme. Voting rights are weighted according to the share an owner has of the common property (based on the value of their lot) and some owners are better able to garner support for decisions. As a result of these challenges, the increase in strata ownership in Australia is beginning to bring into question broader social understandings and experiences of home ownership.

The Potential for Social Change

Relph (1976: 45) explains that the identity of something (including the identity of a place) is:

> inseparable from identity with other things . . . identity is founded both in the individual person or object and in the culture to which they belong. It is not static and unchangeable, but varies as circumstances and attitudes change.

The significant social and economic changes described in this chapter are reducing the control that people have over the places in which they live. They impact upon people's ability to identify with places as home. However, there is a possibility for positive change to result from the reduction in the control people hold over their dwelling places.

The first step in looking at how the housing system can be improved is to look at the social and cultural norms that underpin it. We are at an interesting time in Australia, as there have been important changes in the housing system that have the potential to lead to a broader-scale questioning of long-standing social and cultural norms, notably increases in long-term private rental and strata property ownership. Both changes point to a loss of control over dwellings. As control is an important aspect influencing the ability of people to feel at home in their dwellings, does this mean that more and more Australians will find it difficult to feel at home in the places in which they live? The answer is: possibly, but not necessarily. It might be that these changes are enough to enable a reconsideration of the role of ownership (and by extension, private rental) in Australian society. In order to achieve this, the status quo must be challenged—namely the commodification of residential property and the normalization of detached housing as the ideal form for home ownership—and then alternative approaches considered in the light of these dominant ideas about ownership.

First, the commodification of dwellings has impacted on the ability of many people to feel attached to their dwellings, and to relate to them as home. As Stone et al. (2013: 7) note:

> The rental sector is increasingly being understood more as an investment sector and less as a home for renters, with policy much more focused on the investment side than with creating a secure and stable living environment for tenants.

The prioritization of landlords' rights to realize a profit by rapidly increasing rents or selling a property quickly in Australia has a significant impact on whether tenants can feel secure in their ability to remain in a place, and their willingness to become involved with and committed to a place that they may be forced to leave.

This might be turned around. If dwellings were to be considered as places to dwell first and foremost, and items to invest in second—and if tenancy legislation and associated government policies were to follow suit by providing better security of tenure and more control to tenants over their dwellings—then many private renters may find that they are better able to feel attached, involved, and committed to the places in which they live. Such a change could include improved rights for, and legislation regarding, tenants that recognize the importance of making dwellings home. Part of this would be recognizing the importance of being able to better experience a place as an insider by affording more opportunities for tenants to become involved with their dwellings. This might come in the form of providing more security of tenancy (for example, by abolishing no-grounds terminations) to facilitate attachment and enabling tenants to make improvements to their dwellings (becoming more involved and committed to their dwellings). This might also include a greater realization of the potential for improved cooperation between tenants and their landlords in regards to the upkeep of their properties to the benefit of both parties. An example would be the introduction of practices, policies, and associated legislation that encourage tenants to share in the responsibilities and costs associated with making improvements to their rental properties, while ensuring that their investment is recognized at the end of their lease.

Second, the dominant understanding of home ownership in Australia to date, based primarily on owner occupation of a detached house, has led to significant confusion and dispute among those owners who have purchased strata titled properties believing that they would have the same type of control over their dwellings, but find that they do not. Multiple disputes in these buildings revolve around an individual owner finding that they cannot do as they please with their dwelling—for example, that they cannot smoke, make renovations without permissions, or delay repairs for personal financial reasons. But change is possible. This could include a shift among strata property owners towards recognition of their responsibilities as collective owners, as well as the potential benefits of collective ownership, governance, and management, including cost-sharing. The strata system already provides a legislative framework to make this possible (Randolph and Easthope 2014). The challenge is to change the cultural norms associated with home ownership.

Conclusion

The dream of ownership of a house is no longer achievable for many Australians. In one sense this is a pity, but in another it provides hope. The hope is that we might see the beginning of a cultural shift in the way that people relate to their dwellings. Such a shift might recognize that dwellings are important sites to which people can become attached, and that people can and should be afforded the possibility of experiencing their dwellings as insiders. This would enable them to become involved and committed to those dwellings irrespective of whether (in the case of tenants) or how (in the case of strata owners) they own those dwellings as commodities.

This will require a fundamental social shift away from prioritizing the commodification of dwellings over their use value. Such a shift will also require a change in cultural ideas about the meaning of home ownership. Such a cultural change has the potential to open up possibilities for developing and nurturing people's relationships with their dwellings, and their neighbors. However, a change in cultural ideas about the meaning of home ownership will be no easy task.

Relph (1976: 60–61) argued that mass place identity, as perpetuated by the media, is inauthentic and the easiest type of place identity to break down. But dominant Australian cultural ideas about the importance of home ownership in understanding the dwelling as home are not (or at least are no longer) simply the outcome of media imagery or political rhetoric. They have been internalized by many ordinary citizens and are experienced very 'authentically.' However, they are now being challenged by the realities of increasing long-term private rental and increasing strata property ownership. This provides an opportunity for change—this change can come from the 'bottom'—from the individuals affected by a loss of control over their dwellings—and it can come from the 'top'—from politicians and opinion-makers recognizing the fundamental importance of people being able to feel in control and at home in their dwellings for the wellbeing of individuals and society as a whole. The possibility of 're-embedding' with places is important in the face of rapid social change and globalization. The dwelling is one of the most important places with which people can 're-embed,' become an insider, and feel at home. This chapter has argued that the rapid social changes that are occurring right now in regards to our relationships with our dwellings provide a unique opportunity for this process to occur.

Notes

1 Renting for 10 or more years.
2 Figure includes rented from real estate agent, person not in the same household, other landlord type, and landlord type not stated, and excludes rented from state or territory housing authority and housing cooperative/community/church group (ABS 2012, Basic Community Profile, Australia).
3 In most jurisdictions in Australia rent increases are allowed every 6 months at market rents. (Hulse et al. 2011: 44).

References

ABS [Australian Bureau of Statistics] (2012) *Community Profile, Australia*, www. abs.gov.au/websitedbs/censushome.nsf/home/communityprofiles, accessed October 7, 2014.

Bridge, C., P. Flatau, S. Whelan, G. Wood and J. Yates (2003) *Housing Assistance and Non-Shelter Outcomes*, AHURI Final Report No. 40, Melbourne: AHURI.

Bugden, G. (2005) "Strata and Community Title in Australia—Issue 1 current challenges," paper presented at *The Strata and Community Title in Australia for the 21st Century Conference*, 31 August—3 September 2005, Gold Coast.

Clapham, D. (2010) "Happiness, Well-being and Housing Policy," *Policy & Politics* 38(2), 253–267.

Dockery, A., G. Kendall, J. Li, A. Mahendran, R. Ong and L. Strazdins (2010) *Housing and Children's Development and Wellbeing: A Scoping Study*, AHURI Final Report No. 149, Melbourne: AHURI.

Dupuis, A. and D. Thorns (1998) "Home, Home Ownership and the Search for Ontological Security," *Sociological Review* 46, 24–47.

Easthope, H., B. Randolph and S. Judd (2012) *Governing the Compact City: The Role and Effectiveness of Strata Management, Final Report*, Sydney: City Futures Research Centre.

Easthope, H. (2014) "Making a Rental Property Home," *Housing Studies*, DOI: 10.1080/02673037.2013.873115

Giddens, A. (1991) *The Consequences of Modernity*, Cambridge: Polity Press.

Giuliani, M. (1991) "Towards an Analysis of Mental Representations of Attachment to the Home," *Journal of Architectural and Planning Research* 8, 133–146.

Guilding, C., A. Ardill, E. Fredline and J. Warnken (2005) "An Agency Theory Perspective on the Owner/Manager Relationship in Tourism-based Condominiums," *Tourism Management* 26, 409–420.

Harvey, D. (1996) *Justice, Nature and the Geography of Difference*, Oxford: Blackwell.

Hiscock, R., A. Kearns, S. MacIntyre and A. Ellaway (2001) "Ontological Security and Psycho-social Benefits From the Home: Qualitative Evidence on Issues of Tenure," *Housing, Theory and Society* 18, 50–66.

Hulse, K. and L. Saugeres (2008) *Housing Insecurity and Precarious Living: An Australian Study*, AHURI Final Report No. 124, Melbourne: AHURI.

Hulse, K., V. Milligan and H. Easthope (2011) *Secure Occupancy in Rental Housing: Conceptual Foundations and Comparative Perspectives*, Australian Housing and Urban Research Institute Final Report No. 170, Melbourne: AHURI.

Mallett, S. (2004) "Understanding Home: A Critical Review of the Literature," *The Sociological Review* 52, 62–89.

Massey, D. (1995) "The Conceptualization of Place," in D. Massey and P. Jess (Eds.) *A Place in the World?: Places, Cultures and Globalization*, Oxford: Oxford University Press, 45–85.

Menzies, R. (1942) *The Forgotten People—a Speech by Robert Menzies on 22 May 1942*, www.liberals.net/theforgottenpeople.htm, accessed October 7, 2014.

OECD (The Organization for Economic Co-operation and Development) (2012) *Compact City Policies: A comparative assessment*, OECD Publishing.

Parsell, C. (2012) "Home is Where the House is: The meaning of home for people sleeping rough," *Housing Studies* 27, 159–173.

Randolph, B. and H. Easthope (2014) "The Rise of Micro-Government: Strata Title, Reluctant Democrats and the New Urban Vertical Polity," in B. Gleeson and B. Beza (Eds.) *The Public City: Essays in Honor of Paul Mees*, Melbourne: Melbourne University Press, 210–224.

Relph, E. (1976) "On the Identity of Places," in M. Carmona & S. Tiesdel (Eds.) (2007) *Urban Design Reader*, Oxford: Architectural Press, 103–107.

Ruonavaara, H. (2012) "Tenure as an Institution," in S. Smith (Ed.) *International Encyclopedia of Housing and Home*, Amsterdam: Elsevier Science & Technology, 185–189.

Saunders, P. and P. Williams (1988) "The Constitution of the Home: Towards a Research Agenda," *Housing Studies* 3, 81–93.

Saunders, P. (1989) "The Meaning of 'Home' in Contemporary English Culture," *Housing Studies* 4, 177–192.

Saunders, P. (1990) *A Nation of Home Owners*, London: Unwin Hyman.

Singer, J. (2000) *Entitlement: The Paradoxes of Property*, New Haven: Yale University Press.

Somerville, P. (1997) "The Social Construction of Home," *Journal of Architectural and Planning Research* 14, 226–245.

Stone, W., T. Burke, K. Hulse, K. and L. Ralston (2013) *Long-term Private Rental in a Changing Australian Private Rental Sector*, AHURI Final Report No. 209, Melbourne: AHURI.

Stones, R. (2012) "Disembedding" in G. Ritzer (Ed.) *The Wiley Blackwell Encyclopedia of Globalization*, Volume 2, Wiley Blackwell, 449–450.

Wise, J. (2000) "Home: Territory and Identity," *Cultural Studies* 14, 295–310.

Yip, N.-M. and Forrest, R. (2002) "Property Owning Democracies? Home owner corporations in Hong Kong." *Housing Studies* 17, 703–720.

8 Tuning In and Out of Place

Rachel Cogger

Introduction

With more than half the global population living in cities, improving the livability of urban environments is becoming one of the most important challenges of the 21st century. Increasing attention is being paid to the human dimension to ensure that cities and towns are environmentally sustainable, socially healthy, and economically vibrant places in which to live work and play (Gehl 2010). However, city visions, plans, and developments have tended to place a stronger focus on visual aesthetics rather than considering all of the senses and their impacts on people's experiences.

This chapter provides a brief overview of the place-based approach being used in contemporary urban-planning theory and practice. The importance of all the human senses (sight, smell, touch, taste, and hearing) in the experience of place is presented by revisiting early theoretical explorations of environmental experience. This provides the framework for understanding people's experience of place and placelessness (Relph 1976). In particular, the concept of soundscapes, that is, people's aural relationship with place, highlights the role of the acoustic environment in people's engagement or disengagement.

In the second half of the chapter, my theoretical discussion is complemented by empirical research. This research included conducting qualitative interviews with residents in Sydney, Australia about urban soundscapes and sense of place. Insights from these interviews have been tapped to add a qualitative dimension to reflect individual perceptions and experiences of the soundscape in local urban neighborhoods.[1] Sounds encountered in these neighborhoods (whether natural, mechanical, or man-made) are typical to many cities.

Place-Based Planning

The practice of urban planning has undergone significant changes in the past few decades, shifting paradigms from a modern, to postmodern, and now a place-based approach. The ideology of high modernism produced cities where uniformity and inhumanity were ever present, and urban environments were characterized by a "degree of monotony, sterility and vulgarity" (Jacobs 1961: 7). The modernist approach to planning had a lot to do with utopian attitudes imposing homogenous, machine-like order and large-scale, technocratic urban plans, where a sense of place and a sense of community were eroded (Hirt 2005). It can be argued that during this period the importance of place as a center of meaning in people's everyday experience was neglected, resulting in placeless landscapes devoid of meaning (Relph 1976).

Place-based urban planning emerged in response to the shortcomings of the modernist approach, acknowledging that the 'one-size-fits-all' planning template ignored the uniqueness of each landscape and situation and the "emotional ties and feelings of connectedness that people have for places—and the intangible meanings and values people ascribe to places (Kruger 2008: 2). There has been a return to the human scale—adopting a small-scale approach, characterized by sensitivity, inclusiveness, building social capital, and reinforcing people-place bonds. Places are now considered at the micro-level, with more attention paid to the subjective, emotional, and symbolic meanings people ascribe to place and the experiences that they make possible. A greater focus on the needs and aspirations of the people who use cities is emerging through the practice of place-based planning (Gehl 2010).

The place-based planning approach refocuses attention on the character, quality, and feel of places we encounter. Association with places that facilitate and enable a meaningful experience is a deep human need (Relph 1976). Urban planners and other built-environment practitioners now strive to create places characterized by distinctiveness rather than sameness, with a "growing concern with perceptual and aesthetic preferences" (Untaru 2002: 78). Unfortunately, those visions tend to place a disproportionate focus on visual aesthetics, and the full sensory experience is rarely taken into account. The bias in favor of the visual has been maintained throughout Western modernity, particularly within the disciplines of architecture and urban planning.

According to pre-eminent human geographer Yi-Fu Tuan (1979: 413), "blindness makes a geographical career virtually impossible." But our perception of the world and the environment we live in is engendered by the integration of all the stimuli we perceive. The human sensory system is a holistic system that goes far beyond visual–spatial perception and refers to a more complex geographical experience. The urban experience is by nature multi-sensorial and, as Rodaway (1994: 37) has described, the five senses are "geographical in that they contribute to orientation in space, an awareness of spatial relationships and an appreciation of the specific qualities of different places." While in recent years there has been a resurgence in sensory studies (e.g. Landry 2012; Borer 2013; Howes and Classen 2014), planning practice has been slow in recognizing the influence that sensory stimulation has on the urban experience, and therefore the impact it has on the relationship between people and place.

Experience of Place through the Senses

The way we understand and make meaning of a city is directly connected to our experiences. In the late 1960s, theorizations of place in geographical enquiry drew strong connections between space, experience, and meaning. Explorations of the people-and-place relationship sought to uncover the meaningful connections people form with everyday places through the realm of experience and to provide insights into the emotions and feelings of the places we encounter daily. Lukermann (1964: 167) explained that "knowledge of place is a simple fact of experience." Tuan (1977: 213) argues that "place is not only a fact to be explained in the broader frame of space, but it is also a reality to be clarified and understood from the perspective of the people who give it meaning." Godkin (1980: 73) suggests that the places in a person's world are much more than the entities described by the spatial conception; they are "profound centers of meanings and symbols of experience," not simply a physical stage where life's dramas are played out.

Edward Relph (1976: 7) in *Place and Placelessness* explains that the phenomenological approach he adopts to explore 'place' as an experiential phenomenon stems from "an acceptance both of the wholeness and indivisibility of human experience, and of the fact that meaning defined by human intentions is central to all our existence. The lived-world and its geography are thus taken as being irrefutable and profoundly human and meaningful." Places are the "focus of meaning or intention, either culturally or individually defined" (Relph 1976: 55) and they "incarnate the experience and aspirations of people" (Tuan 1971: 281). Places lie at the core of human existence. Malpas (1999: 31–32) argues that the "crucial point about the connection between place and experience is not . . . that place is properly something only encountered 'in' experience, but rather that place is integral to the very structure and possibility of experience." Such an understanding of place rejects the ideology of high modernism where the focus on functionalism and efficiency excludes the human scale and unique character of places and their importance in people's every day experiences in cities.

Ultimately, the experience of place is made possible through our senses. For Relph (2008: 314), a sense of place is a "synaesthetic faculty that combines sight, hearing, smell, movement, touch, imagination, purpose, and anticipation." He explains that "in our everyday lives places are not experienced as independent, clearly defined entities that can be described simply in terms of their location or appearance. Rather, they are senses in a chiaroscuro of setting, landscape, ritual, routine, other people, personal experiences, care and concern for home, and in the context of other places" (Relph 1976: 29).

Place can hold both personal experiences and meanings; however, it is the sensory feelings that connect a person to their surrounds (Tuan 1975). Lynch (1976: 8–9) argued that the senses allow us to determine the perceived quality of a place and encompass "what one can see, and how it feels underfoot, and the smell of the air and the sounds of bells and motorcycles, and how that quality affects our immediate well-being, our actions, our feelings, and our understandings." Through the senses, knowledge, and awareness of a place, the character of a place, the atmosphere and its ambience can be determined and understood.

The senses are integral to our everyday experience. Through their structure and the way we use them, the senses mediate that experience. Information gathered gives rise to a mental representation of the perceived environment and any judgments made about that place will be based upon this multi-sensorial representation. Understanding how people perceive, experience, respond to, and assign meaning to urban places should be of central concern to urban planning. The sights, sounds, and scents of urban life surround us at all times and as Feld (1996: 91) suggests, "as place is sensed, senses are placed; as places make sense, senses make place."

Sensory Urban Environments

Cities are rich sensory environments. The vast array of external stimuli we encounter mediates our experiences and understanding of everyday places. Places that infuse a rich sensory experience and evoke a positive emotional response for the individual contribute to a heightened sense of place. Such places encourage people to linger and connect with one another. They provide opportunities for social interactions and are important to the health and wellbeing of urban society. If a place evokes a unique sensory experience, or gains an individual's attention, this can increase spatial awareness, resonate in fond memories of a place, and the individual may bestow value upon the location. Affective bonds to such a place can develop.

On the contrary, if a place has the inability to evoke a positive sensory response, this can result in places conveying little meaning, and the individual may succumb to the forces of placelessness (Relph 1976). Urban settings that lack distinctive personality erode opportunities for high quality experiences. The loss of significant places and their meanings have negative implications for an individual's connection and attachment to place, psychological well-being, and quality of life. Landry (2007) suggests that many cities and towns are boring, staid, and unattractive. Although moments of delight may exist, people are often left disappointed with their experience, due to the lack of the finely crafted 'whole.' Relph (1976) argued that designers who ignore the meanings that places bring to people's minds destroy *authentic* places and make *inauthentic* ones. Lynch (1960) also noted that the sameness of urban places diminishes a sense of place.

Exploring the human interaction with place is a worthwhile endeavor because places have fundamental significance to human beings and relationships with places are almost as important as relationships with people (Relph 1976). Feld and Basso (1996: 9) have argued that "place is the most fundamental form of embodied experience—the site of a powerful fusion of self, space, and time." For Casey (1993: 33), "what matters most is the experience of *being* in that place and, more particularly, *becoming part of the place*" (original emphasis). The experience of place is grounded in the experience of the body (Buttimer and Seamon 1980) and can become deeply meaningful "since perception has an inevitable individual component" (Cossette 2014: 93). The following section briefly explores the role of each of the human senses in the experience of place, before turning specifically to the auditory sense.

The Senses and Environmental Experience

The way we experience a city is by nature multi-sensorial, and each of the senses plays a connected role in how people perceive, interpret, and respond to environmental stimuli. Each of the senses contributes to our comprehension of the world around us, whether we are aware of it or not. Sensory perception refers to "the insights that people gain into the physical and socially constructed environment by attaching meaning through association, following the potential detection and identification of sensory information" (Henshaw and Bruce 2012: 450). The following section summarizes each of the senses in environmental experience.

Vision

Tuan (1977: 16) suggests that "the organization of human space is uniquely dependent on sight." While visual cues are a dominant part of our making sense of the world around us, and are one of the most familiar dimensions of our experience of place, the visual does not play an exclusive role in our environmental experience. Information from the other senses, memory, past experience, and even our expectations also play a role. Sight allows us to differentiate elements of the environment in terms of color, shape, texture, form, distance, size, and arrangement in space. As Berger (1972: 9) suggests, "we never look just at one thing; we are always looking at the relation between things and ourselves."

Touch

As we move through the environment we unavoidably touch and feel the places we encounter, and this plays a vital role in our structuring of space and relations to the physical environment and to other people (Porteous 1990). The sense of touch allows us to determine features of the environment such as size, shape, weight, texture, vibration, energy, and temperature. Referring to the tactile receptivity of the body, the sense of touch has been relatively neglected in considerations of environmental experience. Tuan (1993) suggests that while we may lose one or more of the other senses, to lose the ability to feel (touch) is to lose all sense of being in the world.

Taste

The sense of taste is rarely considered in the epistemology of sense perception, let alone in people's experience of place. Tuan (1977) proposes that taste cannot make us individually aware of a spacious external world inhabited by objects but that tastes combined with the other senses can "greatly enrich our apprehension of the world's spatial and geometrical character" (Tuan 1977: 12). While it is difficult to determine the role that the sense of taste plays in the environmental experience, the symbolic meanings associated with food are clear. Food plays a significant role in our identity construction, religious practices, and social patterns of behavior (Korsmeyer 2002; Thompson 2005).

Smell

Immensely meaningful to humans, odors can provide us with information about the character and identity of an environment and are closely linked to emotion and memory (Marshall 2009). Borer (2013: 973) suggests that the "production of odors and the meanings that individuals endow odors with are context-dependent . . . and in the context of the city, they become necessarily place-based." Smells are arousing, emotional and are established by direct contact between body and environment and, as stated by Lefebvre (1991: 197), "where an intimacy occurs between subject and object, it must surely be the world of smell and the places where they reside."

Sound

Sound dramatizes the individual's spatial experience (Tuan 1977) and can deeply enrich our feelings toward a place, influencing the listener's moods and emotions. The world of sound would appear to be spatially structured, though not with the sharpness of the visual world. Sound can expand and enrich visual space as it enlarges one's spatial awareness to include areas that cannot be seen. Through sound, an environment can come alive. When humans listen, they create an intimate connection to the dynamic activities of life (Blesser and Salter 2007). The environment plays a key role in what and how we hear. The physical form (such as open or enclosed spaces and building materials), the wind, moisture, time of day, number of different sound sources, direction, and so forth all modify the character of the sounds heard.

The urban experience is thus dynamic, direct, and different for everyone. Encounters with place can either stimulate our senses and increase awareness of our surrounds, or cause us to miss them altogether (Gieseking et al. 2014). Urban planning plays a fundamental role in the design, creation, and management of the urban landscape, however sound (as opposed to noise) has rarely been considered as a factor of urban quality.

The Concept of Soundscapes

Analogous to the concept of landscape, the soundscape is the relationship as mediated through sound, between living beings and their environment. The soundscape is the totality of all sounds within a location, with an emphasis on the relationship between an individual's or society's perception of, understanding of, and interaction with the sonic environment (Truax 2001; Schulte-Fortkamp and Dubois 2006). Like a landscape, a soundscape is simultaneously a physical environment and a way of perceiving that environment (Thompson 2002). People bring their own cognitions to the listening situation. "These cognitions represent memories, ideas, feelings, attitudes, values, preferences, meanings, and conceptions of behavior and experience which relate to the variety and complexity of the physical settings that define the day-to-day existance of every human being" (Proshansky et al. 1983: 59).

The soundscape is an integral component of the environment, and contributes to the identity and specificity of that environment (Raimbault and Dubois 2005). Soundscapes have the capacity to affect us, as they contribute meaningfully to our comprehension of time and space through various and complex perceptual systems. Furthermore, soundscapes can also reinforce the relationship between people and their surroundings, because in an acoustic environment, we are always at the center, listening 'out' with the ear.

Soundscape recognizes that "when humans enter an environment, they have an immediate effect on the sounds; the soundscape is human-made and in that sense, composed" (Westerkamp 1991: 4). Westerkamp (1991) explains that soundscapes are an acoustic manifestation of 'place,' where the sounds give an inhabitant a 'sense of place' and the place's acoustic quality is shaped by the inhabitant's activities and behavior. The meaning of a place and its sounds are created precisely because of this interaction between the soundscape and people.

While there is an increasing amount of research that has been conducted regarding sounds, the environment, and the human experience of place, the discipline of urban planning has been slow to address the role that sound plays in the experience of an urban setting. With a focus on the physical properties of noise, the human dimension is often neglected.

Controlling the Soundscape

Urbanized environments create multiple sources of sound in order to function, whether those sounds are natural, mechanical, or man-made. People can be deeply affected by the sounds they encounter. With an increased focus on usability, livability. and experiential values in urban environments, attention to the soundscape becomes of central importance. Unfortunately, the current paradigm for managing unwanted sound (i.e. noise) in the environment is concerned with the negative aspects of the human response to sound, and does not consider the full spectrum of the human acoustic experience.

When the acoustic components of urban environments are investigated, they often have only a negative focus, documenting noise pollution and the adverse effects on health. The problem with this approach is that the subjective human interpretation of the sound is ignored. Truax (1978: vi–vii) states that "in any of these measuring systems, no matter how sophisticated, one sound is treated similar to any other sound. In other words, any such device or system treats sound as a signal to be processed, instead of information to be understood." Porteous and Mastin (1985: 170) support this view by suggesting that the sonic environment "is taken to comprise a vast array of stimuli, each representing a wealth of information capable of producing a variety of environmental experiences."

Soundscapes that are meaningful and valued by people are not solely assessed in terms of volume. Quiet or loud spaces will not necessarily provide or protect high quality soundscapes as suggested in Figure 8.1. Schafer (1994: 4), who pioneered soundscape research in the 1970s, states that "noise pollution results when [humans do] not listen carefully. Noises are sounds we have learnt to ignore." Böhme (2000: 16) argues that "city planning can no longer be content with noise control and abatement, but must pay attention to the character of the acoustic atmosphere" in order to create healthy and attractive sonic environments. There is a need to overcome the scientific approach that remains, at best, capable of grasping noise as a function of decibels. Urban planners must seek a way to make environmental acoustics a key factor of urban quality. The advantage of the soundscape approach is that it covers not only the negative aspects of the sonic environment, but also acknowledges the positive aspects (Adams et al. 2006; Davies et al. 2007).

The quality of sound environments should be considered beyond offensive noise levels. Some sounds should be preserved, encouraged, and multiplied, while others should be minimized, masked, or avoided altogether (Gillespie 2009). Only a total appreciation of the acoustic environment can give us the resources for improving the orchestration of the 'world soundscape' (Schafer 1977) and ultimately enhance an individual's experience and sense of place. The increasing presence of artistic sound installations in public spaces is one such way that urban soundscapes are being altered. Such artworks contribute to the identity and character of a place, in addition to providing opportunities for people to engage with place and one another. Figure 8.2 entitled '21 Balançoires' (21 Swings) is an interactive musical installation in Montreal, Canada designed by *Daily tous les jours* that plays music when the swings are in motion. The musical composition is dependent on the cooperation and interaction of members of the public.

Schafer (1996) suggests that every culture is unique, and one of the ways it remains so is through the unique quality of its sounds. Ensuring that the public has access to quality sound environments not only enriches the design

Figure 8.1 Noise abatement poster focused on lowering sound levels
Source: Author, 2014.

Figure 8.2 Interactive sound insta_ation: '*21 Balançoires*' (21 swings)
Source: Reitman, 2015.

possibilities in a contemporary urban environment but it can also improve the quality of city life. Urban practitioners should be striving to "produce an urban fabric which will delight those who experience it" (Porteous 1996: 217). A place lacking in quality acoustic features may appear to be boring and unengaging. A place dominated by negative sounds may appear somewhat unattractive even though visually it may be pleasing to the eye. Awareness of this is instrumental, as how a place 'looks' does not alone determine the perceived quality of a place.

(De)Valuing the Soundscape: Sydney Stories

Expectation plays an important role in enhancing a sense of place. Chueng and Marsden (2002) suggest that when auditory spaces meet expectation, people's sense of presence is increased. Sounds that are congruent with expectations can yield a more accurate representation of the environment, hence increasing a place's identity. My field interviews in Sydney in 2014 suggest that people bestow value on the places where they expect to have high quality acoustic experiences. (Respondents' names have been changed for privacy reasons.)

When an acoustic environment meets expectations, people will value and choose some places over others. "These little places are definitely an oasis from the noise, where you get to really hear and connect with the beautiful birds and the water and the social conversation" (Peter 2014, pers. comm.). Sarah (2014, pers. comm.) states that "if it is somewhere that I have enjoyed, then I seek it out and go back, and you grow attachment through that familiarity, and if its somewhere that has bothered you, you won't ever really want to go back there again, because you . . . don't like that. When it's pleasing or soothing or enjoyable . . . that's what you do, you seek it out and you grow an attachment to it." When a strong sense of place exists, it can foster connectedness and stewardship, and increases feelings of belonging.

Urban environments with high acoustical qualities are scarce resources that need to be creatively planned, designed, and maintained to enable an urban experience that is fulfilling and enchanting. Figure 8.3 entitled 'Forgotten Songs' is an installation by Michael Hill that commemorates the songs of 50 birds that once populated central Sydney, before they were eradicated by European settlement. This artwork was part of a revitalization strategy designed to reactivate a number of Sydney's historical laneways. Such design interventions are generally popular and appreciated. This is reflected in one interview respondent stating: "I couldn't stress enough how much public spaces need to be planned to allow . . . sanctuary from the chaos of the city, and being thoughtful in providing some sounds, by encouraging birds, that can then bring that atmosphere as it definitely has soothing effects" (Anna 2014, pers. comm.). On the other hand, in Douglas Barrett's (2004) considerations of what public spaces should sound like, land use and activities mismatched with soundscapes may result in underutilized places, annoyances, and interruptions. Simon (2014. pers. comm.) stated that this is all part of the planning process: "you need to plan for what will happen with the land use and the noise impact from land use. I think it should receive greater attention . . . otherwise give people headphones."

Noises encountered and expected in particular places can lead to people avoiding such places: "I hate any kind of thug noises, so I avoid this little stretch . . . and the music that comes from restaurants, that particularly stands out . . . it's quite jarring, I notice just how jarring it is, and I realize how much I don't like it" (Isabel 2014, pers. comm.). Sound, or noise encounters, can also influence and alter the way in which people negotiate their environments. "It's unpleasant to walk along and just hear traffic sounds. That's pretty much all you hear, so I go the back way where there are less busy roads" (Simon 2014, pers. comm.). Noise can also influence how people emotionally and physically respond to an environment: "if it's too noisy I try to get away as quickly as I can; I get really irritated; frustrated with noise . . . I will leave places if it's really noisy, I will very ostentatiously stick my fingers in my ears" (Kate 2014, pers. comm.).

In recognizing how the soundscape can influence the urban experience, urban practitioners should be striving to create, preserve, and maintain

Figure 8.3 Forgotten songs: Sound installation incorporated into the city of
Sydney's laneway revitalization strategy
Source: Author, 2015.

Figure 8.4 Place activation through music, Liberty Place, Sydney
Source: Author, 2015.

quality sound environments that contain unique characteristics, contribute to the identity of a place and are meaningful for the people experiencing them. For one respondent, the relationship between place, sound, and self is highlighted in these terms: "I like sounds that reassure me that I am a part of where I am . . . unless there is an overlay of natural sounds or social sounds, then the sound closes in on me . . . I don't like no sound, so I think I have a sense of reassurance from social and natural sounds, and I like the complexity" (Naomi 2014, pers. comm.).

Relph (1976: 90) suggests that "the weakening of the identity of places to the point where they not only look and feel alike and offer the same bland possibilities for experience." Such places can be described as placeless, devoid of meaning and identity, as opposed to places that provide meaningful experiences and possess distinctive character in which the soundscape can play an integral role. Busking and street performances are creative ways that places can be activated to enhance the individual experience (Figure 8.4).

'Tuning Out' from Place

The lack of quality urban soundscapes is leading to urban inhabitants disengaging from their surrounds as they reconfigure their relationship to the environment (Bull 2005; Simun 2009). Millions of city dwellers 'tune out' of their environment through the use of earphones and music, then navigate their way through the urban setting, reorganizing the sounds of the city to their liking (Bull 2005). One respondent stated: "I can manipulate the multisensory experience to what I want, I can get into the right mood from what I am hearing, by playing a song . . . I adapt my mood to what I am hearing instead of what I am hearing is adapted to my mood . . . I am more inclined to wear it if I know the area and I am going to less enjoy the sound" (Peter 2014, pers. comm.). This self-induced isolation is changing social behavior within society (Figure 8.5). Users of portable music players are able to "deconstruct and re-construct meanings of the city, and in doing so, they reconfigure not only their relationship to the city, but also the city itself" (Simun 2009: 931). The use of such devices enables the individual to "precisely shape their experience of space, place, others and themselves [and] in doing so . . . experience greater control as they transform urban journeys into private and pleasurable spaces" (Simun 2009: 921).

This modern-day practice comes at the cost of the shared experience of public space, in addition to the individual's awareness of, connection to, and sense of place. This disconnection between people and their surrounds

Figure 8.5 Disengagement from place: People listening to their iPods
Source: Author, 2015.

echoes Relph's notion of *inauthentic places*. Relph (1976: 82) suggests that "an inauthentic attitude to place is essentially no sense of place, for it involves no awareness of the deep and symbolic significances of places and no appreciation of their identities." As previously discussed, the senses are integral to an individual's sense of place, and perceived quality of a place; however, when an individual 'tunes' out from the soundscape, their links to place are compromised. Questions about the quality of the urban soundscape become even more pressing as we try to understand why people are choosing to "shut out and step out of their surroundings [and] exclude the outside world from their experiences" (Byrne 2009: n.p.). Anna (2014, pers. comm.) states that she always wears an iPod when traversing the cityscape: "even when I run out of battery I will still wear it, I like the noise cancelling . . . I wear it just to be in my own world."

Places lacking in quality acoustic features and that are full of noise do not provide a rich soundscape experience for the individual and can lead to a sense of disconnection between people and place. Such a disconnection can result in places that convey little meaning, and urban settings that lack distinctive personalities can result in people suffering from a sense of placelessness. As Relph (2013: 267) suggests, this is "replacing diversity with uniformity." As he wrote in the 1970s, "the casual eradication of distinctive places and the making of standardized landscapes" stems from "insensitivity to the significance of place" (Relph 1976: Preface).

Conclusion

The sensory experience of space leads to the production of place—that is, places of meaning and significance. A deeper understanding is needed for the way each of the human senses is integral to the way the urban environment is encountered, experienced, and perceived. Places are not "abstractions or concepts, but are directly experienced phenomena of the lived-world and hence are full with meanings, with real objects, and with ongoing activities" (Relph 2013: 267). Places provide the context for the soundscape to be experienced, to be heard, and to provide the listener with acoustic information about the world around them.

To ensure that people's experience of place is one that provides sensory nourishment, enhances quality of life, and connects people to their surrounds in a meaningful way, the soundscape warrants attention from those who create and facilitate the development of place. It is not about the lowering of sound levels. It is about the preservation of wanted and valued sounds, thereby enabling and fostering acoustic diversity and richness. It is about enhancing the acoustic experience of place, to ensure that not all places become homogenized, indistinctive, and sound the same, exacerbating the negative connotations of placelessness. It is about tuning into, not out of, place.

Note

1   These are noted in the text as personal communication (pers. comm.) research respondents. Interviews were conducted by the author in the City of Sydney villages of Kings Cross and Surry Hills between March and July 2014.

References

Adams, M., T. Moore, G. Croxford, B. Refaee and S. Sharples (2006) "Sustainable Soundscapes: Noise Policy and the Urban Experience," *Urban Studies* 43, 2385–2398.

Barrett, D. (2004) *Urban Soundscapes: What Should a Public Space Sound Like?*, Boston: Miller & Hanson Inc.

Berger, J. (1972) *Ways of Seeing.* London: BBC/Harmondsworth: Penguin.

Blesser, B. and L.R. Salter (2007) *Spaces Speak, Are You Listening?*, Cambridge: The MIT Press.

Bohme, G. (2000) "Acoustic Atmospheres: a Contribution to the Study of Ecological Aesthetics," *Soundscape: The Journal of Acoustic Ecology* 1, 14–18.

Borer, M. (2013) "Being in the City: The Sociology of Urban Experience," *Sociology Compass* 7, 965–983.

Bull, M. (2005) "No dead air! The iPod and the Culture of Mobile Listening," *Leisure Studies* 24, 343–355.

Buttimer, A. and D. Seamon (1980) *The Human Experience of Space and Place*, London: Croom Helm.

Byrne, B. (2009) The iPod: Development or Digestion. *Avantewhatever*, available at www.avantwhatever.com/bb/wp-content/uploads/2008/03/the_ipod.pdf, accessed July 22, 2011.

Cain, R., P. Jennings, M. Adams, N. Bruce, A. Carlyle, P. Cusack, W. Davies, K. Hume and C.J. Plack (2008) "Soundscape: A Framework for Characterizing Positive Urban Soundscapes," *Proceedings at the Acoustics Conference* 29 June— 4 July, Paris, France.

Casey, E (1993) *Getting back into place: Toward a renewed understanding of the place-world*, Bloomington: Indiana University Press.

Cossette, J. (2014) " 'How Far is it?' Of Geocaching and Emplacement in Athens, Greece," *Totem: The University of Western Ontario Journal of Anthropology* 22, 78–100.

Chueng, P. and P. Marsden (2002) "Designing Auditory Spaces to Support Sense of Place: the Role of Expectation." paper presented at *The Role of Place in Online Communities Workshop*, 27–29 September, New Orleans, LA.

Davies, W.J., M. Adams, N.S. Bruce, R. Cain, A. Carlyle, R. Cusack, K.I. Hume, P.J. Jennings and C.J. Plack (2007) "The Positive Soundscape Project," paper presented at *The 9th International Conference on Acoustics*, 2–7 September 2007, Madrid, Spain.

Feld, S. (1996) "Waterfalls of Song: An Acoustemology of Place Resounding in Bosavi, Papua New Guinea," in S. Feld and K.H. Basso (Eds.) *Senses of Place*, Santa Fe: School of American Research Press, 91–135.

Feld, S. and K.H. Basso (1996) *Senses of Place*, Santa Fe: School of American Research Press.

Gehl, J. (2010) *Cities for People*, Washington: Island Press.

Gieseking, J.J., W. Mangold, C. Katz, S. Low, and S. Saegert (2014) *The People, Place and Space Reader*, New York: Routledge.

Gillespie, A. (2009) "The No Longer Silent Problem: Confronting Noise Pollution in the 21st Century," *Villanova Environmental Law Journal* 20, 181–216.

Godkin, M.A. (1980) "Identity and Place: Clinical Applications based on Notions of Rootedness and Uprootedness," in A. Buttimer and D. Seamon (Eds.) *The Human Experience of Space and Place*, London: Croon Helm, 73–85.

Henshaw, V. and N. Bruce (2012) "Smell and Sound Expectation and the Ambiances of English Cities," in *Proceedings of the 2nd International Congress on Ambiances*, Montreal, 449–454.

Hirt, S.A. (2005) "Toward Postmodern Urbanism? Evolution of Planning in Cleveland, Ohio," *Journal of Planning Education and Research* 25, 27–42.

Howes, D. and C. Classen (2014) *Ways of Sensing: Understanding the Senses in Society*, New York: Routledge.

Jacobs, J. (1961) *Death and Life of Great American Cities*, New York: Random House.

Korsmeyer, C. (2002) *Making Sense of Taste: Food and Philosophy*, New York: Cornell University Press.

Kruger, L.E. (2008) "An Introduction to Place-Based Planning," in J. Farnum and L.E Kruger (Eds.) *Place-based Planning: Innovations and Applications from four Western Forests*, Gen. Tech. Rep. PNW-GTR-741. Portland: U.S. Department of Agriculture, Forest Service.

Landry, C. (2007) "Creativity and the City: Thinking Through the Steps," *The Urban Reinventors Paper Series, Issue 1*, available at www.eukn.org/binaries/eukn/eukn/research/2008/06/creative-city—-thinking-through-the-steps.pdf, accessed August 16, 2011.

—— (2012) *The Sensory Landscape of Cities*. Gloucestershire: Comedia.

Lefebvre, H. (1991) *The Production of Space*, in N.S. Donald (trans.), London: Blackwell Publishing.

Lukermann, F. (1964) "Geography as a Formal Intellectual Discipline and the Way in Which it Contributes to Human Knowledge," *Canadian Geographer* 3, 167–172.

Lynch, K. (1960) *The Image of the City*, Cambridge: Harvard University Press.

—— (1976) *Managing the Sense of a Region*, Cambridge: MIT Press.

Malpas, J. (1999) *Place and Experience: A Philosophical Topography*, Cambridge: Cambridge University Press.

Marshall, N. (2009) "Retreat from the City: Representations of Sense of Place," paper presented at *The State of Australia Cities Conference*, 25–27 November 2009, Perth, Australia.

Porteous, J.D. and J.F. Mastin (1985) "Soundscape," *Journal of Architectural and Planning Research* 2, 169–186.

Porteous, J.D. (1990) *Landscapes of the Mind: Worlds of Sense and Metaphor*, London: University of Toronto Press.

—— (1996) *Environmental Aesthetics: Ideas, Politics and Planning*, London: Routledge.

Proshansky, H.M., A.K. Fabian and R. Kaminoff (1983) "Place-Identity: Physical World Socialization of the Self," *Journal of Environmental Psychology* 3, 57–83.

Raimbault, M. and D. Dubois (2005) "Urban Soundscapes: Experiences and Knowledge," *Cities* 22, 339–350.

Relph, E. (1976) *Place and Placelessness*, London: Pion.

—— (2008) "A Pragmatic Sense of Place," in F. Vanclay, M. Higgins and A. Blackshaw (Eds.), *Making Sense of Place: Exploring Concepts and Expressions of Place Through Different Senses and Lenses*, Canberra: National Museum of Australia Press, 311–323.

—— (2013) "Prospects for Places," in M. Larice and E. Macdonald (Eds.), *The Urban Design Reader*, London: Routledge, 266–271.

Rodaway, P. (1994) *Sensuous Geographies*, London: Routledge.

Schafer, R.M. (1977) *The Tuning of the World*, Toronto: McClelland and Stewart.

—— (1994) *Our Sonic Environment and the Soundscape: The Tuning of the World*, Rochester: Destiny Books.

—— (1996) "Soundscape: A Theme in which Everyone Can Participate," *New Soundscape Newsletter*, 1, August 1996, available at www.wfae.proscenia.net/library/new_newsletter/NSNL01 html, accessed July 8, 2012

Schulte-Fortkamp, B. and D. Dubois (2006) "Preface: Recent Advances in Soundscape Research," *Acta Acoustica United with Acustica* 92, 5–8.

Simun, M. (2009) "My Music, My World: Using the MP3 Player to Shape Experience in London," *New Media & Society* 11, 921–941.

Thompson, E. (2002) *The Soundscape of Modernity: Architectural Acoustics and the Culture of Listening in America, 1900–1933*, Cambridge, MA.: MIT Press.

Thompson, S.M. (2005) "Digestible Difference: Food, Ethnicity and Spatial Claims in the City," in E. Guild and J. van Selm, (Eds.), *International Migration and Security: Culture, Identity, Opportunities and Challenges*, London: Routledge, 217–237.

Truax, B. (1978) *Handbook for Acoustic Ecology*, 5, Music of the Environment Series, World Soundscape Project, Vancouver: ARC Publications.

Truax, B. (2001) *Acoustic Communication*, Westport: Ablex Publishing.

Tuan, Y-F. (1971) "Geography, Phenomenology and the Study of Human Nature," *Canadian Geographer* 14, 193–201.

—— (1975) "Place: An Experiential Perspective," *Geographical Review* 65:2, 151–165.

—— (1977) *Space and Place: The Perspective of Experience*, London: University of Minnesota Press.

—— (1979), "Space and Place: Humanistic Perspective," in S. Gale and G. Olsson (Eds.), *Philosophy in Geography* Boston: Reidel Publishing Company, 387–427.

—— (1993) *Passing Strange and Wonderful: Aesthetics, Nature, and Culture*, Washington D.C: Island Press.

Untaru, S. (2002) "Regulatory Frameworks for Place-based Planning," *Urban Policy and Research* 11, 169–186.

Westerkamp, H. (1991) "The World Soundscape Project," *The Soundscape Newsletter*, 1, available at www.wfae.proscenia.net/library/articles/westerkamp_world.pdf, accessed September 15, 2011.

9   The Risk of Placelessness for Children and Young People in 21st century Cities

Kate Bishop

Introduction

Children and young people growing up in the contemporary cities of developed nations are at greater risk of experiencing both social and environmental placelessness than ever before. The proportion of children and young people as groups in these societies is falling (UN 2013) and they are losing ground on most political agendas in the face of the needs and challenges of ageing populations. Their social voice is a quiet one, and growing quieter. In understanding why this is the case, we need to look at a patchwork of social and environmental influences impacting on children's experience of place in cities in these societies. These include changes in social demographics and, in particular, the decreasing proportion of children in these populations, increased social risk aversion, decreasing environmental opportunity, combined with limited civic influence, participation, and power. Together, this cocktail of considerations undermines children's social status and priority, which in turn influences environmental provision for their needs within communities.

Communities have always struggled to embrace the presence of adolescents in public space, and increasingly children are also less tolerated. In populations where societies are experiencing the lowest birth rates on record (UN 2013), the implications for children and young people and their position and welcome in society are shifting. While parents are becoming more risk averse and overly protective of their children, society in general is becoming less tolerant towards the antics and nature of children and young people (Mackay 2008). We already have child-free developments being proposed (Gleeson and Sipe 2006; Gleeson 2007). It is not unreasonable to suggest that social intolerance will lead to a sense of social placelessness for children and young people ultimately, and that this will lead to experiences of actual placelessness in many communities. At present, children and adolescents already struggle to receive particular attention in the provision of environmental opportunities in most communities. In the face of the social changes taking place in modern societies, this is only likely to get worse. In this chapter, children are defined as being from newborn to 12 years old, and adolescents or young people are defined as being 13–18 years of age.

This chapter is organized in several parts. The next section examines the development of children, childhood, and adolescence as social and cultural constructs, leading to a discussion on children's and young people's continued lack of social status and power and the implications for children's environmental experience. Following is a discussion on the nature of urban childhood experience in particular and the increasing pressures at work in cities, influencing children's environmental and social opportunities in urban neighborhoods. This leads to some concluding reflections on the potential for children to experience placelessness in 21st century cities.

Children, Childhood, and Adolescence as Social and Cultural Constructs

This discussion of children's experience of place and placelessness is based on the theoretical propositions that have emerged from contemporary childhood sociology: that childhood is culturally and spatially segregated from adults' places in the developed world, and that children's "gradual emergence into wider, adult space is only by accident, by degrees, as an award or privilege or as part of a gradualist rite of passage" (James et al. 1998: 37). This description of childhood represents the progression of ideas and attitudes that started in the 17th century, when children were first recognized as being developmentally different from adults (Airès 1962). Neither children nor childhood existed conceptually as a social construct until the 18th century, and since this time this social group and this stage of life have commanded social attention as 'distinct' and 'special,' with particular needs that are different from adults' (Airès 1962). The same conceptual progression is true for adolescence, which is a more modern concept emerging as a social construct in the early 20th century (Hall 1916).

Within Western cultures there has been a long-standing classification of children as 'minors,' not yet adult and therefore not yet competent, responsible, or reliable (Casas 1996). This perception undermines children's opportunities to participate in social processes such as community development. Approaches to children's participation are linked to fundamental beliefs about children and childhood that are culturally engendered. It can be these beliefs that often restrict children's ability to participate effectively, because they encompass views on competence, generations, power relations, and status (Alderson 2001; Mayall 2002).

Children's experience in all areas of life, including their environmental experience, has received greater attention as the needs of children and adolescents have been better understood and given greater social value. Since the United Nations Convention on the Rights of the Child (UNCRC) (1989), there has been a steady increase in participatory research with children and youth. Contemporary social researchers now begin with the assumption that childhood and adolescence have an intrinsic social status and value that commands recognition and respect, and that both need to be understood as particular entities in themselves, with their own cultures, and not merely as part of a larger continuum of development (Graue and Walsh 1998; James et al. 1998; Christensen and James 2000; Lewis and Lindsay 2000).

Respecting childhood and adolescence as being distinct periods of life and having distinctive associated cultures is relatively recent, emerging in full only since World War Two, with increased economic prosperity (Fornas and Bolin 1995; Nilan et al. 2007). It emerged most powerfully in children and youth research following the UNCRC (1989). But what ground has truly been gained for children's and young people's social status? There is no doubt that the UNCRC (1989) has helped to raise awareness of children's rights, needs, and capacities to participate in social processes that affect their lives, and this has certainly penetrated the way we now research children's and young people's lives. But has it really penetrated the social psyche beyond that in terms of civic and social processes such as community design and planning? The evidence discussed in this chapter would suggest it has not.

No Social Status, No Civic Power

Children and young people still have very little social and civic status and power in most developed societies (Chawla 2002; de Visscher and Bouverne-De Bie 2008). Participatory projects with them are still rare, and bespoke rather than the result of embedded institutional procedures and policies. In a capitalist society where human beings are often valued in relation to their capacity to work and produce wealth, children are valued in relation to what they can become—a workforce of the future. As Woolcock et al. (2010: 181) state, "children have not made the balance sheet" in terms of the conventions of economic rationalism. Drawing on Qvortrup et al.'s (1994: 4) phrase, we have not managed to see them as "human beings rather than human becomings," and this is the case in many developed societies.

In fact, societal tolerance for children and childhood in developed nations is breaking down as more of the population chooses not to have children, and those that do have just one or two (Mackay 2008). This, coupled with an increase in parental risk aversion in these societies, ensures that children are increasingly absent from public life and space. Parents' increased risk aversion results in a lack of permission for children to explore their neighborhoods by themselves. This is in contrast to previous generations who consistently explored their neighborhoods independently (Tandy 1999; Mackett et al. 2007). This in turn undermines children's capacity to develop social connections and networks within their neighborhoods, which in turn undermines their social status within their communities (Chawla 2002).

For adolescents, social acceptance has always been problematic, especially for young boys (Eubanks Owens 1999). They have long been seen as a threat to social order (Malone 1999) and, in a climate of growing intolerance for young people, this is increasingly formalized in loitering ordinances, curfews, and the advent of devices such as *The Mosquito* (a device installed in public spaces that emits a high pitched sound that only young people can hear, to drive them out of the space). This age group has always struggled to find its social and environmental place in developed societies and their cities. Young people are portrayed through media and police campaigns as deviant, barbaric, unclean, and a threat to social order (Malone 1999; Matthews and Limb 1999; Tranter and Sharpe 2007). However, they are also seen as in need of protection and as vulnerable to a range of "risks" posed by modern societies (Hillman 1999). The conflict in these attitudes undermines the consistent inclusion of this social group in civic processes.

Urban Childhood is on the Rise and the Nature of it is Changing

The world's population is increasingly urban (UN 2014), and therefore it follows that modern childhood for many nations will be an urban one. Currently in Australia, for example, approximately 90% of the population under 14 years of age lives in urban and major regional centers (AIHW 2012). In the developing nations the rural–urban drift means that childhood is also increasingly urban (UN 2014). Most of the world's children will grow up in urban environments from this time forward.

Much debate surrounds children and childhood concerning the impact of changes in social trends in the developed world on environmental experiences. Childhood is perceived as being increasingly spatially segregated from adult lives and lived in private rather than public spaces (Nieuwenhuys 2003). After home and school, neighborhoods are the most significant spaces for children to be physically active (Wridt 2010; Carroll et al. 2015). They are also one of the most potent settings in influencing the relationship between children and society, because the neighborhood is one of the main settings in which children can get to know the meanings, rules, and values of their community. Neighborhoods are also the place where children get to experience different social positions and processes and potentially influence them (de Visscher and Bouverne-De Bie 2008). Research to date indicates that if children are not given permission to go out, this affects the development of their emotional bonds to place, especially natural settings (Kong 2000), the acquisition of spatial skills (Risotto and Giuliani 2006), and their sense of responsibility for the environment (Palmberg and Kuro 2000). Contact with natural places as a child has also been positively linked to children's health and development through providing: space for exploratory and dramatic play; places to interact socially; opportunities to develop imagination, creativity and resourcefulness; and places to manage emotional self-regulation and restoration (Hart 1979; Faber et al. 1998; Korpela 1992; Valentine and McKendrick 1997; Korpela et al. 2001; Ward Thompson 2007). The research that exists clearly indicates that children's connection to place—socially and emotionally—is undermined by changes in social attitudes. A greater recognition of the *social* value of public and community spaces and places in children's lives is needed in formal planning and design processes.

Children, Cities and Place

Designing cities which are inclusive for, and cognizant of, children and adolescents is becoming imperative. Over the past decade the interest in the implications of children's environmental experience has greatly increased in social and health science research (Jackson 2003; Papas et al. 2007; Feng et al. 2010). This is largely due to changes in social attitudes to childhood, perceived loss of environmental opportunities in urban settings, and increases in the prevalence of health problems such as obesity and mental illness within the populations of many developed nations. Increasingly, disciplines such as medicine are recognizing the role of the physical environment in shaping the outcomes that the discipline cares about, such as community health. This has produced new areas of interdisciplinary research concerned with the nature and quality of the urban built environment for promoting healthy life styles and supporting community wellbeing (Giles Corti 2006). The experience of children and youth has been one of the areas targeted in this burgeoning field of research (Evans 2003; Leyden 2003; Gordon-Larsen 2006).

In relation to research into children's experience of cities, key research areas include: the ways children use place and space; their environmental and activity preferences; differences in environmental needs and use based on age and gender; the environmental attributes that need to be present to support children's health, wellbeing and development; the impact of technology; and the need to address environmental provision for children more holistically through movements such as child-friendly cities and to move away from addressing their needs exclusively through educational, recreational, and residential settings. Modern urban childhood still remains rooted principally in a local experience of place. Urban children's experience of place has always been conditioned by social and cultural norms and attitudes, environmental opportunity, and access. Traditionally, most childhoods are very place-centered, with children spending the bulk of their time in a limited number of neighborhood environments. Although mobility and the capacity for communication and information exchange has increased for children, as it has for all members of contemporary developed societies, childhoods are still place-centered. Children's lived experience of local neighborhoods still remains the most powerful in their everyday experience of place (Wridt 2010; Carroll et al. 2015).

What is changing is the actual environmental opportunity that is available for children in these neighborhoods. Children are faced with an actual experience of placelessness in modern urban contexts, because increasingly the availability of environmental opportunity for them is under threat. If we accept that physical environments are an expression of the values of the societies that build them (Relph 1976; Sanoff 2010), not surprisingly, this translates into limited environmental consideration for children and young people in the planning processes of most communities. Children's lack of social status, in combination with the pressures on modern urban planning and design to deliver more residential capacity, increasingly translate into less environmental opportunity within our communities for children and young people. Movements in planning, such as increasing urban densification, are a direct threat to children's environmental opportunity and social acceptance. Described as "child-blind" (Woolcock et al. 2010: 183), this urban planning strategy is on the increase in major urban centers around the world.

Diminishing Environmental Opportunity

As Churchman (2003: 101) states: "we can with a high degree of certainty assert that, on the whole, cities are not planned and managed with children in mind." Historically, the 'place' needs of children and young people have not been recognized comprehensively by planners and designers of cities. Instead, children's environmental needs are usually summarized in three very traditional environments: their homes, schools, and recreational settings such as playgrounds and skate parks (Churchman 2003). This is not meant to devalue these formal places in children's lives. Indeed, they are increasingly important as children's access to their neighborhoods and the informal spaces in most urban communities disappears. What we should be seeing is an increase in the formal and sanctioned spaces in urban environments created for children and adolescents in response to diminishing informal environments in urban neighborhoods, but this is not happening (Moore 1997). Children and young people are literally losing ground in most neighborhoods in developed nations.

The substantial recent change is not the presence of the formal, sanctioned environments in cities but the absence of the additional informal environments such as vacant blocks that used to supplement children's urban environmental opportunity beyond these formal environments. These spaces have disappeared in response to increased residential pressure (Moore 1997). They were some of the real 'proving grounds' of childhood in urban neighborhoods in previous generations (Tandy 1999). Many of these places were natural places, and contact with natural environments has been established in research as being crucial for social and cognitive development. The diversity and quality of environments in which children's activities take place are also important for a young person's physical, social, cognitive, and emotional development (Wridt 2010). So the loss of these places stands to impact all crucial domains of children's and young people's lives.

The Threat of Urban Consolidation: Australia as a Case Study

One of the major planning responses to the pressure of the need for more residential capacity in cities is urban consolidation. It is one of the main urban planning strategies for most major Australian cities (Sydney, Melbourne, Brisbane, Perth, and Adelaide) as it is in other developed nations around the world. In Australia's case, it is implemented through increasing the proportion of medium-to-high-density dwellings, particularly apartments (Easthope and Tice 2011). It is driven by the need to accommodate expanding city populations in ways that limit greenfield sprawl and the need for further city infrastructure. Although families are not the dominant household type living in apartments, at only 25% (ABS 2006), this subgroup is increasing and there is growing concern about the implications of this built form in constraining children's experiences (Gleeson and Sipe 2006; Woolcock et al. 2010; Easthope and Tice 2011). Easthope and Tice (2011: 431) call on local developers and local and state governments "not to forget one of the dominant sub-sectors [i.e. families] of the residential apartment population in Sydney." Even as early as the mid-1990s, Yates (1995) identified that there were two major problems if an urban development project was not developed with children in mind: inadequate facilities and spaces to support children's needs (no play areas, no outdoor access, a lack of family orientated amenities, unsafe design solutions), and an intolerance of children by other residents (with the rules and regulations of a project often not being child friendly).

As Gleeson (2007) has pointed out, many strata-title developments now legislate against children, for example banning play in common areas. Woolcock et al. (2010) also defend the need for more attention to be paid to meeting the needs of children in the new compact city. They discuss the idea that certain urban forms support different social processes, and that the compact city presents children with new challenges in terms of defending any social status they might have. They argue that the new compact city will be developed into "zones based on age, life style, and household composition with town centers for the childless, the suburbs remaining for the minority with children" (Woolcock et al. 2010: 184). Recsei (2005: 76) maintains that the compact city will leave families with an increasingly limited housing choice of either an inner city unit or an outer area house, with more and more families living in group housing, which is not likely to be socially successful. So there are at least two forms of potential placelessness inherent in this policy in relation to urban children's experience. The first is simply social exclusion from whole sections of the city. The second is a form of social blindness, resulting in very poor spatial provision for children in the areas and facilities surrounding residential blocks.

In choosing this form of planning solution, are we actually returning to a housing type that has already been rejected? In discussing the experience of this new planning ideal also being used in Sweden, Björklid and Nordström (2007) observe that modern housing density is even denser than in the 19th century when social and environmental problems led to the housing reform and garden suburb movements. This intense form of city living also leads to increased traffic intensity and a reduction in suitable outdoor areas for children, leading to further restriction of children's independent mobility because of increased parental fear of the traffic danger. These trends all remove children from public places and induce an experience of social and environmental placelessness. They also mean that childhood will be lived increasingly indoors and the experience of social isolation will increase.

Potential of Placelessness for Urban Children

When Relph first described placelessness, his intention was to decry the impact of global corporate cultures on urban cityscapes. He was afraid of the potential loss of urban environmental idiosyncrasy and identity and a creeping sameness across cities resulting in non-places or placelessness for their residents. In passing, he discussed the relationship between people, place, and identity stating:

> The relationship between community and place is indeed a very powerful one in which each reinforces the identity of the other, and in which the landscape is very much an expression of communally held beliefs and values and of interpersonal involvements.
>
> (Relph 1976: 34)

Relph argued that the identities of people and place are intricately linked, and that the landscape of a community reflects this identity, which is ultimately an expression of the local community's values. He argued for these connections as a potent set of interrelationships: "in short people are their place and a place is its people" (Relph 1976: 34).

The implications of the landscape as a fundamental expression of a community's values are worth further exploration in relation to children's experience. If the 'landscape' of a community is interpreted to mean the collective physical settings of a community, Relph's assumptions about the strength of the association between community, landscape, and identity situate contemporary urban children and their sense of place in a very vulnerable position. If children's experience of place is increasingly narrowed and their presence in public life increasingly reduced, then it is possible to anticipate a reduced sense of place for urban children and possibly a reduced sense of community and of belonging in communities whose values increasingly isolate children and childhood from adult space and public life. Relph's (1976) original definition of placelessness did not include an experience of actual placelessness, meaning an experience of 'no place' either socially or environmentally in a community, but this would seem the most useful extension of this concept from children's perspectives in contemporary urban environments.

Increasingly, in urban communities children are accorded less space— socially and environmentally. It is not illogical to suggest that this may lead to an experience of actual placelessness in many urban communities where children's relationship with both the physical and the social environments of their communities is not strong and they experience little opportunity to influence the values and decisions of their communities. In reality, it is hard to imagine that communities will decide not to provide playgrounds, at the very least, for children. However, the experience of placelessness does not need to be a literal one; it can also be perceptual. If children perceive a lack of welcome in their communities, which translates into a poor sense of belonging or a poor sense of social place within their communities, then a sense of social placelessness, at least, will not be far behind. If, as Relph (1976) suggests, community landscapes are indeed a reflection of a community's social values then a sense of social placelessness may readily translate into an experience of physical placelessness within communities for children.

Conclusion

Policy settings are powerful in children's and young people's social and environmental outcomes. It is necessary to give children a place in urban planning and design to ensure they are considered as population groups with real needs. As Chawla (2002) argues, people-centered development requires a shift in focus from products and construction to people and process. This represents a significant cultural shift in many planning and design processes. There are of course many potential points of breakdown from children's and young people's perspectives in all processes that create the built environment, and children need champions in key places in the development process (Chawla 2002).

If the first two decades of life were given greater social status and value, and children and young people were regularly included in community planning and development processes, environmental opportunities would be greatly improved (Hart 1997; Horelli 1998; 2006; Driskell 2002). Institu-tionalizing children's engagement and participation in the planning and design of their environments, and enabling adults to see children in terms of their competencies, provides benefits for society as well as for children themselves (Chawla 2002). As Chawla (2002: 21) states, "a focus on chil-dren in development planning leads to attention to human development, community quality and basic needs, health-promoting environmental standards and the long-term consequences of decisions . . . which increase[s] social and environmental well-being for all ages, now and in the future."

Children's social place is directly linked to their ultimate environmental opportunity in most communities. They have little power to change their own social status and are at the mercy of adult priorities. If our definition of what constitutes suitable environmental opportunity for children and young people is limited, then this may be all that children are left with as a basis for their experience of place in any community. A limited definition of what is suitable environmental provision for children and young people, coupled with the disappearance of informal spaces in most neighborhoods, ensures that children are literally losing ground. They will never be entirely without places, but their places are increasingly restricted in cities. A sense of social and environmental placelessness will not be far behind.

References

Alderson, P. (2001) "Research by Children," *International Journal of Social Research Methodology* 4, 139–153.

Ariès, P. (1962) *Centuries of Childhood: A Social History of Family Life*, Robert Baldick (trans.), New York: Vintage.

Australian Bureau of Statistics (2006) *Census of Population and Housing*, Canberra, ABS

—— (2009) *Children's Participation in Cultural and Leisure Activities, Australia*, Canberra, ABS

Australian Institute of Health and Welfare (2012) *A Picture of Australia's Children*, Canberra, AIHW

Björklid, P., and M. Nordström (2007) "Environmental Child-Friendliness: Collaboration and Future," *Children, Youth and Environments* 17, 388–401.

Carroll, P., K. Witten, R. Kearns and P. Donvan (2015) "Kids in the City: Children's Use and Experiences of Urban Neighborhoods in Auckland, New Zealand," *Journal of Urban Design*, 20, 417–436.

Casas, F. (1996) "Children's Rights and Children's Quality of Life: Conceptual and Practical Issues," *Social Indicators Research* 42, 283–298.

Chawla, L. (2002) "Insight, Creativity and Thoughts on the Environment: Integrating Youth into Human Settlement Development," *Environment and Urbanization* 14, 11–21.

Christensen, P. and A. James (2000) *Research with Children: Perspectives and Practices*, London: Falmer Press.

Churchman, A. (2003) "Is There a Place for Children in the City?" *Journal of Urban Design* 8, 99–111.

De Visscher, S. and B. Bouverne-De (2008) "Children's Presence in the Neighborhood: A Social-Pedagogical Perspective," *Children & Society* 22, 470–481.

Driskell, D. (2002) *Creating Better Cities with Children and Youth: A Manual for Participation*, London: Earthscan.

Easthope, H. and Tice, A. (2011) "Children in Apartments: Implications for the Compact City," *Urban Policy and Research* 29, 415–434.

Eubanks Owens, P. (1999) "No Teens Allowed: The Exclusion of Adolescents from Public Space," *Bulletin of People-Environment Studies* 14, 21–24.

Evans, G.W. (2003) "The Built Environment and Mental Health," *Journal of Urban Health* 80, 536–555.

Faber, T.A., A. Wiley, F. Kuo and W.C. Sullivan (1998) "Growing Up in the Inner City: Green Spaces as Spaces to Grow," *Environment and Behavior* 30, 3–27.

Feng, J., T.A. Glass, F.C. Curriero, W.F. Stewart and B.S. Schwartz (2010) "The Built Environment and Obesity: A Systematic Review of the Epidemiologic Evidence," *Health & Place* 16, 175–190.

Fornas, J. and G. Bolin (1995) (Eds). *Youth Culture in Late Modernity*, London: Sage.

Giles-Corti, B. (2006) "The Impact of Urban Form on Public Health," paper prepared for the 2006 *Australian State of the Environment Committee*, Canberra: Department of the Environment and Heritage.

Gleeson, B. and N. Sipe (Eds.) (2006) *Creating Child-Friendly Cities: Reinstating Kids in the City*, London: Routledge.

Gleeson, B. (2007) "Child-Friendly Cities," in R. Atkinson, T. Dalton, B. Norman and G. Wood (Eds.). *Urban 45: New Ideas for Australia's Cities*, Melbourne: RMIT University, 31–34.

Gordon-Larsen, P., N.D. Nelson, P. Page and B.M. Popkin (2006) "Inequality in the Built Environment Underlies Key Health Disparities in Physical Activity and Obesity," *Pediatrics* 117, 417–424.

Graue, M.E. and D.J. Walsh (1998) *Studying Children in Context: Theories, Methods, and Ethics*, Thousand Oaks: Sage.

Hall, G.S. (1916) *Adolescence: Its Psychology and its Relations to Physiology, Anthropology, Sociology, Sex, Crime, Religion and Education*, Volume Two, New York: Appleton and Co.

Hart, R.A. (1979) *Children's Experience of Place*, New York: Irvington.

—— (1997) *Children's Participation*, London: Earthscan.

Hillman, M. (1999) "The Impact of Transport Policy on Children's Development," *Canterbury Safe Routes to Schools Project Seminar, Canterbury Christ Church University College*, 29 May, available at www.spokeseastkent.org.uk/mayer.htm, accessed September 5, 2010.

Horelli, L. (1998) "Creating Child-Friendly Environments—Case Studies on Children's Participation in Three European Countries," *Childhood* 5, 225–239.

Horelli, L. (2006) "A Learning-Based Network Approach to Urban Planning with Young People," in C. Spencer and M. Blades (Eds.) *Children and their environments: Learning using and designing spaces*, Cambridge: Cambridge University Press, 238–255.

Jackson, R.J. (2003) "The Impact of the Built Environment on Health: An Emerging Field," *American Journal of Public Health* 93, 1382–1384

James, A., C. Jenks and A. Prout (1998) *Theorizing Childhood*, Cambridge: Polity Press

Kong, L. (2000) "Nature's Dangers, Nature's Pleasures: Urban Children and the Natural World," in S.L. Holloway and G. Valentine (Eds.) *Children's Geographies: Playing, Living, Learning*, London: Routledge, 257–271.

Korpela, K. (1992) "Adolescents' Favorite Places and Environmental Self-Regulation," *Journal of Environmental Psychology* 12, 249–258.

Korpela, K., T. Hartig, F.G. Kaiser and U. Fuhrer (2001) "Restorative Experience and Self-Regulation in Favorite Places," *Environment and Behavior* 33, 572–589.

Lewis, A and G. Lindsay (2000) *Researching Children's Perspectives*, Buckingham, England: Open University Press.

Leyden, K.M. (2003) "Social Capital and the Built Environment: The Importance of Walkable Neighborhoods," *American Journal of Public Health* 93, 1546–1551.

Mackay, H. (2008) "Tomorrow's Society," *Australian Chief Executive* February, 49–53.

Mackett, R., B. Brown, Y. Gong. K. Kitazawa and J. Paskins (2007) "Children's Independent Movement in the Local Environment," *Built Environment* 33, 454–468.

Malone, K. (1999) "Growing Up in Cities as a Model of Participatory Planning and 'Place Making' with Young People," *Youth Studies Australia*, 18, 17–23.

Matthews, H. and M. Limb (1999) "Defining an Agenda for the Geography of Children: Agenda and Prospect." *Progress in Human Geography* 23, 61–90.

Mayall, B. (2002) *Towards a Sociology of Childhood: Thinking from Children's Lives*, Buckingham, England: Open University Press.

Moore, R.C. (1997) "The Need for nature: A Childhood Right," *Social Justice* 24, 203–221.

Nieuwenhuys, O. (2003) "Places of Work and Non-Places of Childhood," in K. Fog Olwig and E. Gulløv (Eds.) *Children's Places: Cross cultural perspectives*, London: Routledge, 99–118.

Nilan, P., R. Julian and J. Germov (2007) *Australian Youth: Social and Cultural Issues*, Sydney: Pearson Education Australia.

Palmberg, I. and J. Kuro (2000) "Outdoor Activities as a Basis for Environmental Responsibility," *Journal of Environmental Education* 31, 32–36.

Papas, M.A., A.J. Alberg, R. Ewing, K.J. Helzlsouer, T.L. Gary and A.C. Klassen (2007) "The Built Environment and Obesity," *Epidemiology Review* 29, 129–143.

Qvortrup, J., M. Bardy, G. Sgritta and H. Wintersberger (1994) *Childhood Matters: Social Theory, Practice and Politics*, Aldershot, England: Avebury.

Recsei, T. (2005) "Pipe Dreams: The Shortcomings of Ideologically Based Planning," *People and Place* 13, 68–81

Relph, E. (1976) *Place and Placelessness*, London: Pion

Risotto, A. and Giuliani, M.V. (2006) "Learning Neighborhood Environments: The Loss of Experience in a Modern World," in C. Spencer and M. Blades (Eds.) *Children and their environments: Learning, Using and Designing spaces*, Cambridge: Cambridge University Press, 75–90.

Sanoff, H. (2010) *Community Participation Methods in Design and Planning*, New York: John Wiley & Sons.

Tandy, C.A. (1999) "Children's Diminishing Play Space: A Study of Intergenerational Change in Children's Use of Their Neighborhoods," *Australian Geographical Studies* 37, 154–164.

Tranter, P. and S. Sharpe (2007) "Children and Peak Oil: An Opportunity in Crisis," *International Journal of Children's Rights*. 15,181–197.

United Nations, Department of Economic and Social Affairs, Population Division (2013) *World Population Ageing 2013*, ST/ESA/SER.A/348.

—— (2014) *World Urbanization Prospects: The 2014 Revision*, ST/ESA/SER.A/352.

Valentine, G. and J. McKendrick (1997) "Children's Outdoor Play: Exploring Parental Concerns About Children's Safety and the Changing Nature of Childhood," *Geoforum* 28, 219–235.

Ward Thompson, C. (2007) "Playful Nature: What Makes the Difference Between Some People Going Outside and Others Not?" in C. Ward Thompson and P. Travlou (Eds.) *Open Space: People Space*, London: Taylor and Francis, 12–23.

Woolcock, G., B. Gleeson and B. Randolph (2010) "Urban Research and Child-Friendly Cities: A New Australian Outline," *Children's Geographies* 8, 177–192.

Wridt, P. (2010) "A Qualitative GIC Approach to Mapping Urban Neighborhoods with Children to Promote Physical Activity and Child-Friendly Community Planning," *Environment and Planning B: Planning and Design* 37, 129–147.

Yates, R. (1995) *Child-Friendly Housing: A Guide for Housing Professionals*, Vancouver: Society for Children and Youth of British Columbia.

Part 3

Place/lessness in Practice

10 Examining Place-making in Practice

Observations from the Revitalization of Downtown Detroit

Laura Crommelin

Introduction

In the 40 years since *Place and Placelessness* was published, place-making has become an established urban design and revitalization strategy, spawning an international industry of place-making practitioners and consultancies. This chapter provides a case study of a recent place-making project in downtown Detroit, Michigan, to examine how Edward Relph's concept of place-making has been applied in a city grappling with major economic transition. The case highlights some of the tensions created by the evolution of place-making into an increasingly global and corporatized practice, replicated around the world and adopted by governments and developers alike.

After a brief overview of downtown Detroit's recent history and the development of the project, this chapter examines how place-making in Detroit has been shaped by influences at multiple scales, and considers the way these influences have translated into specific outcomes on the ground. The aim of the chapter is not to assess the physical and social impact of the project—a goal that seems premature given its implementation was yet to be completed at the time of writing. Instead, the Detroit project is examined as an example of how place-making has evolved as a practice. Through this analysis, the chapter raises questions about the value of defined processes to 'make' place, and contemplates who such place-making processes are most likely to benefit in practice.[1]

The Rise of Place-making: From Concept to Reality

Among the many concerns associated with globalization has been the fear that our cities will become largely indistinguishable, as increasingly "the places we build appear as clones of places elsewhere: suburban tracts, shopping malls, freeway interchanges, office complexes, and gussied up old neighborhoods vary less and less" (Gieryn 2000: 463). With international networks facilitating processes like inter-urban competition and policy transfer, the same practitioners and ideas now shape urban revitalization efforts around the globe (McCann and Ward 2011). The resulting developments are often critiqued as embodying the "uniformity, standardization and disconnection from context" associated with placelessness, rather than the "ideas of community and locality" associated with place (Relph 2008: 312). Yet as Relph (2008) points out, place and placelessness are never mutually exclusive; everywhere combines elements of both the local and the global, of distinctiveness and homogeneity.

One response to this perceived rise of placeless urban development has been the growth of 'place-making' as a concept and a practice. While the term is used across different disciplines, of particular interest in this chapter is the emergence of place-making as an urban design and revitalization strategy. Underpinning the movement is Relph's vision of place-making, outlined at the end of *Place and Placelessness*, in which he calls for design that is "responsive to local structures of meaning and significance, to particular situations and to the variety of levels of meaning of place" (Relph 1976: 146). Translated into contemporary urban design practice, place-making is understood as the provision of urban spaces that alleviate homogeneity and encourage greater public use (Krieger 2009). In this capacity, place-making has become increasingly popular with urban governments, often in association with broader economic development and physical revitalization strategies. In part this popularity reflects the fact that place-making frequently involves the use of low-cost, short-term interventions that require little technical expertise, and can be implemented without the need for formal approval processes.

The growing enthusiasm for place-making has been reflected in the emergence of a new industry of place-making practitioners and consultancies, including the well-known non-profit organization Project for Public Spaces (PPS). Since 1975, PPS has worked in over 3000 communities across 43 countries. In line with Relph's concept, PPS stresses that place-making is more than a set of design principles; it is "a process and a philosophy" that "capitalizes on a local community's assets, inspiration, and potential" (PPS n.d.a). Among the qualities defining PPS's place-making approach are inclusivity, collaboration, and cultural awareness.

In addition to its project work, PPS now convenes a Place-making Leadership Council with more than 700 members worldwide. This first met in Detroit in 2013 to share ideas about "achieving a common understanding of the issues and challenges facing Place-making—and our goals and opportunities for the future" (Place-making Leadership Council 2013: 1). The international nature of PPS's activities highlights how a worldwide network of place-making practitioners and enthusiasts is now redefining place-making philosophy and practice on a global scale, even as place-making projects remain focused on local engagement and small-scale interventions.

As well as hosting the Place-making Leadership Council, Detroit has recently been the site of a major place-making project, which offers a particularly interesting case study of how place-making has evolved since the 1970s. The project was developed by PPS in collaboration with billionaire Dan Gilbert, one of Detroit's largest property owners and a key figure in the city's revitalization (Austen 2014). In 2012, with the city on the verge of municipal bankruptcy, PPS and Gilbert's company Rock Ventures LLC launched the project to revitalize key public spaces in the downtown area. Given the central roles played by PPS and a major corporation in its design, this place-making project offers some telling insights into the development of place-making into both a globally networked movement and a practice with growing corporate involvement.

Detroit: Rebooting the Heart of the Motor City

Detroit is best known as the home of the American automotive industry, which in the 20th century "determined the city's fate and defined its character" (Hyde 2001: 57). Between 1910 and 1920 Detroit jumped from the ninth to the fourth most populous US city, with new residents drawn by factory jobs offering middle-class prosperity. This economic golden era was not to last, however, and the second half of the century saw the city grappling with declining employment, tax, and population levels, as suburban development flourished and auto-making facilities closed or relocated.

From its mid-20th century peak of nearly two million residents, today the City of Detroit's shrinking population of just under 700,000 is spread over 139 square miles. The result is widespread property vacancy, with a recent comprehensive survey identifying over 110,000 vacant lots and 40,000 blighted structures requiring demolition (Blight Removal Task Force 2014). The reduced tax base has exacerbated the city's economic and social challenges, while the suburban population shift has resulted in significant segregation between the predominantly black Detroit and the predominantly white suburbs, entrenching racial and political divisions across the metropolitan region. As Sugrue (2005) convincingly argues, the city's difficult racial history has played a key role in many of its ongoing challenges, from high poverty rates to inadequate public services.

Detroit's financial challenges came to a head in July 2013, with the city's emergency financial manager instituting bankruptcy proceedings. It was the biggest municipal bankruptcy in US history and has been characterized as both a low point and a turning point for the city (Helms et al. 2013). Yet even as the bankruptcy occurred, some parts of the city were experiencing economic growth, most notably a spurt of redevelopment downtown. The area has seen over $9 billion[2] in real estate investment since 2006, reducing commercial vacancies from 27% in 2010 to 16% in 2014 (Hudson-Webber Foundation 2015).

Much of this activity is the result of efforts by businessman Dan Gilbert through his various corporate interests, which include companies involved in mortgage lending (Quicken Loans), real estate (Bedrock Real Estate Services) and venture capital funding (Detroit Venture Partners), most of which sit under the umbrella company Rock Ventures LLC.[3] Through these interests Gilbert claims to have invested more than $1.7 billion in the revitalization of downtown Detroit, purchasing more than 70 properties, bringing 12,500 staff downtown and developing the 'Opportunity Detroit' rebranding campaign (Quicken Loans 2015). The campaign has promoted a positive image of downtown Detroit in various ways, including a 60-second TV commercial during the 2012 World Series baseball playoffs, a website showing where to 'Live, Work and Play' in Detroit, a weekly podcast, banners displayed around the city (Figure 10.1), and a social media presence. The Opportunity Detroit tagline was also used on a full-page advertisement in national newspapers after Detroit's bankruptcy filing, highlighting 28 major Michigan-based companies involved in the city's revitalization.

Through these investments, Gilbert is undoubtedly playing a significant part in reshaping downtown Detroit physically and economically. Rock Ventures' efforts are also clearly designed to reshape downtown Detroit's image, and Gilbert is highly visible in mainstream media reports about the

Figure 10.1 Opportunity Detroit banners on Woodward Avenue
Source: Author, 2013.

city (e.g. Segal 2013; Austen 2014). Gilbert is also Vice President of the non-profit consortium developing Detroit's new M-1 streetcar project, which will link downtown to the cultural district, while Rock Ventures' President Matt Cullen is M-1's President and CEO. These roles indicate the breadth of Rock Ventures' involvement in the revitalization of downtown Detroit, where Gilbert is now both a major private investor and a key player in what might traditionally have been public infrastructure projects.

The Place-making Vision: Making a Place to Drive to Instead of Drive Through

On 28 March 2013, PPS and Rock Ventures launched "A Place-making Vision for Downtown Detroit" (Opportunity Detroit 2013) after more than seven months of planning. Three other urban consulting firms were also involved in this planning process, while the place-making vision ('the vision') lists seven organizations as 'key stakeholders': Rock Ventures LLC, Illitch Holdings Inc., M-1 Rail, the Detroit Economic Growth Corporation (DEGC), the City of Detroit, the Detroit Entertainment District Association, and the Downtown Detroit Partnership. The planning phase was facilitated by D:Hive, a foundation-funded economic development organization and welcome center in downtown Detroit, which provided space for focus groups, workshops, and interactive public displays. Over 1,000 community members contributed to the planning through these mechanisms, which were designed to develop a 'collective vision' to guide the three-year revitalization process. The resulting vision (Opportunity Detroit 2013: 1) outlines:

> how the public spaces, and particularly the three major downtown parks, can be transformed . . . so that they support [the] exciting commercial and residential rebirth in the downtown, and also become destinations in their own right.

As this goal suggests, the vision is designed to complement the redevelopment projects of Rock Ventures and other private investors in the downtown area. As a press release at the time of the launch explained, the vision "ties together the threads" (PR Newswire 2013) of Gilbert's commercial and residential investments over the past five years. It is also explicitly linked with the Opportunity Detroit campaign, bearing its symbol on the cover and throughout the document, and being made available from the Opportunity Detroit website. While the City of Detroit is a key stakeholder and the vision is focused on the revitalization of public spaces, both its development and implementation have been led by Gilbert and Rock Ventures. Key city officials have nonetheless been supportive, with then mayor Dave Bing saying at the time of the launch that "My job . . . is to knock down as many barriers as possible and get out of the way" (Segal 2013). Likewise, current mayor Mike Duggan told the *New York Times* he

had no issue with the private sector playing such a significant part in the city's revitalization (Austen 2014).

The three downtown parks at the heart of the vision are Campus Martius, Capitol Park, and Grand Circus Park. To revitalize these parks, the vision adopts a number of PPS's established place-making principles, including the 'Lighter, Quicker, Cheaper' ('LQC') concept and the 'Power of 10' model. As the vision explains, the LQC concept proposes that place-making be initiated by developing "a moderate cost, high-impact framework for short-term, experimental intervention in public spaces" (Opportunity Detroit 2013: 12), which provides momentum and tests out ideas while longer-term change is implemented. The Power of 10 model dictates that to attract public interest and keep visitors engaged, a CBD needs a minimum of ten 'great destinations,' each containing at least ten 'places.' These 'places' are smaller areas within the destinations, offering such attractions as seating, food stalls, play equipment, and public art. Using these concepts, and drawing on feedback received during the planning phase, the vision identified a series of projects to be implemented over two years, ranging from short-term changes such as temporary seating and games equipment, to long-term im-provements such as redesigning surrounding roads and developing annual events programming.

The three parks at the center of the vision are some of the most signifi-cant public spaces in downtown Detroit. Not surprisingly, therefore, a number of events associated with the parks in recent years have highlighted some of the tensions created by the unique mix of public and private involvement in downtown Detroit's revitalization.

Arguably a model for the current place-making strategy, Campus Martius was redeveloped and is managed by a non-profit corporation called the Detroit 300 Conservancy, through a contract with the City of Detroit. Both city government and corporate representatives sit on the board of the Conservancy, which attracted the funding for the park's revitalization in the early 2000s, and continues to provide event programming, upgrades, and private security. This public/private approach has recently attracted some scrutiny after the American Civil Liberties Union (ACLU) lodged a lawsuit against the Conservancy, claiming that the park's private security force illegally prevented protesters from exercising their First Amendment rights to demonstrate peacefully in a public space. In response, the City of Detroit has adopted new rules explicitly allowing peaceful protests in the park (Guillen 2015).

Somewhat more entertainingly, perhaps, Grand Circus Park was the subject of an unofficial rebranding effort by Rock Ventures, which sought to emphasize the city's tech-friendly culture by renaming key downtown sites: Woodward Avenue as 'Webward Avenue,' the Madison Building as 'the M@dison,' and Grand Circus Park as 'Grand Circuit Park' (Beshouri 2013). While only 'the M@dison' has stuck (the building is home to Rock Ventures' tech startup hub), the other rebranding efforts can nonetheless be seen as evidence of Gilbert's desire to reshape the city's public spaces in line with his broader revitalization efforts.

In the vision, Capitol Park is designated as the centerpiece of a new 'arts district' for downtown Detroit. Not long after the vision's release, however, artists were reportedly being evicted from a Bedrock–purchased building overlooking Capitol Park. While Bedrock cited seemingly legitimate safety issues with the dilapidated building, the move nonetheless triggered debate about how Gilbert's efforts might facilitate gentrification, and whether only a certain kind of art fits the place-making vision (Felton 2014) (Figure 10.2).

Notwithstanding these tensions, much of the local press coverage at the time of the vision's release was positive. PPS subsequently claimed that an evaluation of the first summer's LQC initiatives "showed a huge increase in foot traffic in the area, and much heavier use of public spaces with a mix of people that truly represented the entirety of the Detroit region" (PPS, n.d.b). A subsequent survey by another of the vision's key stakeholders also showed improving local perceptions of downtown as a whole, particularly its recreational facilities, and noted Campus Martius as a key downtown destination (Downtown Detroit Partnership 2014). John Gallagher, a well-known Detroit urban affairs reporter and author, recently concluded that

Figure 10.2 Graffiti on a building overlooking Capitol Park. Renderings of Capitol Park in the vision show a graffiti-free building

Source: Author, 2013.

the "programming and flexibility" of PPS's place-making strategies had made Campus Martius a success, with similar features needed to revive another major downtown park, Hart Plaza (Gallagher 2015).

While such positive assessments of place-making's impact on Detroit are heartening, it remains to be seen how long-lasting the project's benefits will be. In the meantime, the Detroit experience offers some valuable insights into how place-making has evolved as a practice. In particular, two aspects of the vision raise questions about the extent to which Relph's 1976 conceptualization of place-making remains relevant: its global influences, and the degree of corporate involvement. The remainder of the chapter will consider these two aspects of the vision in more detail.

Place-making in Practice: the Local Movement is Global

As noted above, PPS is at the center of a growing global network of place-making practitioners, activists, and consultancies. Reflecting the "local globalness" of urban policy-making more broadly (McCann and Ward 2011: xvi), this international perspective has informed the vision in various ways. For example, in explaining the approach to be adopted in Detroit, the vision notes that "[a]t a 2010 PPS forum in Vancouver, BC . . . several principles emerged that provide a context to better understand the opportunities for downtown Detroit" (Opportunity Detroit 2013: 16). Beyond the sharing of key principles, PPS's global experience is also reflected in the tangible changes proposed for downtown Detroit. One of the first place-making installations to be implemented—the temporary beach in Campus Martius—replicates the Paris Plages project by the Seine River, as PPS Senior Vice President Ethan Kent noted (quoted in Steuteville 2014):

> That idea was inspired by what is going on in Paris . . . In Detroit, it is a similar idea—the people who can't afford to go to the lakes of northern Michigan now have a beach right there in the center of Detroit.

Likewise, the vision indicates that some of the more significant, long-term changes proposed are directly inspired by international examples of successful urban design. These include making the northern part of Woodward Ave 'the place to be seen,' like the Champs-Elysées in Paris, and transforming the southern part into an esplanade, similar to Las Ramblas in Barcelona or Helsinki's Esplanadi.

Certainly, PPS is not alone in looking globally for design inspiration, even in the context of efforts intended to reflect local needs and desires. In a related context, Mimi Zeiger (2012) has critiqued the increasing homogeneity of the Do-It-Yourself (DIY) urban design movement, which involves residents making unsanctioned, functional, and civic-minded alterations to urban space (Douglas 2014). While these interventions are generally small-scale and highly localized, they are increasingly influenced by a global flow of design ideas shared primarily through social media. An early proponent of the movement, Zeiger (2012) has since become more circumspect:

> As each project is created, then adopted by subsequent groups and formally repeated (every iteration fleetingly distributed across the Internet), a set of visual aesthetics codifies around it. Modes of DIY making and participatory actions are rendered in bright colors and repurposed shipping pallets, as if low-tech craftsmanship and nonformal design are just the thing needed to deflate any pomposity attached to notions of high art or architecture. More importantly, and perhaps more critically, as a group these tactical projects collect into a set of programmatic aesthetics. There's a series of program typologies at work: microparks, urban farms, pop-up shops, and community-gathering spaces. Solo, each one is a much-needed intervention, but taken together they unwittingly champion traditional city-beautiful values—and as such present a more conservative urban-planning position.

Much the same argument can be made about some place-making projects, which replicate not only principles like LQC but also aesthetics (as an example, Figure 10.3 shows the similar installations in Detroit and Paris). In doing so the design of these installations reflects the "uniformity, standardization and disconnection from context" that Relph associates with placelessness, rather than capturing any quality of local distinctiveness.

While such projects may still prove effective at activating these spaces and fostering economic revitalization, this generic design has prompted some more pointed questions about the real drivers behind these place-making projects. For example, Cleveland-based writer Richey Piiparinen (2013) examined Gilbert's revitalization projects in both Cleveland and Detroit, and offered a fairly damning assessment of the vision's aesthetic and cultural approach:

> So, why this path? Why pretty Detroit? Why make it culturally less distinct? Why embark on a plan of hyper-modern ephemerality when your distinction is resilience, making things, and hard work?

Piiparinen (2013) answers these questions by labeling the vision "copycat urbanism," which is less about making place than it is about making Gilbert money, by attracting the creative class to live and work in his downtown real estate acquisitions. Whether or not this is a fair criticism of Gilbert's motives, it highlights important questions about the role and impact of corporate involvement in place-making projects. Is such corporate involvement a positive sign that place-making is achieving the broad recognition it deserves? Or is it a sign that the concept has become as much about image-making as place-making, thus supporting the broader shift towards urban entrepreneurialism rather than enhancing local connections to place?

Figure 10.3 The Seasonal Beach in Detroit and Paris. Campus Martius, Detroit, 2014 (top) and similar LQC design approaches used for the Paris Plages, 2012 (bottom)

Source: *Top*: Author, 2014; *Bottom*: Sharat Ganapati, Flickr: Paris Plage, 2012, via Wikimedia Commons [CC BY 2.0].

Place-making in Practice: the Corporations Come to Town

While Detroit may be one of the most extreme examples of private involvement in civic place-making efforts, corporations are now an increasingly common feature of place-making more broadly. Kim Dovey (2010: 3) has previously been critical of how the complex concept of place-making is at times simplified into "manipulative corporate formulae," rolled out in standardized developments across the globe. In Detroit, the significant involvement of Rock Ventures is not the only way place-making has been intertwined with corporate strategies; Southwest Airlines also sponsored Campus Martius' beach transformation in 2013, working with PPS and the Downtown Detroit Partnership through its 'Heart of the Community' grants program. Interestingly, this was PPS's first corporate collaboration, labeled "a breakout moment for Place-making" (PPS 2014).

Yet it is the role of Gilbert in the place-making process that raises the most challenging questions. As local planning consultant Richard Carlisle noted about the vision, "what you have here is the marketplace at work . . . This is a private entrepreneur that has a combination of two key things, vision and resources, beyond the scope of most governments" (quoted in Pinho and Walsh 2013). This approach to place-making prompts two key questions: to what extent is the vision inclusive of the desires of the whole community, and to what extent will the redesigned public spaces be available and beneficial to all Detroiters?

On both fronts there are some grounds for concern. On the first question, it is worth noting again that PPS and D:Hive facilitated the involvement of 1,000 local residents in the vision's development, through workshops, casual get-togethers, and a public voting process. Yet at the same time, it is significant that the majority of the vision's key stakeholders were organizations with an established pro-growth agenda, including property developers and the city's economic growth corporation. Much of the community participation was also quite limited: more than 800 of the participants engaged by voting in place-making huts in Campus Martius, choosing eight preferences from a pre-prepared list of activities and amenities, while also being able to offer other revitalization ideas.[4] While the simplicity of this engagement process was a virtue in terms of facilitating high participation rates, it did not allow for detailed engagement with the complex concerns of a full cross-section of local participants and organizations. Meanwhile, the association between the place-making vision and the Opportunity Detroit branding campaign—itself explicitly informed by the goal of repositioning Detroit as an emerging tech hub—reinforces the perception that the views of a particular segment of the Detroit community most significantly informed the vision.

On the second question, there is some unease in Detroit about how Gilbert's companies are now assuming responsibilities normally associated with local government—most notably security. Rock Ventures has installed security cameras throughout downtown Detroit, and has security agents patrolling the streets and watching camera feeds from the 'Qube' building across from Campus Martius. A *Detroit Free Press* journalist recently raised concerns about the extent and legitimacy of Rock Ventures' activities at this "intersection of private security and public space" (Kaffer 2015), prompting reassurances that the company simply monitors downtown activity and refers all incidents to the Detroit Police Department. Rock Ventures is certainly not the only private company providing such security, and the *Detroit Free Press* (2015) noted that many residents support these efforts, including some who feel downtown has become more inclusive as residents' safety concerns have declined.

Yet as the ACLU's Campus Martius case indicates, there are risks associated with allowing private interests to define what is considered appropriate behavior in public space. It is also worth noting that when listing "issues" to be addressed in Grand Circus Park, the place-making vision states that "[t]he park is occupied primarily by the homeless, discouraging its use by local residents and office workers" (Opportunity Detroit 2013: 56). Certainly, others might also consider this an "issue"—as the vision points out, almost all of the park's seating has since been removed, presumably by the city seeking to reduce the park's appeal to the homeless community. Nonetheless, such language seems at odds with the ideals underpinning place-making philosophy, as does another aspect of Rock Ventures' efforts (Kaffer 2015):

> [Rock Ventures LLC] has stepped outside a strict corporate role, working actively to incarnate Gilbert et al.'s vision of downtown, filling storefronts with restaurants and retail, adding benches and recreational space, and inexplicably affixing speakers blaring eclectic musical selections onto downtown streets.

While the musical selections may seem inexplicable, this description brings to mind the strategy of deterring 'antisocial behavior' by playing unappealing music in areas where young people congregate (Maley 2006). Again, such efforts may meet with approval from many local residents, who would otherwise be discouraged from using downtown spaces. But what does it mean for place-making as a practice—one built around the goal of inclusiveness, at least in the PPS model—if such practices and perspectives are part of the way downtown Detroit is being remade through place-making? This is an issue not just for the Detroit project but the broader place-making movement, which Mehta (2012) argues has not focused closely enough on equity when assessing the outcomes of place-making projects.

Conclusion

Looking at the Detroit place-making vision as a whole, then, there is evidence to support concerns about how the contemporary practice of place-making has evolved. There are various aspects of the Detroit vision that can be criticized as generic, imported, and designed primarily to serve major corporate interests—all qualities more commonly associated with creating placelessness than place. Yet it remains the case that making sandcastles in Campus Martius does not feel the same as lounging in a beach chair by the Seine in Paris; these experiences are shaped by the distinctive spirit of place of these cities, even as globally replicated interventions like temporary beaches make them more physically alike. In this way, Relph's observations about everywhere embodying both place and placelessness are reinforced. In other words, the enduring significance of place as a concept is again made apparent: even where attempts to manufacture place may do little to enhance local distinctiveness, place persists.

At the same time, the Detroit experience can also be seen as a powerful example of place-making as a political process, rather than a design strategy. There are few—if any—other cities where such forces might combine: a city with the historical and architectural significance to attract a property investor with Dan Gilbert's resources, yet with financial challenges significantly restricting government involvement; a public sufficiently jaded by failed revitalization promises that a private investor's ability to implement significant change fast is viewed by many as a positive development, even if it means some private encroachment into the public sphere; and challenges on such a scale that a plan to simultaneously redesign multiple downtown public spaces might rank low on the city's list of concerns. In bringing to light these features of Detroit as a city, the vision might therefore be viewed as a quintessential example of place-making as an inevitably political exercise, as with all processes of urban change. In other words, the Detroit place-making vision might best be seen as a case that captures the essence of Wortham-Galvin's (2008: 39) succinct observation: that "place is always a remaking process, never a product."

Notes

1   The author would like to thank Colby King and Patrick Cooper-McCann for their helpful feedback on an earlier draft. Any errors remaining are my own.
2   All dollar amounts in this chapter are in USD.
3   For simplicity Gilbert's corporate interests will be collectively referred to using the name of the umbrella company. Rock Ventures, although Bedrock is actually a separate entity.
4   Participation in this voting exercise was not limited to established local residents; as an international visitor living temporarily in the nearby city of Ann Arbor, I participated during a brief visit to the city.

References

Austen, B. (2014) "The Post-Post-Apocalyptic Detroit," *New York Times*, 11 July, available at www.nytimes.com/2014/07/13/magazine/the-post-post-apocalyptic-detroit.html, accessed September 12, 2014.

Beshouri, P. (2013) "Bedrock Exec Rebrands Grand Circus Park, Mentions Two Residential Towers for Hudson's Site," *Curbed Detroit*, 22 March, available at www.detroit.curbed.com/archives/2013/03/grand-circuit-park.php, accessed September 14, 2014.

Blight Removal Task Force (2014) *Detroit Blight Removal Task Force Plan*, available at www.report.timetoendblight.org/index.html, accessed August 31, 2015.

Detroit Free Press (2015) "Readers: We'll take safety over privacy in Detroit," *Detroit Free Press*, 18 May, available at www.freep.com/story/opinion/2015/05/18/dan-gilbert-security/27541239/, accessed May 28, 2015.

Douglas, G.C.C. (2014) "Do-It-Yourself Urban Design: The Social Practice of Informal 'Improvement' Through Unauthorized Alteration," *City & Community* 13, 5–25.

Dovey, K. (2010) *Becoming Places: Urbanism/Architecture/Identity/Power*, London: Routledge.

Downtown Detroit Partnership (2014) "Destination: Excellence—2014 Downtown Detroit Perceptions Survey," *Downtown Detroit Partnership*, available at www.downtowndetroit.org/wp-content/uploads/2014/04/2014-Downtown-Detroit-Perceptions-Survey-Executive-Summary.pdf, accessed May 29, 2015.

Felton, R. (2014) "Capitol Park Artists Get the Boot," *Metrotimes*, 12 February, available at www.metrotimes.com/news/capitol-park-artists-get-the-boot-1.163 2841?pgno=1, accessed September 14, 2014.

Gieryn, T.F. (2000) "A Space for Place in Sociology." *Annual Review of Sociology*, 26, 463–496.

Guillen, J. (2015) "Lawsuit: Campus Martius security violated free speech." *Detroit Free Press*, 28 January, available at www.freep.com/story/news/local/michigan/detroit/2015/01/28/aclu-campus-martius/22472923/, accessed May 29, 2015.

Helms, M., N. Kaffer and S. Henderson (2013) "Detroit files for bankruptcy, setting off battles with creditors, pensions, unions." *Detroit Free Press*, 19 July, available at www.freep.com/article/20130718/NEWS01/307180107/Detroit-files-Chapter-9-bankruptcy-amid-staggering-debts, accessed September 14, 2014.

Hudson-Webber Foundation (2015) "7.2 Sq Mi: A Report on Greater Downtown Detroit," *Detroit Seven Point Two*, February (2nd Ed.), available at www.detroitsevenpointtwo.com/resources/7.2SQ_MI_Book_FINAL_LoRes.pdf, accessed May 29, 2015.

Hyde, C.K. (2001) " 'Detroit the Dynamic': The Industrial History of Detroit from Cigars to Cars," *Michigan Historical Review* 27, 57–73.

Kaffer, N. (2015) "Watching Dan Gilbert's watchmen," *Detroit Free Press*, 18 May, available at www.freep.com/story/opinion/columnists/nancy-kaffer/2015/05/18/quicken-detroit-security/27521889/, accessed May 28, 2015.

Krieger, A. (2009) "Where and how does urban design happen?" in A. Krieger and W.S. Saunders (Eds.) *Urban Design*, Minneapolis: University of Minnesota Press, 113–130.

Maley, J. (2006) "Forget Asbos. Australia uses Barry Manilow," *The Guardian*, 6 June, available at www.theguardian.com/world/2006/jun/06/arts.australia, accessed May 31, 2015.

McCann, E. and K. Ward (Eds.) (2011) *Mobile urbanism: cities and policymaking in the global age*, Minneapolis: University of Minnesota Press.

Mehta, N. (2012) "The Question All Creative Placemakers Should Ask," *Next American City*, 16 October, available at www.americancity.org/daily/entry/the-question-all-creative-placemakers-should-ask, accessed August 31, 2015.

Opportunity Detroit (2013) "A Place-making Vision for Downtown Detroit," *Opportunity Detroit*, available at www.opportunitydetroit.com/wp-content/themes/OppDet_v2/assets/Place-makingBook-PDFSm.pdf, accessed November 15, 2014.

Piiparinen, R. (2013) "Don't bet on Dan Gilbert for a Rust Belt comeback," *Cool Cleveland*, 8 May, available at www.coolcleveland.com/blog/2013/05/don%E2%80%99t-bet-on-dan-gilbert-for-a-rust-belt-comeback/, accessed June 1, 2015.

Pinho, K. and D. Walsh (2013) "Change quickens: Gilbert's downtown plan," *Crain's Business Detroit*, 31 March, available at www.crainsdetroit.com/article/20130331/NEWS/303319980/change-quickens-gilberts-downtown-plan, accessed May 31, 2015.

Place-making Leadership Council (2013) "Creating a Common Agenda for Place-making: The View from Detroit," *Project for Public Spaces*, available at www.pps.org/wp-content/uploads/2013/08/Creating-a-Common-Agenda.pdf, accessed November 17, 2014.

PPS (n.d.a) "What is place-making?" *Project for Public Spaces*, available at www.pps.org/articles/what_is_place-making/, accessed June 1, 2015.

—— (n.d.b) "PPS Involvement in the Place-Led Regeneration of Detroit," *Project for Public Spaces*, available at www.pps.org/projects/pps-involvement-in-the-place-led-regeneration-of-detroit/, accessed May 29, 2015.

—— (2014) "Heart of the Community: Investing in People and Places with Southwest Airlines," *Project for Public Spaces Blog*, 3 April, available at www.pps.org/blog/heart-of-the-community-investing-in-people-and-places-with-southwest-airlines/, accessed May 31, 2015.

PR Newswire (2013) "Detroit Leaders Launch Opportunity Detroit's Place-making and Retail Vision for City's Urban Core," Press release, 29 March.

Quicken Loans (2015) "Rock Ventures & Bedrock: Detroit Fast Facts," *Quicken Loans*, 13 May, available at www.quickenloans.com/press-room/wp-content/uploads/2015/05/05.13.2015-Detroit-Fast-Facts.pdf, accessed May 28, 2015.

Relph, E. (1976) *Place and Placelessness*, London: Pion.

—— (2008) "A pragmatic sense of place," in F. Vanclay, M. Higgins and A. Blackshaw, (Eds.) *Making Sense of Place*, Canberra: National Museum of Australia, 311–323.

Segal, D. (2013) "A Missionary's Quest to Remake Motor City," *New York Times*, 13 April, available at www.nytimes.com/2013/04/14/business/dan-gilberts-quest-to-remake-downtown-detroit.html, accessed September 14, 2014.

Steuteville, R. (2014) "Place-making initiative is a departure for Southwest," *Better Cities & Towns*, 30 June, available at www.bettercities.net/article/place-making-initiative-departure-southwest-21191, accessed May 31, 2015.

Sugrue, T.J. (2005) *The origins of the urban crisis: race and inequality in postwar Detroit*, Princeton: Princeton University Press.

Wortham-Galvin, B.D. (2008) "Mythologies of Place-making," *Places* 20, 32–39.

Zeiger, M. (2012) "An Aesthetics of Participation," *LabLog*, 2 March, available at www.blog.bmwguggenheimlab.org/2012/03/an-aesthetics-of-participation/#more-5676, accessed September 12, 2014.

11 Place-making in the Rise of the Airport City

Robert Freestone and Ilan Wiesel

Introduction

At the dawn of commercial aviation in the 1920s, airports were distinctive places of excitement, opportunity, and visitation contributing to the growing global craze of 'air mindedness' (Adey 2006). By the 1970s following the popularizing of air-travel, airports had transformed into an "increasingly maligned aspect of modern culture" (Budd 2011: 151). They had come to epitomize the notion of placelessness—a homogenized built environment with universal 'look-alike' architecture devoid of local identity or connection. The design of airport departure lounges and arrival halls, in particular, seemed to sacrifice any sense of place in the name of mobility and the functionalities of air-travel (Budd 2011). The experience of inhabiting such spaces was increasingly described in terms of stillness and suspension, timelessness, and emptiness—a space of transit to be moved through as quickly as possible (Relph 1987; Abranches 2013).

Some commentators have distanced themselves from this critique, arguing that the 'placeless-airport' narrative glosses over the complexity of the airport as a land-use ecosystem and the diversity of subjectivities and emotive experiences (Cresswell 2006; Adey 2011; Cidell 2013). The rigid distinction between 'place' and 'mobility' underpinning the notion of placeless airports has also been critiqued for forgetting how the circulation of people, material, and ideas can be intrinsic to a sense of place (Thrift 1996; Urry 2007; Abranches 2013).

What is also overlooked is the changing nature of airports themselves in the last few decades. Contemporary airports are no longer simply installations to facilitate air travel. They fulfill many other roles, such as major retail, business, and institutional centers for their cities. The current landscape of airports includes both aeronautical and non-aeronautical features as diverse as art exhibitions (e.g. the Rijksmuseum at Schiphol Airport, Amsterdam) and pleasure gardens (e.g. butterflies, flowers, and cacti gardens at Changi Airport, Singapore). No longer just travel stations serving cities, airports have become miniature cities in their own right, as captured in the concept of the 'airport-city' (Güller and Güller 2003). As noted by Budd

(2011: 156), "arguably, the only things cities possess which airports do not are resident populations."

Little has been written about whether and how place and placelessness in airports have been affected by this transformation and the design awakening that has come with it. Responding to this newer environment of airport development, the first part of this chapter presents a review of existing literature on placelessness applied to airports, with a focus on the classic treatment by Edward Relph (1976, 1981, 1987), the critique within the mobility turn in geography and urban studies (Cresswell 2006; Adey 2007; Urry 2007) and the 'airport-city' literature (Güller and Güller 2003; Kasarda and Lindsay 2011). The second part focuses on three small/medium-sized Australasian airports and describes the impact of recent transformations on their character as places invested with more than anodyne functionalist qualities.[1] The intent is to destabilize the polarity of place and placelessness in the airport realm, contest the notion of airports as placeless through the primary lens of airport land development, and illustrate place-making initiatives through case studies that raise issues of their own.

Placeless Airports

In *Place and Placelessness*, Relph (1976: 24) identified airports as exemplars of placelessness—bland, hyper-planned spaces lacking unique identity. He linked airports to other mobility infrastructure such as roads and railways, and argued that these are typically imposed on the landscape, as opposed to 'lived-in' places developing more organically in their environment. Relph argued further that airports are not only placeless in themselves, but have facilitated the global spread of placelessness by making possible the mass movement of people.

Subsequently, Relph (1981: 102–3) likened airports to shopping malls, virtually indistinguishable and soulless modern megastructures:

> International airports are also a creation of the last thirty years bearing a certain topographical similarity to shopping malls—built islands in a sea of concrete and asphalt. Airports represent enormous expenditures, of time, expertise and money and are as much symbols of the modern age as the glass and steel high-rise offices of downtown. Their visual and other qualities are both ahuman and anti-nature—they are machine landscapes of vast expanses of windswept, sun-baked concrete, filled with ear-shattering noise, multi-storey parking lots covered in grime and automobiles, chain-link fences and buildings, scaled to machines rather than people, all undergoing ceaseless reconstruction.

He argued that placelessness connotes not only the physical shape of airports, but also the standardized, dehumanizing, and disorientating lived experience of traveling through them, "being questioned, searched, crowded, herded, delayed and harassed in surroundings which have no redeeming features" (Relph 1981: 103).

This critique has since been echoed in the work of other commentators (e.g. Whitelegg 2005; Miles 2010, 2012). Most notably, Augé's (1995: 52) writing on "non-places" offered a similar critique of airports. Augé described airports as archetypical non-places characterized by "solitary contractuality" and alienation between individuals and the space they occupy.

The Mobility Turn

The prospect of more fine-grained interpretations of airport spaces was captured by the so-called 'mobility turn' in the social sciences, offering more distinctive perspectives on place, placelessness, and of course mobility. Some of the mobilities literature still alludes to placelessness in airports, such as Dixit's (2010: 31) description of the international airport as a "continuum" in a global network of flows rather than a finite destination in its own right. Other writers have sought to bridge the two views of airports as nodes in networks of mobility and as places in their own right. Urry (2007: 148) used the notion of "airspaces" to describe airports as places of "dwelling in mobility," sites of rest, activity, meeting, and consumption. Mobility studies often view airports as places where mobility flows interconnect—similar to railway stations and motorway service areas, but also urban squares and parks—resulting in diversity and frequency of human contacts (Bertolini and Dijst 2003; Urry 2007).

Similarly, Adey's work has critiqued the tendency to overlook the micro-space of the airport itself and its embeddedness within local and national cultures, histories, and uses (Adey et al. 2007: 780). Articulating a similar view and using Schiphol as an example, Cresswell (2006: 220) described international airports as "the space par-excellence of postmodern, post-national flow." But rather than placeless spaces, Creswell (2006: 257) emphasized the cultural distinctiveness evident: "Schiphol may be a node in a global space of flows, but it is still uniquely Schiphol—still a place." Alain de Botton's (2009) diary of his stay in Heathrow similarly captured the richness rather than sterility of a global hub airport.

Airports are now viewed as complexes integral to the new world order of globalization. They act as 'terraformers' reconfiguring their surroundings by facilitating the mobility of global capital (Fuller and Harley 2004). In turn, the capacity of airports to process such globalized flows of people and materials depends on their unique characteristics as places: their history, governance, politics, and geography (Cidell 2006). The intertwining of aeromobility and globalization inevitably produces varied and hybrid outcomes. Globalization begets competitive branding and differentiating impulses as much as uniformity and sameness; as Short (2004: 68) observed: "global cities, like their airports, are all very different, yet the same."

The Airport City

Although never purely aviation facilities (Edge 2009), in the 1970s airports were primarily specialist transport facilities controlled by public bureaucracies—"a branch of government" as put by Doganis (1992: xii)—with predominantly aviation- and industrial-land uses regulated through strict zoning (Roeseler 1971: 258). The design of the traditional airport aimed, first and foremost, to facilitate the efficient movement of passengers through the terminal, from kerb to gate, keeping impediments to a minimum and adjusting to new aeronautical technologies (Edge 2009).

Yet, since Relph (1976) crystallized the stereotype of the placeless airport, the nature of airports has changed fundamentally. They have transformed "from a mono-modal 'field' to a multimodal transport hub ... to a multifunctional commercialized global hub" becoming "ambivalent places, of multiple forms of transport, commerce, entertainment, experience, meetings and events" (Urry 2007: 138, 139). As summarized by Graham (2001), three key developments since the late 20th century have revolutionized airports worldwide. First, a process of commercialization transformed airports from public utilities to business enterprises adopting more corporate management philosophies. Second, this process was enhanced by the privatization of the management and, in some cases, ownership of airports. Third, the airport industry has globalized with the emergence of a small number of global airport companies operating at an increasing number of airports around the world, the Schiphol Group for example.

The new airport landscape evolving through these transformations is very different from the modernist utilitarian airport of the late 1970s. The most conspicuous expression has been the explosion of terminal airport retailing including food and beverages, second only to the internet as the fastest growing retail network globally (Letourneur and Frayn 2009). Retail growth has been associated with business-minded airports' pursuit of non-aeronautical revenues to cushion the vicissitudes and uncertainties of sole reliance on aviation income. It has capitalized upon the increase in passengers' 'dwell time' within terminals—an estimated average of over one hour due to the tightening of security following the 9/11 airplane hijackings (Appold and Kasarda 2006). Alongside diversification of retail and restaurant mix has been the far greater attention to design treatments and installations attempting to capture the distinctiveness and heritage of the airport, its locality and wider geographic and national context, but all within the complex trade-offs imposed by a surveilled environment (Nikolaeva 2012).

Commercialization on the one hand, and securitization on the other, have turned the airport into a unique kind of place. Kellerman (2008) argued that the authoritarian nature of airports is comparable only to prisons and army bases, with the explicit coercive exercise of authority by different bodies—international, national, local, and commercial—controlling the terminal environment, its operations and flows. Authority is exercised through standardization of equipment and procedures, required by the large volumes of passengers and by growing airline acquisitions and code-sharing agreements. This contributes to the sense of sameness and disorientation, described by other writers as placelessness. At the same time, Kellerman noted a tension between the standardization of airport terminals and the diversification of commercial and entertainment activity: "International airport terminals have become, thus, simultaneously the most guarded and most varied consumption complexes under one roof" (Kellerman 2008: 176).

Rather than a place that has evolved organically, the new airport has been described as representing the first generation of market-researched architecture; and rather than a truly authentic sense of place, Edge (2009: 236) described the new airport as an "imposter city" of "demographically correct citizen-consumers." Lloyd (2003: 106) depicted the terminal architecture of the redeveloped Sydney International Airport as "an organization of distraction" attempting to "refashion" non-place into place by incorporating liminal spaces of distraction and consumption.

But shopping malls can be different too. There has been a notable shift in some revitalizing airports towards retail outlets offering distinctive regional food, less reliance on national and global chains, and micro-department stores offering a more authentic experience (Letourneur and Frayn 2009). Furthermore, in addition to diversifying retail and restaurant options, some of the larger airport terminals provide other services: karaoke lounge, sauna, swimming pool (Changi); bowling alley, cinemas (including an erotic cinema), wedding chapel, furrier (Frankfurt); casino, tanning booth, branch of the Rijksmuseum (Schiphol); full service medical clinic (Chicago); library (San Francisco), and so on (Edge 2009). The proliferation of terminal amenities was fueled in part by regional as much as international competition between major airports.

Urban sociologist Gottdiener (2001, 2005) acknowledged early the impact of these changes on meanings of place in airports. Alluding to Relph's notion of placelessness, Gottdiener noted the persistence of "nowhere architecture," in airports which seem the same "just about everywhere." But he also identified elements of place in the new airport landscape, with some of the "best airport" described as "places in their own right," allowing people to enjoy, relax, and interact within an environment capturing the imaginative realm of flight. Thus, "airports are a new kind of space that provides portals to the realms of both place and placelessness" (Gottdiener 2001: 61). Similarly, Rowley and Slack (1999: 375), argued that airports exude "a softened, but not entirely absent sense of place and time."

The transformation of airports in recent decades is perhaps best captured by the notion of the 'airport-city.' While originally coined in the 1980s as a marketing concept referring, primarily, to the increased diversity of commercial activities in passenger terminals, the concept today carries broader meanings. Airports outside their terminals have become centers for diverse economic activities, including business parks, free-trade and custom-free business zones, logistics distribution centres, hubs for international cargo carriers, and high-technology research and development clusters (Kwon and Park 2003). Growth in airport retailing is occurring beyond the terminals as airports capitalize upon their accessibility advantages to service wider metropolitan catchments. Leisure and recreational uses are also increasingly common on airports enjoying generous landbanks or encompassing precincts of environmental fragility. The legacy stereotype of 'placeless' is a coarse and misleading trope (Table 11.1).

Airport cities differ from one another in their mix of economic activity; each has its own 'signature collection' of businesses (Prosperi 2008). The combination of land uses in any given airport can also change over time, and some of the less profitable features are potentially only temporary land uses until demand grows for more profitable development.

What has become evident recently is that the jumble of activities typical of last century's airports has been displaced by attempts at more coherent master-planning, even where this is not required statutorily. Part of that involves a greater emphasis on place-making through incorporation of urban design strategies comparable to those reshaping the wider urban environment (Global Airport Cities 2012). In response to criticism of placelessness, place-making approaches are being applied to various aspects and scales of airport planning and design, through naming, public art, zoning, and signage (Appold and Kasarda 2011). In Zurich and Vienna airports, for example, place-making principles have been applied in the design of more playful signage (Rawsthron 2012). Airport terminals are increasingly being designed by 'starchitects' such as Norman Foster (Beijing, Hong Kong), Helmut Jahn

Table 11.1 Diversifying land uses in global airport cities

Airport	Land use variety (existing and planned)
Hong Kong	Office tower; 4D cinema; 'Skycity' (1 million m²) including: retailing; entertainment and tourist facilities; golf course; hotels; exhibition center; office blocks; ferry and bus station.
Dubai	'Dubai World Central' (140,000 m²), eight districts under development Al Maktoum International Airport, aviation, logistics, humanitarian, residential, commercial, leisure, exhibition, and commercial.
Incheon (Seoul)	Free Trade Zone; museums and exhibition halls within terminal; 'Air City' with theme park and tourist, healthcare, sports, and fashion complexes
Kuala Lumpur	Golf courses, convention center, theme park, shopping center, hotels, wetlands nature reserve, car racing track.
Dallas/Fort Worth	Hotels; art exhibitions; leisure and retail facilities; business park, private warehouse, and distribution centers; golf courses; natural gas drilling.

Sources: Siebert and Kasarda (2008); www.globalairportcities.com/; Airport websites.

(Bangkok), Renzo Piano (Osaka), Richard Rodgers (Madrid), and Santiago Calatrava (Bilbao) (de Neufville 2006). Critics, however, have argued that the commissioning of a relatively small number of firms to guide the design of multiple airports across the globe has resulted in a degree of replication rather than singularity, as well as misrepresentation of local identities by foreign designers, in some instances resulting in 'orientalism' (ABC 2014; Heathcote 2014).

Australasian Airport Cities

Driven by economic forces similar to those observed internationally—commercialization, privatization, and deregulation—all of Australia's major airports have transformed from mono-modal airports into airport-cities (Freestone and Wiesel 2014a). The impact on the airport landscape has been profound, with a plethora of new land uses often with little or no relation to aviation, including office parks, retail malls, automotive showrooms, and other highly specialized businesses provided either on site or in proximity. This transformation was facilitated by a bespoke Commonwealth regulatory regime established in 1996 to quarantine aviation and land development on privatized federal airports from the normal planning and development laws of the state governments (Freestone and Wiesel 2014a). Australia's major airports have duly become major employment centers, some with growth rates well above metropolitan averages (BITRE 2013). New Zealand airports have been similarly impacted by commercial pressures to both improve facilities and secure higher rates of return on investment to leaven pressures on the public purse (Lyon and Francis 2006). Although still largely with some local authority ownership, they have been given considerable discretion to pursue growth-generating initiatives.

In the following subsections we briefly consider the question of place and placelessness with respect to two Australian airports, Canberra and Essendon, and one New Zealand airport, Auckland. While relatively small airports serving predominantly domestic and general aviation (GA) markets respectively, the Australian airports serve as powerful examples of the transformation from airport to airport city and its implications for place. Auckland Airport as the gateway to New Zealand's most globally connected city has taken advantage of a considerable landbank held in unrestricted freehold to similarly diversify its commercial portfolio. All three airports are notable in the leavening, if not guidance, of property development by public-realm development and design strategies sensitive to place values. We draw here on recent studies of Canberra and Essendon (Freestone and Wiesel 2014b; 2015), as well as interviews conducted with executives at all three airports.

Canberra Airport

In 1998 Canberra airport was leased by the Australian Government to a family-owned local development company. The company's full control over the land-development process, exemption from local planning restrictions that have applied to other property companies working in Canberra and aggregate investment of $600 million (Australian dollars) have enabled a radical metamorphosis. Canberra airport has been transformed from a small, purely functional facility surrounded by rural paddocks into a modern aviation-commercial complex, which won the Australian Airport Association's Capital City Airport of the Year award in 2013. The revitalization of the privatized federal airport has not been without controversy surrounding its dramatic growth paying little heed to the official metropolitan planning strategy (Freestone and Wiesel 2015).

The new owners have had three investment targets: the airport runway and aviation facilities; the main passenger terminal; and a ring of employment precincts. The terminal capacity was augmented to project a major increase on the current three million passengers per annum. The new $480m (Australian dollars) terminal, announced in the 2005 masterplan and completed in March 2013, is a three-level glazed structure of over 55,000m² floor space designed by Guida Moseley Brown Architects (selected in a design competition). Retail outlets and restaurants are relatively few and modest— partly because the airport serves primarily domestic flights, which require little 'dwell time,' but a significant area (7,000 m²) is dedicated to private-lounge areas reserved for airline frequent flyers. Amenities such as terrazzo flooring, granite security benches, stone check-in counters, leather seats, and bronze art sculptures contribute to a sense of luxury. The atrium with its high, glazed walls overlooking the tarmac and landscape beyond serves as the building's focal point. The natural light (through high, glazed walls as well as linear-louvered skylights) and the outside views connect passengers to a specific time and place. Yet such features have been criticized by some as highly generic to new airport terminals (Heathcote 2014).

There are three employment precincts on site challenging traditional ideas of airports. The Brindabella Business Park (Figure 11.1) consists of 18 commercial buildings totaling 100,000m² as well as a childcare facility, service station, gymnasium, cafes, and sporting fields. It is a high-quality, campus-style office park designed by architects Daryl Jackson and Alastair Swayn. The buildings are designed to be 'modern, sharp' (interview with Airport Executive 2014) and reference aviation themes (e.g. wing-shaped structures and the use of aeronautical materials). Mid-rise office buildings predominantly clustered within a circuit road and interconnected by an internal pedestrian access spine with public spaces, cafes, recreation areas, and landscaping also recall Canberra's history as a garden city. By 2011 Brindabella had won 15 design, building, and environmental performance awards, including a prestigious prize for urban design in 2009. A second precinct, Majura Park, also by Jackson and Swayn, accommodates 26,000m² of commercial offices as well as 44,500m² of retail floor space now dominated by retail giants such as Costco, Woolworths, and Big W. The third precinct at Fairbairn is the most characterful, taking its design cues from a series of heritage buildings that relate to the airport's early history as a Royal Australian Air Force base. The ambience of the new infill buildings, with several major tenants including the Department of Defence, is respectful of Canberra's wider garden-city setting with tree-lined streets and plentiful open space. To animate public open spaces in the airport's various precincts, and to build a sense of community among people working at the airport, Canberra Airport organizes occasional events and social gatherings for tenants.

Canberra's airport city evinces high design standards, incorporates employment and retail destinations disconnected from the primary airport function and, while the ambience trends to archetypal 'pastoral capitalism' (Mozingo 2011), it is recognizably a multi-faceted place, startlingly different from a 1970s placeless airport. Local planners are, nonetheless, still critical of the lack of connectivity between the various precincts; and although there is some legacy housing stock at Fairbairn, the absence of residential development is also seen as ultimately constraining the airport's potential to flourish as a genuine mixed-use activity center of the kind favored by the metropolitan strategy. The same could be said of Essendon Fields.

Figure 11.1 Brindabella Business Park, Canberra Airport
Source: Authors, 2014.

Essendon Fields

Serving as Melbourne's international airport until the 1970s, Essendon Fields is now a General Aviation airport, accommodating mainly executive, police, and emergency flights. Since its privatization in 2001, the lessee company—a partnership comprising transport and property interests—has redeveloped the airport into a multi-functional precinct combining aviation, retail, and commercial real estate. From a dilapidated site with buildings unsuitable for general commercial use, the company's investment strategy has facilitated substantial refurbishment and new development.

The developers' vision for the business park was "to create a Melbourne culture ... where you had density ... with lots of little cafes or retail outlets and other activities going around the buildings and people walking through a nice landscaped environment" (quoted in Freestone and Wiesel 2014b). This vision was ultimately underpinned by commercial interests—differentiating Essendon Fields as a high-quality office park to attract commercial tenants. Essendon Fields is situated in the north-west sub-region of Melbourne, which historically has been a less competitive commercial development market compared to the south-east, but more recently was identified as a high-growth area, expected to experience a massive population boom over the next 20 years.

Developing a strong place identity for Essendon Fields was described by airport executives as a key strategy to grab prospective commercial tenants' attention, in the context of a metropolitan commercial real-estate market that has been slow to recover from the Global Financial Crisis of 2007–2008. At the same time, place-making was a strategy to strengthen retail activity, by creating an attractive environment that consumers would favor as their preferred shopping destination. Quinquennial master plans, required under the Airports Act 1996, have guided precinct-based commercial development. The airport's English Street Precinct and smaller Bulla Precinct have become the most developed areas, integrating office buildings and shopping outlets with aviation facilities such as a terminal and hangars. An independent and successful whole-foods supermarket in an adaptively reused building adds local flavor. In contrast, a retail factory outlet center (a favorite of privatized federal airports because of their low-cost, high-yield business model)—while lauded by airport executives as a 'destination in its own right' for consumers—resembles the "nowhere architecture" of strip malls elsewhere in Melbourne. Similarly, at the northern end of the airport, the 'Autocentro' precinct is a hub for some of Melbourne's major car dealerships and, although a commercial success, from a design perspective it is dominated by car parks and outward facing signs aiming to attract attention from freeway drivers. The scene is tidy but generic.

Much of Essendon's character as a place derives from the conservation of historical hangars and buildings, which serve as references to the airport's history as one of Australia's oldest aviation facilities dating back to the 1920s

(Figure 11.2). An aviation-historical-society museum is located in one old building, and plans are in preparation to relocate it to the large terminal, which once served all of Melbourne's international and domestic departures and now sits mostly idle, catering for only 20,000 passengers a year. It is hoped that the museum, along with a new cafe and office development inside the terminal will restore a sense of vibrancy to the heritage building. A heritage walk leads pedestrians through some of the airport's primary aviation and commercial precincts with signage providing information about the airport's history (Figure 11.3).

Like Canberra Airport, Essendon Fields activates its outdoor communal spaces through organized events such as bike races, car shows, and social gatherings. An award from the Property Council of Australia in 2010 serves as evidence of the generally high quality standard of development. Despite the airport's growing significance as a center of employment and commerce, its claim for the status of a recognized metropolitan 'activity center' has been questioned by strategic planners. The relatively limited range of community services considered essential, and—as in the case of Canberra Airport— an absence of residential development prevents Essendon Fields from turning into a fully-fledged 'activity center' with the mix of residential- and

Figure 11.2 Heritage Park at Essendon Fields with historic control tower
Source: Authors, 2014.

Figure 11.3 Entering one of Essendon's heritage zones. Old hangars have been recycled into warehouses, youth clubs, and an indoor trampoline park
Source: Authors, 2014.

commercial-land uses required in planning strategies (Freestone and Wiesel 2014b). Like Canberra it has evolved into an interesting place in its own right, with an admixture of streetscapes and experiences combining both the derivative and the distinctive.

Auckland

Auckland International Airport was privatized in 1998 and became the first airport in the Asia Pacific region to be floated on a stock exchange (Lyon and Francis 2006). In its first decade as a private airport, land development was slow and engineering-led. Hubs of retail, office, freight, and clean industrial activity were then seeded. The airport's offices were relocated from the main terminal to a new building designed to sustainable environmental standards and intended to set the character for future office development away from the earlier campus model.

From 2008, a comprehensive urban design strategy has guided a creative approach to property development. Although urban design was always a secondary objective to the airport's core business of aviation, it was nevertheless a key strategy in uplifting real-estate values. The design strategy sought to create a mix of built and natural landscape to enrich existing elements of place, including the Maori and European heritage of the site, its unique natural environment (including a maritime outlook to the Manukau Heads), and its aviation history variously emphasizing the 'romance of travel' and the 'theatre of the airport.' Another principle underpinning the design strategy is the concept of creating a 'place for people' through a pedestrian-focused environment that is legible, easily navigable, vibrant, comfortable, and stimulating with minimal 'left-over spaces' lacking purpose or character. The distinctive character of the airport can be described as a mix of semi-rural landscapes (Figure 11.4) and 'downtown urbanism' with streets, plazas, parks, squares, and public art (Figure 11.5). Diverse architectural styles are held together by shared story-telling narratives of local heritage and a palette of local materials (e.g. basalt). The airport's landscaping similarly uses local agricultural patterns and planting features characteristic of the cultures of indigenous and European settlers. Conspicuous high earth mounds have been controversial but place-shaping in evoking the arrival of people—from Maoris to Europeans—and their impact on the land. Where possible, in the various development precincts view corridors are maintained to aviation activity on the airport tarmac.

Figure 11.4 Auckland Airport's rural landscape. This view looks across the common to the Abbeville Estate Conference Center

Source: Authors, 2014.

Figure 11.5 Auckland Airport's downtown urbanism. Leonard Isitt Avenue with Ibis Hotel at right

Source: Authors, 2014.

Heritage buildings have been conserved at the airport, with two relocated to enable runway expansion to form part of a boutique conference center with a rural feel connecting to the past history of the site (Figure 11.4). The complex is linked in to the commercial core of the airport through The Common, a broad swathe of green capturing attention to the public realm and a demonstrable attempt not to over-develop. An 'Art Walk' of installations threads through The Common and makes use of a small lake (an extant stormwater pond). There is also a traditional Maori Marae, a mountain-biking track, a golf course, and a sports field.

The design strategy purposefully included high-level principles as opposed to a more rigid blueprint, recognizing the need for longer-term adaptability. The strategy's underlying motivation was also unapologetically commercial, to compete more effectively with other business precincts in Auckland (interview with Auckland airport executive 2014). While the core business of the airport predominates, the effort to create a high-quality complementary civic environment for subsidiary activity is laudable. The tacit objective remains enhancement of property values in a competitive market place, yet the role assigned to design, landscape, and art in creating attractive and usable spaces is one of the more successful examples of distinctive place-making in any major Australasian airport.

Conclusion

Canberra, Essendon, and Auckland airports today are the products of the privatization and commercialization processes that have turned Australasian airports into 'airport cities.' From primarily transit facilities, these airports are now multi-functional sites and the impact on their character as places has been profound. There has been significant private investment in high quality and creative urban design, implemented by a new generation of design firms to challenge the critique of placelessness effectively.

With control by a single private long-term lessee (in Essendon and Canberra) and freehold ownership (in Auckland) and the use of urban designers and architects, the three airports are a far cry from Garreau's (2011) chaotic "edge cities." But they also fall short of mannered 'hyper-planning' (Relph 1981) and still face challenges in retrofitting design sensibility into highly dynamic, complex, and constrained built landscapes. The planning for all these places has been directed almost autonomously by the airport lessees or owners themselves, and are embedded within self-generated design frameworks rather than broader sub-regional strategies.

As opposed to the image of 1970s placeless airports connected to global networks but detached from their own environments, these airports are integral, if at times contested, elements in the day-to-day lives of their cities, not only as transport facilities, but increasingly as economic centers, work-places, and sites for general commercial and entertainment activity. However, elements of placelessness remain. Essendon and Canberra airports are both fragmented sites, lacking internal connectivity and inter-precinct walkability, while much of the terrain of Auckland is overwhelmed by surface car parking. The commercial drive underpinning all new development also constrains possibilities for other non-commercial elements of place-making. When opportunities have been presented, however, there is a demonstrable com-mitment to high-quality building stitched together through wider urban design frameworks seeking to engender a sense of place for visitors.

After Relph (1976: 118) linked airports to "uniformity and standardiza-tion," many other commentators have similarly seen them as archetypes of placelessness and non-places, "look-alike" nodes within what Castells (1996: 421) termed "spaces of flows," apparently devoid of any unique identity as places in their own right. A major strand in the mobilities literature has challenged this stereotype (Cresswell 2006). Furthermore, airports today are very different from what they were. Processes of privatization and com-mercialization have turned them into airport cities that are embedded not only in global networks but also, more deeply, into the social and economic fabrics of their own cities, as multifarious commercial real-estate sites responding to diverse market opportunities (Freestone and Wiesel 2014a, 2015).

Both in and outside the core aviation precinct, airports are receiving major makeovers, with terminals infused with "local identity and symbolism" just as surrounding development is made more interpretable, navigable, and welcoming through urban design (Global Airport Cities 2012). Through diversification of land uses, attention to the public realm, heritage, and customized place-making strategies using design and "story telling" techniques, the experience of travelling, working, or visiting airports has changed in profound ways.

However, the focus on commercial and retail development and the absence of residential development and a wider suite of community-oriented amenities still ultimately constrains their distinctiveness as authentic, lived-in places and any authenticity is mediated through commercial imperatives. Furthermore, as airports emulate each other and follow international trends, new forms of 'look-alike' architecture emerge. But Relph (2000: 618) himself has conceded that the simple definitional verities of the 1970s have become blurred and today "each place has to be assessed carefully and on its own terms." Airports today invite further exploration and interpretation of their new found sense of place.

Note

1 Our thanks to Peter Alexander, Steve Appold, David Holm, Campbell Jensen, Noel McCann, Kathryn Scarano, Mark Thomson and Rob Whitwell for sharing their insights on airport development. The interpretations remain ours alone.

References

ABC (2014) *Airport conundrums* (audio podcast), available at www.abc.net.au/radionational/programs/latenightlive/airports/5587926, accessed August 20, 2014.

Abranches, M. (2013) "When People Stay and Things Make Their Way: Airports, Mobilities and Materialities of a Transnational Landscape," *Mobilities* 8: 506–527.

Adey, P. (2006) "Airports and Air-Mindedness: Spacing, Timing and Using the Liverpool Airport, 1929–1939." *Social and Cultural Geography* 7, 343–363.

—— (2007) "Airports, Mobility and the Calculative Architecture of Affective Control," *Geoforum* 39, 438–451.

—— (2011) "Airports: Terminal Vector," in P. Merriman and T. Creswell (Eds.) *Geographies of Mobilities: Practices, Spaces, Subjects*, Farnham: Ashgate, 137–150.

Adey, P., L. Budd and P. Hubbard (2007) "Flying Lessons: Exploring the Social and Cultural Geographies of Global Air Travel," *Progress in Human Geography* 31, 773–791.

Appold, S.J. and J.D. Kasarda (2006) "The Appropriate Scale of US Airport Retail Activities," *Journal of Air Transport Management* 12, 277–287.

—— (2011) "Are Airports Non Places?" *Airport Consulting* Summer 2011, 14–16.

Augé, M. (1995) *Non-places: An anthropology of supermodernity*, London: Verso.

Bertolini, L. and M. Dijst (2003) "Mobility Environments and Network Cities," *Journal of Urban Design* 8, 27–43.

Budd, L.C.S. (2011) "Airports: From Flying Fields to 21st Century Aerocities," in B. Derudder, M. Hoyler, P.J. Taylor and F. Witlox (Eds.) *International Handbook of Globalization and World Cities*, Cheltenham: Edward Elgar, 151–161.

Bureau of Infrastructure, Transport and Regional Economics (BITRE) (2013) *Employment Generation and Airports*, Canberra: BITRE.

Castells, M. (1996) *The Rise of the Network Society*, Vol. 1, Oxford: Blackwell.

Cidell, J. (2006) "Air Transportation, Airports and the Discourses And Practices of Globalization," *Urban Geography* 27, 651–663.

Cidell, J. (2013) "When Runways Move but People Don't: The O'Hare Modernization Program and the Relative Immobilities of Air Travel," *Mobilities* 8, 528–541.

Cresswell, T. (2006) *On The Move: Mobility in the Modern Western World*, London: Routledge.

de Botton, A. (2009) *A Week at the Airport: A Heathrow Diary*, London: Profile.

de Neufville, R. (2006) "Planning Airport Access in an Era of Low-Cost Airlines," *Journal of the American Planning Association* 72, 347–356.

Dixit, M. (2010) "Departure Gate Urbanism," *Log* 18, 29–36.

Doganis, R. (1992) *The Airport Business*, London: Routledge.

Edge, K.F. (2009) "Buy, Sell, Roam: The Airport Calculus of Retail," in M. Orvell and K. Benesch (Eds.) *Public Space and the Ideology of Place in American Culture*. New York: Rodopi, 219–242.

Freestone, R. and I. Wiesel (2014a) "The Rise of the Airport Property Market in Australia," in S. Conventz and A. Thierstein (Eds.) *Airports, Cities and Regions*, London: Routledge, 218–241.

—— (2014b) "The Making of an Australian 'Airport City,'" *Geographical Research* 52, 280–295.

—— (2015) "Privatization, Property, and Planning: The Remaking of Canberra Airport," *Policy Studies* 36, 35–54.

Fuller, G. and R. Harley (2004) *Aviopolis: A Book about Airports*. London: Black Dog.

Gallagher, J. (2015) "A Tale of Two Parks: Campus Martius vs. Hart Plaza," *Detroit Free Press*, 9 August, available at www.freep.com/story/money/business/michigan/2015/08/08/campusmartius-detroit-architecture-design-parks-fredkent/31226477/, accessed September 28, 2015.

Garreau, J. (2011) *Edge City: Life on the New Frontier*. New York: Anchor Books.

Global Airport Cities (2012) "Airport place-making through design," available at www.globalairportcities.com/page.cfm/action=library/libID=1/libEntryID=495#sthash.huGZj3hP.dpuf, accessed September 25, 2012.

Gottdiener, M. (2001) *Life in the Air: Surviving the New Culture of Air Travel*, Lanham, MD: Rowman and Littlefield.

Gottdiener, M. (2005) "Deterritorialization and the Airport," in S. Graham (Ed.) *The Cybercities Reader*, London: Routledge, 185–189.

Graham, A. (2001) *Managing Airports: An International Perspective*. Oxford: Butterworth Heinemann.

Güller, M. and M. Güller (2003) *From Airport to Airport City*, Barcelona: Gustavo Gilli.

Heathcote, E. (2014) "Airport Architecture: Flights of Fancy," available at www.ft.com/intl/cms/s/2/14bac424–004e–11e4–a3f2–00144feab7de.html#slide0, accessed August 20, 2014.

Kasarda, J. and G. Lindsay (2011) *Aerotropolis: The Way We'll Live Next*. London: Allen Lane.

Kellerman, A. (2008) "International Airports: Passengers in an Environment of 'Authorities,'" *Mobilities* 3, 161–178.

Kwon, O.K. and Y. Park (2003) "Airport Development and Air Cargo Logistics: Korea's Initiatives in Northeast Asia," paper presented at the PECC International Roundtable, Role of Airports and Airlines in Trade Liberalization and Economic Growth.

LeTourneur, C. and A. Frayn (2009) "The Perfect Market?," *Global Airport Cities* 4, 26–30.

Lloyd, J. (2003) "Airport Technology, Travel and Consumption," *Space and Culture*, 6, 93–109.

Lyon, D. and G. Francis (2006) "Managing New Zealand's Airports in the Face of Commercial Challenges," *Journal of Air Transport Management* 12, 220–226.

Miles, S. (2010) *Spaces for Consumption*, London: Sage.

Miles, S. (2012) "The Neoliberal City and the Pro-Active Complicity of the Citizen Consumer," *Journal of Consumer Culture* 12, 216–230.

Nikolaeva, A. (2012) "Designing Public Space for Mobility: Contestation, Negotiation and Experiment at Amsterdam Airport Schiphol," *Tijdschrift voor Economische en Sociale Geografie* 103: 542–554.

Prosperi, D.C. (2008) "Airports as Centers of Economic Activity: Empirical Evidence from Three US Metropolitan Areas," paper presented to the REAL CORP Conference, Vienna, May 2007.

Rawsthron, A. (2012) "When the Directions Aren't Clear," *New York Times*, 22 October 2012.

Relph, E. (1976) *Place and Placelessness*, London: Pion.

—— (1981) *Rational Landscapes and Humanistic Geography*, London: Croom Helm.

—— (1987) *The Modern Urban Landscape*, London: Croom Helm.

—— (2000) "Author's Response: Place and Placelessness in a New Context," *Progress in Human Geography* 24, 617–619.

Roeseler, W.G. (1971) "Airport Development Districts: The Kansas City Experience," *Urban Law* 3, 254–262.

Rowley, J. and F. Slack (1999) "The Retail Experience in Airport Departure Lounges: Reaching for Timelessness and Placelessness," *International Marketing Review* 16, 363–375.

Short, J.R. (2004) *Global Metropolitan: Globalizing cities in a capitalist world*, London: Routledge.

Siebert, L. and J.D. Kasarda (2008) *Airport Cities: The Evolution*, Twickenham: Insight Media.

Thrift, N. (1996) *Spatial formations*, London: Sage.

Urry, J. (2007) *Mobilities*, Cambridge: Polity.

Whitelegg, D. (2005) "Places and Spaces I've Been: Geographies of female flight attendants in the United States," *Gender, Place and Culture* 12, 251–266.

12 Urban Squares
A Place for Social Life

Nancy Marshall

Introduction

Public life in contemporary cities is acknowledged by urban commentators as being threatened by modern social forces and philosophies such as economic rationalism that prioritize economic outcomes over social outcomes. This is not the first time public life has been under siege. There are key points in urban planning history during which urban experts, such as Jane Jacobs in the 1960s, have rallied for the cause of public life and the re-establishment of public space (Jacobs 1961). At certain points in time, public life and the existence of quality public space as a core component of city planning have been threatened.

This chapter discusses the importance of public social life in the 21st century city. Edward Relph's (1976) seminal concepts of *place* and *placelessness* are used to argue why social life is important, and the benefits of having a robust and diverse public social life activated in urban centers. The chapter starts with a discussion of some of the sociocultural factors that influence public social life in a contemporary city. If public life is acknowledged and valued by both the community and the city-makers, it will be supported by the physical and social environment. Open spaces, including green parklands, grey streets, and urban squares, are where much public life will occur. Additionally, the benefits of a robust and inclusive public life contribute to positive social outcomes and the overall social sustainability of a city.

In contrast, the chapter then argues that if a public social life is not socially and culturally valued, it is unlikely to be supported in the design and development of the built environment. Relph's (1976) rather exclusive characterization of sense of place is challenged to ensure an inclusive view of the public, and people's different relationships to urban places are valued. Public social life could become placeless. Case studies of urban squares, as one key component of a city's ground floor, are discussed as *places* that can facilitate the sociability of public life or as *placeless* spaces that fail to add social value.

Public Social Life and the Sociocultural Factors that Influence It

Many scholars have defined the terms of 'public life,' 'community life,' 'social life,' and the terms 'public space,' 'social space,' 'open space,' and 'public realm' across decades. For the purposes of this chapter, 'public social life' denotes the movements, activities, meetings, and random, shared contacts that occur between people in the public realm, that is, in urban spaces. This is informed by the work of many observers, but most particularly Lofland's (1998) work on the public realm, Landry's (2008) work on the art of city living, Sandercock's (2003) work on difference and diversity, and Gehl's (2010) emphasis on city life.

Public life is always changing and will always need public open space to represent and enact civic ideology. "Public life was not given much treatment in the 20th century's dominant planning ideology, modernism, or its counterparts in the form of post-modernism or new rationalism" (Gehl and Svarre 2013: 51). Proponents such as Jacobs (1961) agreed when they decried that city planners were not adequately addressing urban form for livability or a lively community life.

There is no single 'public': "the public is a constantly shifting multiplicity of affiliations, interests and alliances" (Marshall and Roberts 2008: 116). There is great diversity in the people who may or may not participate in public life—they differ by fundamental characteristics such as age, gender, or ethnicity among others. A less traditional way of identifying people is by urban subcultures, such as the homeless, gangs, skateboarders, tourists, the 'emos,' 'goths,' 'dog-walkers,' and 'guerrilla urbanists,' to name a few. Different groups emerge in different contexts and times, they grow and shrink in numbers, and they have different views and value sets about what is 'good and bad' or 'right and wrong' and acceptable in public life. This mix of traditional and non-traditional subcultures collectively makes up a public.

Public social life is a reflection of the current and trending social values and interests of society. How it influences and is reflected in the built form changes with the times. As Gehl (2010: 20) points out, 'necessary' and 'purposeful' social life is associated with economic activities and the functions of daily life in a city. This functional use of public space is a constricted view of public life that was particularly prevalent in the late 1800s. Gehl (2010) further argues that there was a disregard for the quality of public space during that period—as long as it functioned well enough; the quality of public spaces was immaterial to public life. Now, in the 21st century, public life has evolved to include more "optional social life," which is associated with active recreation and passive socializing (Gehl 2010: 20). People are using the city for formal and informal sport and leisure activities, as meeting places, for spending time, and to participate in shared experiences such as rallies, parades, demonstrations, or mourning. The quality of public space is now central to public life and is expected to be of higher quality than in previous decades.

Contemporary cities have increasingly pluralistic and diverse publics; Sandercock (2003) calls them 'mongrel cities.' With this richness of difference comes a range of expectations, interest in, and patterns of use of public space that offer challenges and opportunities to city-makers (Banerjee 2001). The public can be seen to have differences or similarities based on stage in the life cycle, physical ability, gender, socioeconomic status, religion, ethnicity, and other personal characteristics such as sexuality, personality traits, and interests. Amin (2002) would call these 'micro-publics,' who negotiate to share and contest public space.

Another determinant in the sociability of public life is linked to changes in social demographics, especially of developed nations. As birth rates fall and the number of one- and two-person households increases rapidly in developed societies, the need for a new 'herd' created with groups outside the family unit has increased (Mackay 2010). Also, increased mobility sees members of the same family unit being dispersed, sometimes globally. This distance from the traditional family social unit and the change in demographics contributes to burgeoning book clubs, cycling groups, and other social interest groups that often use public space (Mackay 2010).

The private household backyard, in some nations, is used to provide extensive open space for a family and community social life. However, the reality of urbanization and higher-density living encourages an extension of life out from the private home and into public parks, plazas, playgrounds, and 'third spaces' (discussed later). High rise and higher-density living simply does not offer the space some people want or need for a private social life (Mackay 2010). Hence, some private aspects of social life now occur in public space and are incorporated into the collective public social life of a city.

Another contributor to ever-changing public social life is the healthy built environment movement, which is contributing to the development of different types and functions of public space. It is well known that many of the determinants of health and wellbeing are linked to different features in our neighborhoods—the people, their lifestyles and attitudes, the local economy, activities afforded in the built form, and natural environments. Under such principles, the urban environment should include walkable streets and neighborhoods, good public transport, safe, accessible and equitable public open space, and access to healthy food options (Thompson, Kent, and Capon 2012). People generally know the value of a healthier lifestyle and, ideally, they want their cities to help facilitate that.

Another major factor in influencing current public life is technology and how it continues to influence daily social practice. A meteoric rise in the use of computers and mobile personal devices (iPhones and tablets) for accessing social media and for networking has influenced how different populations connect with one another and use public space. People use mobile devices

to organize, share instantly in a very public way (for example on Facebook©
and Twitter©), and revisit their public and private lives (experiences, events,
and moments of significance and insignificance) in both physical and virtual
spaces (Hampton, Livio, and Sessions-Goulet 2010). Alternatively, social
media can fuel difference and create spatial segregation that is acted out in
public places (Castells 2014). As Castells elaborates, an example of an
informal, networked protest that represented significant social ideas, and
held in public spaces, is the *Occupy Movement* from 2011.

This discussion of what public life is, and what influences it, is by no
means exhaustive but it does show that public social life is diverse, functional, complex, personal, and ubiquitous. It is time- and culture-sensitive,
and is influenced by many factors, as mentioned above. It occurs at different
scales: on a global stage (e.g. the street life that occurs in host cities for
an Olympic Games); at a city or regional scale (e.g. a protest against a
government decision); or at a more intimate neighborhood scale (e.g. a local
community festival). Public life occurs at different times in a day, a season,
and across a year. Public life also occurs and is interpreted at an individual
level. That is, individuals may still need the functional use of a public space
(e.g. to walk to and from work) or for more optional group activities (e.g.
meeting a friend for a coffee or to join in sporting celebrations). Figure 12.1
shows a very public, simple summer's day of 'chilling out' in San Francisco.
Figure 12.2 in contrast shows a public group activity in Federation Square,

Figure 12.1 A relaxed sunny day in San Francisco, USA, Yerba Buena
Source: Author, 2013.

Figure 12.2 A special event in Melbourne, Australia, Federation Square
Source: Author, 2012.

which is designed to be an informal and formal space for special events in
the heart of Melbourne.

If Public Life is Valued. . .

The emphasis on the importance of public life and therefore public spaces
is being re-established and restored to a position of central importance in
urban social life (Bishop and Marshall 2014). "Public life in good quality
public spaces is an important part of a democratic life and a full life" (Gehl
2012: 1).

"Today, every city in the world needs to be clear about its value proposition in order to attract people and investment in a highly competitive global
marketplace. Every city needs to provide a sustainable, vibrant community
for its citizens to live, work and enjoy life" (Ernst & Young 2011: 6). The
value proposition can be considered as primarily economic, sociocultural
(most often referred to as social), or environmental (natural or man-made
infrastructure). For the purposes of this chapter, the last two are most
important. A healthy, positive, and inclusive civic life is critical to the success
of cities and the social sustainability of the mongrel city. Social outcomes
are influenced *by* people and shaped *for* people.

"Social sustainability blends traditional social policy areas and principles, such as equity and health, with emerging issues concerning participation, needs, social capital, the economy, the environment, and more recently, with the notions of happiness, wellbeing and quality of life" (Colantonio and Dixon 2009: 4). Indicators of social sustainability include issues that are at the heart of what many planners aim to achieve: equity, cultural value, recognition and protection; political participation by citizens; a sense of community; and community action—to name the key ones (McKenzie 2004). The aims of much planning, designing, and the social programing of public spaces in modern times are to promote social capital and engagement, social participation, and social cohesion (Colantonio and Dixon 2009; Markusen and Gadwa 2010). An understanding of how different people contribute to a socially sustainable city is needed to enhance that society's capacity to offer a public life in public spaces.

Other urban researchers (e.g. Jacobs 1961; Jenson 1998; Putnam 2000) argue that social capital is critical to the social success of cities. It is 'the glue' that binds successful communities together and attracts other people to it. This glue is composed of, for example, cultural amenities, safety, health care, and sociability. For Jenson (1998), social capital is almost "infra-structural." Civil society is one in which actions and investments by government, industry, and the non-profit sectors provide and maintain community infrastructure and services: "These efforts will determine whether a local community is well or poorly endowed with social capital. Thus, a civil society is a place, a space between the individual and the state" (Jenson 1998: 40). Putnam (2000) argues that people have become disconnected from family, friends, and neighbors but also argues the importance of social capital within our communities.

Allied to social capital is the concept of social cohesion. Maxwell (1996: 13), for one, defines social cohesion as involving the "building [of] shared values and communities of interpretation, reducing disparities in wealth and income, and generally enabling people to have a sense that they are engaged in a common enterprise, facing shared challenges, and that they are members of the same community." Jenson's (1998) understanding of social cohesion outlines the greatest social outcomes for its citizens being: a sense of belonging; inclusion; participation; recognition; and legitimacy. These are the attributes that contribute to a cohesive public life.

"Tolerance, in the multicultural communities that most of us live in around the world, is an important starting point for developing a civil society" (Malone 2006: 15). Sennett (1996) believes that engaging in a wide range of urban experiences forces people to engage with "the other" and to go beyond one's own defined boundaries of self, both central to a civilized social life. Sennett (1996) further believes that cities have diverse civic cultures that can offer meaningful, intercultural interactions. Donald (1999) suggests that societies should get beyond difference and indifference to 'co-presence.' This would contribute to Jenson's (1998) social outcomes above

Figure 12.3 Anish Kapoor's *Cloud Gate*, colloquially known as *The Bean* in Chicago, USA, AT+T Plaza

Source: Author, 2013.

Figure 12.4 Pedestrianizing streets for public life in New York, USA, Times Square

Source: Author, 2013.

and feeling part of a vital public life. It can be easily argued that the internationally recognized public art work by Anish Kapoor contributes to civic life in downtown Chicago (Figure 12.3). Figure 12.4 shows the redevelopment of Times Square in New York, becoming more people-friendly.

If Public Life is Not Valued . . .

Many urban researchers and commentators believe that urban life is currently under threat. Gehl (2012: 1) notes "in a society becoming steadily more privatized with private homes, cars, computers, offices and shopping centers, the public component of our lives is disappearing." A similar sentiment has been heard before: Jacobs (1961) was one of the first to lament the loss of community and Putnam (2000: preface) warned us that "our stock of *social capital*—the very fabric of our connections with each other, has plummeted, impoverishing our lives and communities." While the contexts of each critique were different, fundamentally each documented the fluctuating value of public life.

Many world cities are currently governed by the ideologies of contemporary neoliberalism (Campbell, Tait, and Watkins 2014). This pervasive value system is now dominating both public policy and, in turn, built form; and so, the value of public life again must be defended. City-makers need to value public life, or it is at risk of not being accommodated, even by governments. The neoliberal land use and property principle of prioritizing economic gain is often used by public and private developers, but it does not necessarily value highly public open space for social life. Public land uses and open space-type developments typically do not make money and so land that could be used to support public life is, more often than not, put to the 'highest and best economic use.'

Public spaces have historically been provided by public administrations, but now privately owned public open space is becoming more prevalent as cities struggle to fund the provision and maintenance of its open spaces. Governments now often rely on public–private partnerships for key infrastructure provision. Other current approaches to ensure the provision of public spaces include offering development incentives, operating businesses to provide an income stream to fund upkeep, and requiring developers to contribute to public lands and amenity. If public life is not valued or provided for, cities will be dominated by economic rationalism and have reduced urban amenities and ultimately be less convivial and socially robust.

Place: The Provision of Public Space and a Robust Public Life

Urban contexts have both *physical and social spaces* that have the ability to contribute, or not, to urban public life. When these spaces are well-loved, well-used, and evoke meaningful associations for their users, they become *places*. "Places are fusions of human and natural order and are the significant centers of our immediate experiences of the world. They are important sources of individual and communal identity, and are often profound centers of human existence to which people have deep emotional and psychological ties" (Relph 1976: 141).

As noted by Bishop and Marshall (2014: 35), "places have long been understood as being based on three broad interrelating components: the physical setting; the individual's psychological and social processes by which an individual ascribes meaning to the setting; and attributes and the activities undertaken in the setting." This phenomenological understanding of place is generally conceived as being space imbued with meaning gained by being in it, feeling it, smelling it, and experiencing it (Tuan 1977).

The design of these urban physical contexts can facilitate or inhibit public life. Public open spaces (e.g. streets, plazas, parks, waterfronts, playgrounds, and pathways) or lack thereof will influence key social outcomes and sustainability of public life. The city must consciously ensure that publicly accessible urban open spaces are planned, designed, built, and managed to afford a public sociability for all the different 'publics.'

Having a rich and diverse public life that is valued by the citizenry and city-makers will ensure that it is afforded and supported, and the social benefits will be garnered. Socially successful spaces are those "that are socially active, functional and valued by local and visiting user groups" (Bishop and Marshall 2014: 34). Influences on the social success of urban spaces are numerous and span physical, social, sensory, and personal considerations for users. In designing and planning urban spaces, designers are engaging with all of these considerations, whether they are conscious of them or not. Regardless, the experiential qualities of the spaces, and their capacity to sustain social interaction, can generate an emotional response and form the basis of enduring memories for many people. When challenged with poor planning and design decisions or a lack of public spaces for public activity, some public and community processes are trying new and innovative strategies to 'place-make.' This occurs by permanently or temporarily activating space with pop-ups or 'lighter, quicker, cheaper' developments, with or without planning authority consent. When not affording space for certain forms of activity or certain subcultures of the population, they often re-appropriate otherwise fallow city spaces.

To accommodate more technological public life, research by Hampton, Livio, and Sessions-Goulet (2010) indicates that the popularity of an urban open space for wireless technology users is determined by the site's existing reputation, access to free Wi-Fi, the local population density, the actual urban design of the site, surveillance/harassment, and local culture. To consciously plan and design for technology in public spaces is one way to socially construct and support both place and mobile networks (Castells 2014). Supporting both physical and digital network spaces is powerful, as it ensures that people "are together in place with the constant interaction in mobile communication networks" (Castells 2014: 94). This technological public life will continue to change with the times.

Finally, much can be learned about the value of public social life when looking through Oldenburg's concept of 'third space.' The phrase stems from thinking about our homes as our 'first' place, and our work places/offices as our 'second' place (Oldenburg 1997). "Third spaces are a public balance to the increased privatization of home life," which will become increasingly important as cities become more dense and public space becomes even more highly valued (Oldenburg 1997: 6). These informal, public gathering places, especially when used by the local residents, may help unify a neighborhood through contributing to a sense of community, familiarity, and shared experience. They are 'ports of entry' for visitors and places where people meet regularly to relax and enjoy one another's company, especially for people who have similar interests or offer a place for controlled debate—shared spaces. They can also bring different generations together, who might not otherwise meet. For the elderly, "they provide the means for keeping in touch with others and continuing to enjoy the life of the community" (Oldenburg 1997: 9). Finally, in support of Whyte's (1980: 19) famous quotation, these public spaces provide entertainment, which is usually provided by the people themselves: "what attracts people most, it would appear, is other people."

Urban Squares: Public Space that Affords Public Life

Urban squares, also known as 'plazas,' 'piazzas,' 'town centers,' or even 'gardens' or 'courtyards,' are one key component of a city's form. Historically, urban squares were essential to the economic, social, and cultural life of all towns and cities. Having once been the absolute center of medieval towns for trade and daily community life, squares lost their purpose as places for public life with the advent of the car and decentralized city planning from the 1950s to the1970s (Bishop and Marshall 2014). More recently, urban researchers have been providing the evidence for re-valuing what constitutes 'good' public space for social outcomes and public life (Cooper Marcus et al. 1998; Gehl 2010; 2011; Carmona, Tiesdell, Heath, and Oc 2010; Project for Public Spaces 2015).

The re-emergence of the public square as a community center has helped to reactivate public life. Some city-makers and designers would argue that squares (and streets) are the most important open spaces in cities. They constitute the ground floor that largely differentiates one city from another. Each has its own local context, design features, ambient qualities, and patterns of use. Squares are usually a mix of grey and green spaces with differing levels and uses of landscaping and pavement. Sounds, smells, tastes, touch, and sights are based on perception and experience,which determine whether people are critics or fans of the space, and which may change over time.

Squares can help establish the image of a city and contribute to a city's character, place identity, aesthetics, amenity levels, and its sense of place. These spaces can be entirely public or be blended with private interests. Some are specifically built to become 'a heart of a city,' others to revitalize old brownfield sites or historical urban precincts, or simply to add more and better open space as cities become more densely populated, something like an 'outdoor living room.' They can also function as works of art, as expressions of their creators' intent and a commentary on society. Urban squares may also engender a sense of community pride where history is acknowledged and events are memorialized. They may equally help 'place-make' through providing locals or visitors a rich and multi-sensorial experience of local culture. All need to function well in meeting the needs of public life—for traditional and subculture populations—and when they do they are heavily used, loved, and contribute to the enjoyment that people get from urban living. Most are a palimpsest of meaning to be unraveled consciously or felt subconsciously.

Relph would probably designate all of these squares as authentic places, as they all offer unique design characteristics and context. Such *places* "are directly experienced phenomena of the lived-world and hence are full with meanings, with real objects, and with ongoing activities" (Relph 2013: 267). Even though some are more successful than others, the value of public urban

Figure 12.5 100 year ANZAC Day commemorations in Sydney, Australia, Martin Place

Source: Trent, 2015.

Figure 12.6 Love sculpture by Robert Indiana in Philadelphia, USA, John F.
Kennedy Square

Source: Author, 2013.

squares as places that have meaning, evoke emotions, and are the location for public life cannot be underestimated. Figure 12.5 shows quiet moments of the public honoring the centenary of the landing of Australian and New Zealand forces at Gallipoli on the 25 April 1915, in Martin Place in Sydney. On a lighter note, the *Love* sculpture in Philadelphia is fun, light, and playful (Figure 12.6). Both urban squares have human emotions on public display.

"Wherever you go, there you are—and it matters. We are always embedded in a place. Person-place influences are both mutual and crucial. We shape not only buildings but also the land, the waters, the air, and other life forms—and they shape us" (Gifford 2014: 543). Cities have long been recognized as physical expressions of their inhabitants, visitors and a reflection of their social cohesion. As Lynch (1960) would suggest, it is important to enhance the meaning of everyday life and strengthen the identity of the group and the self. "If the public spaces are well placed, well designed, and inviting, evidence from all over the world points to the fact that people continue to appreciate public life in public spaces" (Gehl 2012: 41).

Placelessness: The Lack of Public Space and a Reduced Public Life

With the threat of a reduced public life, or not having enough or appropriate public open spaces for that public life to be acted out, there will be the threat of placelessness. In 1976, Relph initially defined placelessness as "the casual eradication of distinctive places and the making of standardized landscapes that results from and insensitivity to the significance of place" (Relph 1976: preface). A contemporary extension on the term would argue that both *place* (as discussed above) and *placelessness*—that is, the lack of a robust, multifaceted, engaged public life, have significant social outcomes. The following section argues that if a society does not have a place to identify, express, and maintain its public social life, it will be *placeless*.

"Placelessness is an attitude and an expression of that attitude which is becoming increasingly dominant, and that it is less and less possible to have a deeply felt sense of place or to create places authentically" (Relph 1976: 80). Authenticity is more about reflecting the current social life of a society and less about just creating physical places that are distinct and unique. If public open space did not allow all social life to be acted out, even by those of less desirable subcultures, that life would be placeless. By extension, if a society produces places that are 'kitsch' or 'inauthentic,' so be it—these are social constructs that still represent parts of a public and perhaps global social life. Kitsch and planning techniques are "powerful processes of landscape modification which do little or nothing to create and maintain significant and diverse places" (Relph 1976: 90). Relph's argument here is too focused on the creation of a particular kind of place identity—from the "individual or collective existential insiders" and the "empathetic insiders." A kitsch public life or experience for some *is* an authentic one, and a more inclusive sense of place should be considered, especially for very pluralistic global cities.

Relph (1976: 83) believed that "an inauthentic attitude to place is nowhere more clearly expressed than in tourism, for in tourism individual and authentic judgement about places is nearly always subsumed to expert or socially accepted opinion, or the act and means of tourism becomes more important than the places visited." Relph and others thought that tourists experienced homogenized places at a very superficial level and scurried from one big attraction to the next in order to say they have 'seen them or done them.' What this part of Relph's argument overlooks is that in order to attract business and tourists, both as drivers of the local economy and in order to compete against other locales, cities are having to offer not only a welcoming economic environment but also a high level of urban amenity for visitors and new businesses. As cities compete to be global, world cities, they are investing more in hard and soft infrastructure—both unique built forms and programming such as festivals, markets, and other place-making initiatives. This investment in the urban context is seeing an improvement in the provision, quality, maintenance, and recognition of public life for locals and tourists alike. Tourists could be classified as one of the subcultures a city supports and is included in the public life of any city. They could also be more like long-term travelers who do spend longer periods of time visiting locales to actually experience 'the local.'

The general demise of public life has been noted by social commentators but most also acknowledge the need for social gatherings, civic life, and social sustainability (McKenzie 2004). There are many factors, which are discussed above, that influence how people experience city and public life. One of the key factors is that we live in a digital and globalized world, which means that people can have an online life and a virtual presence in the world. Granted, much communication is facilitated through electronic media like the internet, email, and social networking on portable, personal devices; however, this does not mean that face-to-face contact in public places is disappearing, or indeed is less important.

The planning, development, and management of modern Western cities, including public open space and built form, are best seen as a balancing act between government, private and public capital, and the interplay of the processes among them all (Marshall and Roberts 2008). There are critical tensions between these players, fighting for 'the highest and best use' concept of land value versus space for public life that does not stack up on an economic rationalist's spreadsheet. Open space will always struggle to be the best financial option for high-demand property. However, if public life and its social outcomes are not embedded into the values of decision-makers and city power-brokers, the provision for it is threatened. Physical spaces are still needed and will best co-exist alongside digital spaces. Public life needs champions in the power echelons in order to provide public space to facilitate it, to respect it, and protect its various forms.

Urban Squares: Public Space that Does Not Afford Public Life

The general public often suggests that their city does not have enough open space, including squares. Some commentators suggest that urban squares have no purpose or instrumental function designed into them and hence become underutilized (e.g. Carmona et al. 2010). Some locals believe their squares are devoid of or have out-of-date or inappropriate amenities. Some communities criticize urban maintenance in general and campaign for further financial investment from the authorities. Others complain that their landscaping is scant or inappropriate for the climatic conditions or of poor quality (Cooper Marcus et al. 1998). Accessibility is also often an issue with urban squares—either they are poorly located and hence difficult to get to on foot, or they are not designed for all abilities. With the increasing numbers of public–private partnerships providing public open space, some might argue that access is not really *public* or open at all times. Lastly, the general public suggests that safety and lack of amenity/programming are reasons why squares are not well-used. They provide no affordances for potential users, nor are they programmed with enough or appropriate activities—this results in under-utilization of the space or its re-appropriation by undesirable users (Malone 2006). When squares are poorly designed, not used, unloved, homogeneous, and deserted they are not affording a public life—

Figure 12.7 A deserted urban square: Downtown Boston, USA, City Hall Plaza
Source: Author, 2013.

and hence public life is *placeless*. Figure 12.7 is representative of urban squares that exist all around the world that contribute little to urban public life.

Conclusion

Public life is still important, and may be ever more important as the world becomes increasingly global, digital, connected, and disconnected. The art of living in a 21st century city includes engaging with people who come from a range of ethnic, cultural, socioeconomic, and religious backgrounds. The norms, ways of life, ideals, and tastes of people vary from society to society.

People have different value sets, and go about their lives in very different ways. However, to create a socially sustainable city, all people should have rights to the city, have a legitimate place in society, and be able to participate in civic governance and contribute to the sociocultural and economic well-being of a city.

City-makers, such as planners, landscape architects, architects, and politicians need to understand people and their civic relationship to open space and facilitate their public life. This ultimately improves the physical urban amenity and the social sustainability of the 21st century city. The impact of not having these *places*, that is, having a *placeless* public life, is unimaginable.

References

Amin, A. (2002) *Ethnicity and the Multicultural City: Living with Diversity*, Durham: Department of Transport, Local Government and the Regions.
Banerjee, T. (2001) "The Future of Public Space: Beyond Invented Streets and Reinvented Places," *Journal of the American Planning Association* 67, 9–24.
Bishop, K. and N. Marshall (2014) "Towards an Evidence-Based Model for Assessing Urban Squares as Social Places," *The International Journal of Interdisciplinary Social and Community Studies* 9, 32–44.
Campbell, H., M. Tait and C. Watkins (2014) "Is There Space for Better Planning in a Neoliberal World? Implications for Planning Practice and Theory," *Journal of Planning Education and Research* 34, 45–59.
Carmona, M., S. Tiesdell, T. Heath and T. Oc (2010) *Public Places, Urban Spaces: The Dimensions of Urban Design*, New York: Routledge.
Castells, M. (2014) "A Conversation with Manuel Castells," *Berkeley Planning Journal* 27, 93–98.
Colantonio, A. and T. Dixon (2009) *Measuring Socially Sustainable Urban Regeneration in Europe*, Oxford: Oxford Institute for Sustainable Development.
Cooper Marcus, C., C. Francis and R. Russell (1998) "Urban Plazas," in C. Cooper Marcus and C. Francis (Eds.), *People Places: Design Guidelines for Urban Open Space Second Edition*, New York: John Wiley & Sons, 13–84.
Donald, J. (1999) *Imagining the Modern City*, London: The Athlone Press.
Ernst & Young (2011) *Cities for Citizens*. Global Government and Public Sector Centre. Paris: Ernst & Young.

Gehl, J. (2010) *Cities for People*, Washington DC: Island Press.

—— (2011) *Life Between Buildings: Using Public Space*, Washington DC: Island Press.

—— (2012) *What Makes a Great Public Space?* Copenhagen: Gehl Architects.

Gehl, J. and B. Svarre (2013) *How to Study Cities*, Washington DC: Island Press.

Gifford, R. (2014) "Environmental Psychology Matters," *The Annual Review of Psychology* 65, 541–579.

Hampton, K., O. Livio and L. Sessions-Goulet (2010) "The Social Life of Wireless Urban Spaces: Internet Use, Social Networks, and the Public Realm," *Journal of Communication* 60, 701–722.

Jacobs, J. (1961) *Death and Life of Great American Cities*, New York: Vintage Books.

Jenson, J. (1998) *Mapping Social Cohesion* F|03, Ottawa: Canadian Policy Research Networks.

Landry, C. (2008) *The Creative City: A Toolkit For Urban Innovators*, London: Comedia.

Lofland, L.H. (1998) *The Public Realm: Exploring the City's Quintessential Social Territory*, New Jersey: Transaction Publishers.

Lynch, K. (1960) *The Image of the City*, Cambridge. MIT Press.

Mackay, H. (2010) *What Make us Tick? The Ten Desires That Drive Us*, Sydney: Hachette Publishers.

Malone, K. A. (2006) "United Nations: A Key Player In a Global Movement for Child Friendly Cities," in B. Gleeson and N. Sipe (Eds.), *Creating Child Friendly Cities: Reinstating Kids in the City*, Abingdon: Routledge, 13–32.

Markusen A. and A. Gadwa (2010) *Creative Place-making*, Washington DC: National Endowment for the Arts.

Marshall, N. and R. Roberts (2008) "That Thing Called Public Involvement," in J. Grant (Ed.) *A Reader in Canadian Planning*, Scarborough: Thomson Nelson, 116–120.

Maxwell, J. (1996) *Social Dimensions of Economic Growth*, Eric John Hanson Memorial Lecture Series, Volume VIII, Edmonton: University of Alberta.

McKenzie, S. (2004) *Social Sustainability: Towards Some Definitions Working Paper Series No 27*, Adelaide: Hawke Research Institute, University of South Australia.

Oldenburg, R. (1997) "Our Vanishing 'Third Places,'" *Planning Commissioner's Journal* 25, 6–10.

Project for Public Spaces (2015) "Place-making for Communities," available at www.pps.org/, accessed June 10, 2015.

Putnam, R.D. (2000) *Bowling Alone*, New York: Simon & Schuster.

Relph, E. (1976) *Place and Placelessness*, London: Pion Limited.

—— (2007) "On the Identity of Places," in M. Carmona and S. Tiesdell (Eds.), *Urban Design Reader*, New York: Architectural Press, 103–108.

—— (2013) "Prospects for places," in M. Larice and E. Macdonald (Eds.), *The Urban Design Reader*, London: Routledge, 266–271.

Sandercock, L. (2003) *Cosmopolis II: Mongrel Cities of the 21st Century*, New York: Bloomsbury.

Sennett, R. (1996) *Flesh and Stone: The Body and the City in Western Civilization*, New York: W.W. Norton Publishers.

Thompson, S., J. Kent and A. Capon (2012) "Healthy Planning," in S. Thompson and P. Maginn (Eds.), *Planning Australia* Second Edition, Melbourne: Cambridge University Press, 381–408.

Tuan, Y-F. (1977) *Space and Place: The Perspective of Experience*, London: University of Minnesota Press.
Whyte, W.H. (1980) *The Social Life of Small Urban Spaces*, New York: The Conservation Foundation.

13 Placelessness and the Rigid Perception of Place Identities

Public Toilets as Multi-functional Places

Edgar Liu

Introduction

The concepts of place and placelessness were most notably popularized by Canadian geographer Edward Relph in his seminal book, *Place and Placelessness* (1976). Debates on these two concepts, especially the simple dichotomizing of them, have persisted. There is increasing recognition—including from Relph (1996, 2007) himself—that these two concepts are not necessarily polar opposites and, with increasing global mobility and technological advances, they may even in some cases become integrated and hybridized.

This chapter further interrogates the rigid dichotomization of place and placelessness and how this rigidity may ultimately influence people's conceptualization of a place's identity. Using public toilets as a case study, it examines the contents of the graffiti found inside public toilets—or latrinalia. The contexts in which they exist are related to both Relph's (1976) discussions of the three elements that constitute placelessness—(in)authenticity, (lack of) distinctiveness and (dis)connection—and Judith Butler's (1990) theorization of human identities. It draws heavily on Butler's deconstruction of human identities—that they are fluid and ever-evolving—to question if place identities, as much literature suggests, are constant and unchanging.

In this chapter, I interrogate the contents of latrinalia identified across metropolitan Sydney in 2005 and 2014 to highlight: first, the multiple identities of public toilets; second, to question human's role in both the formation and maintenance of place identities; and third, to question if these multiple identities are accepted by the managing authorities and users of these toilet facilities.

Immediately below, I reflect on Butler's deconstruction of human identities, followed by a review of literature on place identities. This leads into a brief discussion of the concept of placelessness in a contemporary context.

The use of public toilets and latrinalia as case studies is explained, and then how latrinalia extends the identities of public toilets. The chapter concludes with a discussion of whether these amenities take on multiple identities depending on the people who use and identify with them.

People/Place Identities

Academic discussion regarding identities has predominantly been the subject of behavioral sciences such as psychology. Discussions outside the behavioral sciences often focus on the emergence of the subject (i.e. individuality) and understandings of who we are as individuals within groups (Pratt 2000). Group identities are often highlighted by common traits, and socio-scientific works often politicize such group identities as a means of achieving social and political recognition (e.g Gregory 2000; Kobayashi 2009; Anderson 2010).

Geographic studies have also discussed the significance of identities in relation to place, with Relph noted as an early proponent within the field of human geography. Some recent works (e.g. Kirk 2005; Smith 2005) more readily link place identity to community participation, so that a place's identity is mostly defined by the interactions that occur *in situ* (and is therefore socially constructed)

Identifying Humans

Butler's (1990) book *Gender Troubles* is a seminal work in the theorization of human identities, their formation and maintenance. Following post-structuralist principles, her arguments focus on the deconstruction of human identities, and particularly the reiterative nature of identity construction and maintenance. Butler (1990) argues that such reiterations are strongly regulated through performativity, which she defines as a set of expressions (performatives) of personal characteristics (such as gender and ethnicity), each with their own set of governing rules. Such rules are defined by historical conventions, although how certain conventions are more readily accepted in favor over others is far less transparent. The most heavily governed performances are commonly understood as norms.

A performative can be the result of multiple performances; it can also be voluntarily or involuntarily expressed. The voluntary aspects of a performative stem from the free will of individuals acting out their 'personality.' Concurrently, identities are also about how we are perceived by others, and these perceptions are regularly influenced by expressions of local, religious, political, and cultural motivations, as well as modes of behavior and taste (Sepe 2013). All these influence how we 'voluntarily' change our performances.

Performatives are also involuntarily governed by cultural and societal rules. These rules reflect cultural and social conventions, and work predominantly within the subconscious. Recent evidence suggests that such involuntary subconsciousness may play a far more significant role in governing identity performance than conscious awareness (Mlodinow 2012).

Furthermore, the boundaries of identities are clearly set out and constrained by the names that they are given, and these names in turn restrict the potential multiplicity of performances, compelling singularity and discounting fluidity and constant evolution. Jackson's (1991) discussion of multiple masculinities, as opposed to the more conventional understanding of archetypal masculinity, is a case in point. Taking a similarly post-structuralist approach to Butler, Jackson (1991) argues that since gender identity performances are cultural and social constructions, the existence of unitary identity performances is unfeasible. Instead, there is more than one 'true' type of masculinity (and likewise, more than one 'true' type of femininity). With this multiplicitous logic, it is therefore nonsensical to talk about effeminate males or masculine females, as 'male effeminacy' is only a version of multiple masculinities, while 'female masculinity' is only a version of multiple femininities. In more conventional means of understanding masculinity and femininity, however, males who depart from the hegemonic masculine ideals, and females who depart from the hegemonic feminine ideals, are stereotyped as deviant non-conformists.

Since identities comprise both voluntary and involuntary performatives, they are necessarily complex and may reflect endless combinations. As such, Butler (1990) explains that performances of identities can never be repeated identically but instead are mutative in nature. In each performance, the identity is renewed, though more often reinterpreted with minor adjustments, largely resembling its predecessor but never exactly the same. Given the reinterpretations, Butler (1990) argues that 'norms' can be best understood as imitative and fictitious, though they are habitually (mis)taken as factual and true. With this considered, however, significant emphasis is often placed on conformity to norms, as Butler (1990: 17) explains: " 'coherence' and 'continuity' are not logical or analytical features of personhood, but rather socially instituted and maintained norms of intelligibility." Failure to conform or comply with the norms often results in alienation or pathologization, where non-compliance must be corrected in order to maintain an accepted normalcy.

Identifying Places

Explorations into place identities have traditionally been the domains of geography and environmental psychology, but are now also more widely discussed within the humanities and social sciences. For the most part, these explorations are generally discussed concurrently with those on place attachment and sense of place. In this vein, place is very much without identity in the absence of human elements. This approach is most clearly demonstrated by Cresswell's (2004: 7) definition of places as "spaces which people have made meaningful."

In discussing how place as a concept should be studied, Cresswell (2004: 37) explains that places are "the result of processes and practices" and as such they:

> need to be studied in terms of the 'dominant institutional projects,' the individual biographies of people negotiating a place and the way in which a sense of place is developed through the interaction of structure and agency.

Such a conceptualization of place identity resonates with that explained by Relph (1976). As a consequence of the interactions between structure and agency, the identity of a place cannot necessarily be "static and unchangeable, but varies as circumstances and attitudes change" (Relph 1976: 45). Further, it is also "not uniform and undifferentiated, but has several components and forms" (Relph 1976: 45). Such a fluid conceptualizing of place identities also aligns with Butler's discussions of human identities.

Discussions pertaining to human identities such as Butler's, however, are seldom applied to places and their identities. For one, and unlike human identities in which cultural perspectives play a significant role in their formation and regulation, the identities of places are socially constructed by the people who occupy and use them. Further, unlike human identities, place identities lack the aspect of 'voluntary expressions,' so that any reinterpretation in place identities is only ever applied externally, for example, in terms of pre- versus post-disaster place identity (Chamlee-Wright and Storr 2009).

As discussed in Cresswell (2004: 39), however, "place is made and remade on a daily basis" and therefore so is its identity. Indeed, in understanding place as a social construct, its identity "is within human power to change" (Cresswell 2004: 30). In spite of this recognition of external influences and their ability to experience change, place identities continue to be conceptualized as relatively constant and unchanging. Indeed, as Dovey (2010: 3) explains, "places are identified with what does not change ... [and] are experienced primarily in terms of stabilized contexts of everyday life," though he also (contradictorily) acknowledges that places are "in states of becoming" and, as such, like human identities, are also constantly evolving. From this, perhaps what changes a place's identity is humanity's added values—"the activities, and the meanings"—rather than its "static physical setting" (Relph 1976: 47).

Placeless Non-places

While place identities may be constantly changing, some changes may not necessarily be received as positive outcomes. Indeed, as Relph (1976: preface) argues, "the casual eradication of distinctive places and making of standardized landscapes that results from an insensitivity to the significance of place" have the impact of eroding a place's identity, in a process he termed placelessness. In the years since Relph's initial discussion of placelessness, many scholars have added to the debate, including Calhoun's (1998) and Augé's (1995) terming of places that are deemed placeless as non-places.

Picking up on Relph's definition of placelessness, which highlights the lack of a distinctive identity and the absence of a sense of being, much research into this concept has predominantly described a strictly negative phenomenon. Calhoun (1998: 374) described placeless non-places as "sites of impersonal anonymity," focusing especially on the lack of identifiable connection between said non-places and their intended (human) users. As I have argued elsewhere (Liu 2013), however, qualities of placelessness, especially the anonymity and disconnection that it connotes, need not necessarily be received purely in a negative manner; in certain cases, they may even be received positively. For instance, the renewal of a troubled public housing estate towards a more placeless identity may facilitate disassociation from a stigmatized past, a shift in identity that may be welcomed by some of the estate's residents.

Drawing on Sennett (1977) and Castells (1996), Calhoun (1998) discusses the functional segregation of cities in the increasing presence of placeless non-places. He explains that such functional segregations are often exacerbated by suburbanization, globalization, and other processes that have fundamentally altered how urban spaces function. As a result of their altered functions, urban spaces are (re)designed to suit these particular, altered needs. Calhoun (1998: 389) argues that many urban spaces around the world have been (re)created to similar designs and patterns—such as the many glass-fronted skyscrapers that dominate contemporary metropolitan cityscapes—so that most can now be "distinguished semiotically only in arbitrary ways." From my own personal travels, riding on the above-ground subway trains through Tokyo's Odaiba district, for example, has very much the same feel (and sometimes views) as travelling on London's Docklands Light Railway through the Isle of Dogs, with both of these districts undergoing transformations from former shipping dockyards to major commercial centers of their respective cities.

Since the late 20th century, structural and lifestyle changes have seen more and more cities worldwide undergo drastic transformations under the guises of urban regeneration and consolidation. HafenCity in Hamburg, for example, is yet another district undergoing similar regenerations to Odaiba and the Isle of Dogs. These processes of regeneration and consolidation are often in part a response to urban (or horizontal) sprawl by redirecting growth vertically. In the Australian context, this is highlighted by the promotion of the compact city agenda (Randolph 2006), which endorses mixed use neighborhoods much akin to small villages of yesteryears, though within mixed use and higher density settings. This is in turn reflected by steady increases in the number of higher-density residential dwelling units across Australia since the turn of the millennium (ABS 2015).

Does this return to mixed use neighborhoods spell the end of the age of functional segregation and instead the rise of the age of non-distinguishable cities, as suggested by Calhoun (1998)? With further consolidation expected to continue, will the need for multi-functional, mixed-use, urban spaces—whether created intentionally or unintentionally—increase in tandem to cater for a larger and more mixed population that live, work, and play within smaller confines? If so, will these multi-functional spaces contribute to the loss of cities' distinctiveness in a different way, and therefore create placeless non-places through a different means, or will they bring about new levels of complexity and diversity that drive these urban spaces away from placelessness? These questions are discussed below in the context of public toilets and how some users attempt to redefine these places' identities by giving them additional functional meanings.

Public Toilets as Places

As most people would understand, public toilets are designed specifically for people to maintain personal hygiene with relative discretion. Most importantly, they are generally designed for single-gender uses through "a rigid, architecturally imposed gender divide" (Cavanagh 2010: 28) that is signified very literally by signs and symbols (Schweder 2009). Though significant to our day-to-day lives, public toilets are often hidden away out of everyday view and are generally considered a taboo subject of conversation, unless tactfully euphemized (Stead 2009). Furthermore, they are often considered an inappropriate or improper subject for academic investigations (Longhurst 2001; Greed 2003). In spite of this, their identity as places is very clear. Mostly functional by design, public toilets are often generically non-distinctive, mundane places with simple layouts that divide the interiors by their intended functions, so that the wash basins are placed away from the cubicles and urinals. Moreover, the same design is often applied en masse if multiple facilities are provided within the same complex, such as in a shopping center or parkland, thus furthering their non-distinctiveness. All these design characteristics are implemented to highlight public toilets as transitory places where users would only remain for short periods and vacate once hygiene is achieved.

As a place, public toilets straddle the invisible—and often, contested—line between what is considered public and what is private. As public spaces, they can be accessed by anyone who is of the 'correct' gender; once a cubicle door is closed, however, a level of privacy is afforded (Liu 2009). The individual cubicles, while offering privacy, also actively discourage connectivity among users by disconnecting each from others both visually and physically.

Like discussions on the place of public toilets in academia, there are limited examples of latrinalia (or graffiti in general) being used for research purposes. This is partly because of the negative connotations of graffiti, usually related to social problems, vandalism, or visible obscenities (White 2001). Such negative connotations are, however, not universally applied to all acts of graffiti. When understood as archaeological antiquities (Baird and Taylor 2011), graffiti are often highly prized for revealing parts of our histories that may have been long forgotten. The Lascaux cave paintings in south-western France, for example, are widely regarded as a snapshot of prehistoric hunter–gatherer life in the region (Cunningham 2011). There is also now an increasing recognition of graffiti as a form of street art, especially if the artists have made a name for themselves in underground subcultures or even transitioned into the mainstream (Young 2010). Banksy is one example of a graffiti artist who now enjoys an international reputation, to the extent that extraordinary measures are taken to protect his 'art pieces' and public uproar, or even criminal prosecution, ensue if they are threatened or damaged (Collins 2001; Puente 2014; Hamburger 2015).

Within the social sciences, research into graffiti is continuing to slowly emerge. In geography, such works have focused less on graffiti as an art form, and instead have often highlighted their role in symbolizing territoriality, particularly in relation to the specific act of tagging (Iveson 2007). Others suggest that graffiti-ing is "a gendered cultural practice" (Carrington 1989: 89), both in terms of the prevalence of the practice and also the type of contents conveyed. The Kinsey et al. (1953) study, for example, suggests that the majority of male graffiti are sexual in nature, and that most are same-sex oriented. In contrast, only a quarter of female latrinalia are erotic in nature. This resonates with Carrington's (1989) study, which highlights that the major difference between male and female graffiti is the expression of emotions. Male graffitists generally communicate through what is known as 'rap graffiti' (such as tagging, where tags are stylized scripting of the graffitist's name or alias), while female graffitists are more involved in emotional graffiti-ing, such as statements of who one loves, who one hates, and who one befriends.

Despite such sterile and disconnecting intentions, public toilets have also historically been places for same-sex-attracted people (especially men) to seek erotic encounters (Muñoz 2009). Such an alternative use of public toilets has featured more prominently in academic debates regarding spatiality and identity, particularly in challenging heteronormative discourse (Cavanagh 2010). As Sechrest and Flores (1969) and Schwartz and Dovidio (1984) highlight, latrinalia is often a clandestine method of communication within marginalized groups such as same-sex-attracted people seeking erotic encounters. This form of clandestine communication is used in this chapter to show how place identities may, like human identities described by Butler (1990) and Jackson (1991), also be multiplicitous.

Extending Public Toilets' Identities Beyond Hygiene

Ninety-five facilities across fourteen university campuses and four public parklands throughout metropolitan Sydney were visited during 2005, and materials found in these toilet facilities are discussed below in relation to place identity. These facilities (toilets in university libraries and toilet facilities of parklands where major sporting stadiums are located) were chosen to reflect two contrasting hegemonic masculine ideals that are deemed desirable: intelligence and physicality. The facilities comprised 42 male toilets, 41 female toilets, 11 non-sex- or gender-specific disabled toilets, and a family room. A total of 136 discrete latrinalia entries with contents that highlighted same-sex attraction were recorded photographically from 10 male toilets and a female toilet; some of these toilet facilities can be classified as gay beats, that is, areas frequented by individuals who seek casual sexual encounters with other people usually of the same sex (Iveson 2007). Some of these male toilets were revisited in 2014 to check if they still operated as gay beats.

The aims of visiting these public toilets were threefold. First, the visits were used to ascertain the presence of latrinalia. Second, they were used to explore how such latrinalia function as a form of clandestine communication. Third, they were used to examine how such latrinalia reflect the identities of their writers/drawers, particularly in relation to their conceptualization of public/private spaces and their 'place' in society. Latrinalia entries are used mainly in a qualitative manner, emphasizing their content and context rather than any statistical correlations between the two.

The majority of the 136 latrinalia entries were written by men who experience same-sex attraction; only three were written by females. These latrinalia entries can be broadly classified into four categories according to their intended purpose—erotic, romantic, social, and anti-homophobic.

Much like Kinsey et al.'s (1953) discoveries, latrinalia of an erotic nature were the most commonly found. To the men who wrote these entries, the identity of the public toilets is one that is erotic as well as hygienic. This relates strongly to Muñoz's (2009) discussion of public toilets as traditional places of erotic encounters for same-sex-attracted men. The erotic latrinalia found often included short descriptions of what (in terms of physicality or the sexual acts) the graffitist seeks in potential suitors (Figure 13.1). Sometimes these descriptions are drawn out in graphic form, instead of literal description. These erotic latrinalia were mostly found in hard-to-see places (such as behind cubicle doors, or on the edges of wall surfaces) so that they are not viewed by all users of the toilet facilities. The placement of these erotic latrinalia can suggest the graffitists' conceptualizing of public toilets' identities in two specific ways: first, they view public toilets as a public place where erotica does not belong; and second, that same-sex interactions, especially those of an erotic nature, are incongruent with the well-defined identity of public toilets, that of maintaining hygiene. This is especially so when erotica are often generally understood as activities that should be reserved for private spaces (van der Meer 1999). As a result, most erotic latrinalia with same-sex contents were found in marginal places within these public toilets.

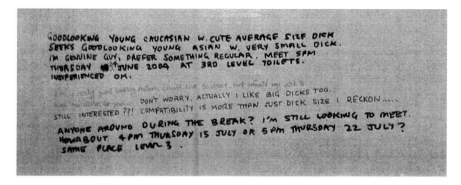

Figure 13.1 Erotica in public toilets, University of New South Wales Library, 2005
Source: Author, 2005.

While less frequently found than those of an erotic nature, romantic same-sex latrinalia, such as exemplified in Figure 13.2, are often drawn in less marginal places and as such may come into the view of more users. Likewise, latrinalia of a social nature (Figure 13.3) were also less commonly found than those of an erotic nature but, again like romantic latrinalia, were predominantly found in very visible places inside the public toilets. On a few occasions, latrinalia with same-sex subject matter could be classified as being anti-homophobic in nature, and again these were more likely to be found in openly visible places inside the public toilets rather than, like those of an erotic nature, in more marginalized, hidden places.

To the same-sex attracted men who write or draw in public toilets, latrinalia was an effective and clandestine method of communication. To these men, the identity of a public toilet is multiple and varied. Public toilets may be variously intimate places for sexual encounters (or for organizing such encounters), social spaces, or places for performing (and sometimes protecting) their personal identities, in addition to maintaining hygiene. At times, these public toilets become well known among same-sex-attracted men, as well as other members of the public, as gay beats or cruising grounds, though such beats are seldom highly visualized or publicly acknowledged. This is especially so as such beats do not generally have any recognizable geo-spatial patterns and are often only known locally or within the non-heterosexual community (Iveson 2007; Muñoz 2009). Such multi-dimensional extensions to the identity of some public toilets thus distinguish them from most others.

An Extension Too Far?

In her critique of the humanistic approach to studying place, Massey (1997) reiterates the bounded nature of identifying places. In particular, she

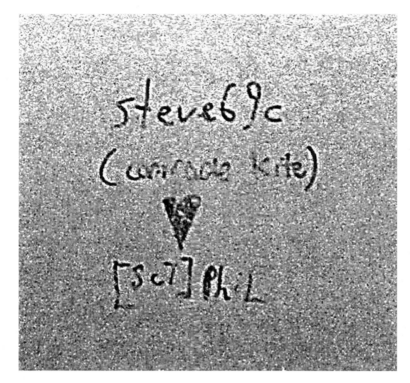

Figure 13.2 Romance in public to.lets, University of New South Wales Library, 2005

Source: Author, 2005.

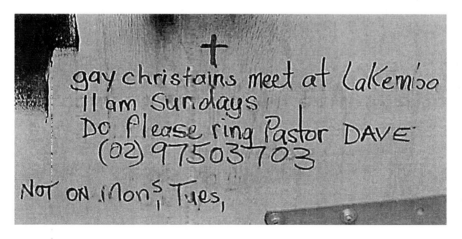

Figure 13.3 Socializing in public toilets, Parramatta Park, 2005

Source: Author, 2005.

highlights the power relations and forces of exclusion that are often at play in the formation of such place identities. Such critical discussions are also emphasized in the works of Harvey (1993) and Sibley (1995). Cresswell (2008) describes the exclusive power relations as a rigid honoring of memories. From this perspective, the presence of latrinalia in public toilets challenges the conventional, heteronormative assumption of public spaces by articulating different types of male-to-male interactions that are not commonly associated with these places, regardless of whether the interactions occur in these toilets or not (Carrington 1989; Muñoz 2009).

These extensions stray from the public toilet's originally intended identity of hygiene. They often do not sit well with other users and the authorities responsible for upkeep of the facilities. This is evident both in terms of personal actions taken by users and design elements implemented by authorities in deterring same-sex interactions, likely to re-establish and restore public toilet's presumed heteronormative identity. These attempts range from derogatory and homophobic latrinalia by other users to pointing out the out-of-placeness of these interactions and even directing them to where these other users think they rightfully belong (Figure 13.4).

Figure 13.4 Re-directing 'Gayness' to where it rightfully belongs, University of New South Wales, 2005

Source: Author, 2005.

Figure 13.5 Reducing legible surfaces in public toilets, Parramatta Park, 2005
Source: Author, 2005.

The authorities also regularly remove the latrinalia, and change the interior surfaces to deter latrinalia writing. These actions include installing glazed tiles to make latrinalia writing difficult and cleaning up easy, and spray-painting the interiors of the facilities with multi-colored stencils to reduce legible surfaces (Figure 13.5). In more extreme cases, entries to these facilities are restricted. For some of the toilet facilities at the parklands visited, their doors were often locked from dusk until dawn to deter erotic and other types of same-sex encounters taking place; in other facilities, cubicle doors were removed to deter these encounters taking place in the cubicles during opening hours. In the most extreme case, a toilet block was demolished completely when the strategies mentioned above failed to achieve the desired outcome of deterring same-sex encounters.

The advancement of technologies and increasing popularity of online geosocial networking applications such as Grindr and Tinder have diminished the role of public toilets as erotic and social places. A reassessment in 2014 of the ten male public toilets where latrinalia with same-sex subject matters were found in 2005 yielded less than a handful of such entries, though evidence of latrinalia of other nature (including attempted humor or political commentaries) still existed.

Conclusion

This chapter demonstrates how human activities can shape the identities of places, and how such identities may change over time as the human activities that occupy these places change. It also demonstrates how the same place may take on different identities for different groups of people and, as a result, conflicts over its 'true' identity(s) may arise. This is discussed in the context of latrinalia and public toilets in metropolitan Sydney.

The presence of latrinalia has assisted in transforming the mostly functional identity of public toilets, places that are generally not notably distinctive from each other. The presence of latrinalia in some public toilets, especially those pertaining to non-heterosexual subject matters, makes some public toilets more distinctive than others. At the same time, they also highlight a level of connection among users that is generally not associated with these places. They are for the most part not mass produced, bringing about a level of authenticity. On these counts, the latrinalia bring these public toilets away from considerations of placeless non-places without replacing their original, intended identity of being generic places for maintaining personal hygiene.

At the same time, however, the presence of latrinalia in these public toilets challenges conventional, heteronormative assumptions of public spaces, and efforts are often made to remove such evidence of difference. Their mainly erotic or sexualized subject matter—which is conventionally conceptualized as a matter for 'private' places—and the fact that such visualizations of same-sex interactions were mainly operationalized by a marginalized group of users may have limited their success in re-identifying these public toilets as anything but public toilets.

The example of public toilets in this chapter is merely a demonstration of how a seemingly ordinary, everyday place may contain multiple identities that evoke different meanings to different groups of users. The same appreciation of place diversity and fluid identities can be (re)interpreted in many different everyday places, be they transitory places of encounters, such as pedestrian malls or public transport, or places such as a community garden where we may invest in its sense of community and connectivity. For example, a bus shelter may be where local commuters wait for their morning bus service but also a place to sleep for a homeless person. The processes through which we, as humans, perceive the identity/ies of these places are, however, more or less the same. Further still, the processes that we employ to maintain these identities in subtle as well as in extreme ways—such as the banning of skateboarding unless in designated areas—only provide additional examples of the ways confined versions of place identities are enforced in much the same way as Butler's (1990) and Jackson's (1991) discussions of human identities.

People and places are obviously very different, though inextricably linked. If indeed their identities can be similarly understood from a more fluid ideological perspective, and especially when we look closely at the more micro- performance-based scale (Cresswell 2004), placeless identities might be harder to come by than one might think. Returning to the questions posed earlier in this chapter—whether multi-functional places contribute to the loss of distinctiveness, and therefore towards placelessness, or whether they bring new levels of complexity and diversity and therefore away from placelessness—perhaps these two perspectives are not polar opposites and instead can shift quite fluidly from one to the other. Recognizing the multiplicitous nature of place identity is the main challenge to places becoming non-places.

References

ABS (2015) *Building Activity, Australia, Dec 2014*, Cat. No. 8752.0. Canberra, Australian Bureau of Statistics, Table 37.

Anderson, M.R. (2010) *Community Identity and Political Behavior*, New York: Palgrave Macmillan.

Augé, M. (1995) *Non-places: An Introduction to Supermodernity*, J. Howe (trans.), London: Verso.

Baird, J.A. and C. Taylor (Eds.) (2011) *Ancient Graffiti in Context*, New York: Routledge.

Birney, A. (1973) "Crack Puns: Text and Context in an Item of Latrinalia," *Western Folklore* 32, 137–140.

Butler, J. (1990) *Gender Trouble: Feminism and the Subversion of Identity*, New York: Routledge.

Calhoun, C.J. (1998) "Community without Propinquity Revisited: Communications Technology and the Transformation of the Urban Public Sphere," *Sociological Inquiry* 68, 373–397.

Carrington, K. (1989) "Girls and Graffiti," *Cultural Studies* 3, 89–100.

Castells, M. (1996) *The Rise of the Networked Society*. Cambridge, MA.: Blackwell.

Cavanagh, S.L. (2010) *Queering Bathrooms: Gender, Sexuality, and the Hygienic Imagination*, Toronto: University of Toronto Press.

Chamlee-Wright, E. and V.H. Storr (2009) " 'There's No Place like New Orleans': Sense of Place and Community Recovery in the Ninth Ward after Hurricane Katrina," *Journal of Urban Affairs* 31, 615–634.

Collins, L. (2007) "Banksy Was Here: The Invisible Man of Graffiti Art," *The New Yorker*, 14, 11 & 18 June 10.

Cresswell, T. (2004) *Place: A Short Introduction*, Malden, MA.: Blackwell.

—— (2008) "Space and Place (1977): Yi-Fu Tuan," in P. Hubbard, R. Kitchen and G. Valentine (Eds.) *Key Texts in Human Geography*, Los Angeles: Sage, 53–59.

Cunningham, D. (2011) "The Oldest Maps of the World: Deciphering the Hand Paintings of Cueva de El Castillo Caves in Spain and Lascaux France," *Midnight Science* 4, 3.

Dovey, K. (2010) *Becoming Places: Urbanism/Architecture/Identity/Power*, London: Routledge.

Greed, C. (2003) *Inclusive Urban Design: Public Toilets*, Amsterdam: Architectural Press.

Gregory, D. (2000) "Identity Politics," in R.J. Johnston, D. Gregory, G. Pratt and M. Watts (Eds.) *The Dictionary of Human Geography*, fourth edition, Malden, MA.: Blackwell, 367–369.

Hamburger, J. (2015) "Glass Protecting Banksy Artwork in Park City Cracks All Over," *Park Record*, available at www.parkrecord.com/ci_28148451/glass-pro tecting-banksy-artwork-park-city-cracks-all, accessed May 19, 2015.

Harvey, D. (1993) "From Space to Place and Back Again: Reflections on the Condition of Postmodernity," in J. Bird, B. Curtis, T. Putnam, G. Robertson and L. Tickner (Eds.) *Mapping the Futures: Local Cultures, Global Change*, London: Routledge, 3–29.

Iveson, K. (2007) *Publics and the City*. Malden, MA.: Blackwell.

Jackson, P. (1991) "The Cultural Politics of Masculinity: Towards a Social Geography," *Transactions of the Institute of British Geographers* 16, 199–213.

Kinsey, A.C., W. Pomeroy, C. Martin, and P. Gebhard (1953) *Sexual Behavior in the Human Female*, Philadelphia: Saunders.

Kirk, K. (2005) "Local Participation and Place Identity," in C. Hague and P. Jenkins (Eds.) *Place Identity, Participation and Planning*, London: Routledge, 139–157.

Kobayashi, A. (2009) "Identity Politics," in R. Kitchin and N. Thrift (Eds.) *International Encyclopedia of Human Geography*, Oxford: Elsevier, 282–286.

Liu, E. (2009) *Neo-normativity, the Sydney Gay and Lesbian Mardi Gras, and Latrinalia: The Demonstration of a Concept on Non-Heterosexual Performativities*. PhD, University of New South Wales.

—— (2013) "The Wander Years: Estate Renewal, Temporary Relocation and Place(less)ness in Bonnyrigg, NSW," *State of Australian Cities Conference*, Sydney.

Longhurst, R. (2001) *Bodies: Exploring fluid boundaries*, London: Routledge.

Massey, D. (1997) "A Global Sense of Place," in T.J. Barnes and D.G. Gregory (Eds.) *Reading Human Geography: The Poetics and Politics of Inquiry*, London: Arnold, 315–323.

Mlodinow, L. (2012) *Subliminal: How Your Unconscious Mind Rules Your Behavior*, New York: Vintage.

Muñoz, J. (2009) *Cruising Utopia: The Then and There of Queer Futurity*, New York: New York University Press.

Pratt, G. (2000) "Focus Group," in R.J. Johnston, D. Gregory, G. Pratt and M. Watts (Eds.) *The Dictionary of Human Geography*, fourth edition, Malden, MA.: Blackwell, 272.

Puente, M. (2014) "Banksy Street Murals Damaged in Park City, Utah," *USA Today*, 3 January 2014, www.usatoday.com/story/life/people/2014/01/03/banksy-street-murals-damaged-in-park-city-utah/4305827/

Randolph, B. (2006) "Delivering the Compact City in Australia: Current Trends and Future Implications," *Urban Policy and Research* 24, 473–490.

Relph, E. (1976) *Place and Placelessness*, Pion.

—— (1996) "Reflections on Place and Placelessness," *Environmental and Architectural Phenomenology Newsletter* 7, 14–15.

—— (2007) "Spirit of Place and Sense of Place in Virtual Realities," *Technè* 10, 17–25.

Schwartz, M.J. and J.F. Dovidio (1984) "Reading Between the Lines: Personality Correlates of Graffiti Writing," *Perceptual and Motor Skills* 59, 395–398.

Schweder, A. (2009) " 'Stalls between the walls:' Segregated sexed spaces," in O. Gershenson and B. Penner (Eds.) *Ladies and Gents: Public Toilets and Gender*, Philadelphia: Temple University Press, 182–188.

Sechrest, L. and L. Flores (1969) "Homosexuality in the Philippines and the United States: The Handwriting on the Wall," *The Journal of Social Psychology* 79, 3–12.

Sennett, R. (1977) *The Fall of Public Man*, New York: Knopf.

Sepe, M. (2013) "Places and Perceptions in Contemporary City," *Urban Design International* 18, 111–113.

Sibley, D. (1995) *Geographies of Exclusion: Society and Difference in the West*, London: Routledge.

Smith, H. (2005) "Place Identity and Participation," in C. Hague and P. Jenkins (Eds.) *Place Identity, Participation and Planning.* London: Routledge, 39–54.

Stead, N. (2009) "Avoidance: On Some Euphemisms for the 'Smallest Room,' " in O. Gershenson and B. Penner (Eds.) *Ladies and Gents: Public Toilets and Gender*, Philadelphia: Temple University Press, 126–134.

van der Meer, T. (1999) "Private Acts, Public Spaces: Defining Boundaries in Nineteenth-Century Holland," in W. Leap (Ed.) *Public Sex/Gay Space*, New York: Columbia University Press, 223–245.

White, R. (2001) "Graffiti, Crime Prevention and Cultural Space," *Current Issues in Criminal Justice* 12, 253–268.

Young, A. (2010) "Negotiated Consent or Zero Tolerance? Responding to Graffiti and Street Art in Melbourne," *City* 14, 99–114.

Part 4
Place/lessness in Question

14 Extraordinary Ordinariness

An Outsider's Perspective on Place and Placelessness in the Japanese City

Matthew Carmona

Introduction

To a visitor, Japanese urbanism may seem to have a split personality, stemming from traditions that still survive and that emphasize order, restraint, and harmony side by side with a dominant contemporary urbanism that is often ultra-modern, brash, and discordant. This split personality echoes the thesis advanced by Edward Relph (1976) and others that in contemporary urbanism there is a place/placelessness divide. From an 'outsiders' perspective, this chapter explores the nature of Japanese cities, and whether Relph's ideas offer a useful lens through which to understand their divergent character.

The discussion draws from a period in early 2012 in which five key cities in Japan—Tokyo, Sapporo, Osaka, Kyoto and Yokohama—were explored by the author in order to take a snapshot of Japanese urbanism at that particular point in time.[1] The project adopted two methods. The first amounted to a sequence of semi-structured walks through each city over a series of days, often with a local guide. During these walks, situations and contexts were observed, photographed and discussed, with notes written up at the end of each day. The processes can be likened to the experimental practice of *dérive* developed in Paris in the 1940s as a method to understand the emotional impact of the geographical environment on individuals. Later adopted and developed by the Situationists, the practice can be thought of as an unstructured drift through the city directed entirely by feelings (Debord 1958). In this case, however, the walks were loosely structured in order to take in episodes of both recent and traditional development in each city, although the method remained a first-hand experiential one[2].

The walks were supplemented by informal engagement with key local experts—academics from local universities and practitioners, including local planners and consultants working in each city—in order to understand the complex planning, design, development, and cultural processes that shape contemporary Japanese cities. Reflecting the informal tone set by the adoption of the *dérive* approach, these were wholly unstructured and were frequently conducted during and as part of the walks, in restaurants, or during other informal gatherings, with notes written up later.

Together, the methods were designed to immerse what Relph (1976) defined as the 'outsider' into the unfamiliar Japanese urban scene. While the 'place' literature contends that a key benefit of a positive 'sense of place' is to engender a sense of belonging within users (Crang 1998)—to be 'insiders'—this requires not only a 'unique address' in Relph's terms, but also a degree of familiarity and rootedness in place. It follows that the 'outsider's' perspective is a distinctive one, and consequently the reflections underpinning this chapter flow directly from this experience. Supported, where appropriate, by the literature, the essentially informal and personally immersive style of the research approach is reflected in the loose, personal, and informal writing style of the chapter. Like the practice of *dérive* itself, or even the Japanese city, this chapter eschews a formal, sequential structure. So while it is in seven sections, these wander around the topic of place/placelessness in the Japanese city, connecting evidence, observation, and supposition where they can be found, and constructing a narrative of the extraordinary ordinariness of place.

An Individual Aesthetic

An obvious polarity can be found between the approaches to landscape and townscape in Japan. From its glorious public parks, to the landscapes of its temples and shrines, to its immaculately designed (often tiny) private gardens, Japanese traditional culture revels in the harmony of its 'captured landscapes.' Across the different scales, each are carefully composed and immaculately tended and treated with great reverence and respect. Fundamentally, this reflects a deep love and respect for nature in a country where densities of living make it very easy to lose touch with the natural environment. A graphic illustration is the national obsession with cherry blossom, which from mid-March to April each year first appears in the south of Japan and then works its way up the country, along with excited national cherry blossom reports that every day update citizens on progress. For the visitor, the arrival of the cherry blossom is met by the strange sight of legions of locals standing under the cherry trees, cameras in hand, ready to take the perfect cherry blossom photo to send to their friends.

Yet, despite the very deep and obvious love for nature that this annual ritual reveals and the extension of this into the cherished open landscapes of the Japanese city, the same cannot be said for the country's townscapes. There, instead of symphony we have soloist after soloist, often beautifully designed and detailed, yet all screaming for attention, like so many discordant sonatas all being played at once. The impression to those unused to such excess is, at first, a sense of shock, but then a sense of energy and excitement that is both invigorating and bewildering in equal measure. The impression is bolstered by layer upon layer of signage all fighting (and failing) to get attention, and by the relentless rush of traffic (human and vehicular) all around. This acceptance of the co-existence and superimposition of urban elements that in the West might be deemed incompatible is a key characteristic of Japanese urbanism (Shelton 2012).

Physically, this seeming disregard for townscape—or the manner in which the physical, built environment is visually composed—is in sharp contrast to the order and coherence of traditional Japanese architecture; there, simplicity and harmony have long been cherished virtues that even border on obsession when it comes to the design of formal interior spaces. Moreover, by virtue of the limited pallet of forms, materials and styles in which traditional Japanese buildings were constructed, these have historically molded seamlessly together to create highly harmonious compositions and townscapes. While many of these characteristics are clearly present in the contemporary as well as the traditional Japanese city, the results on the ground are often very different (Figure 14.1).

So what underpinned this Damascene conversion from harmony to what Radovic (2007: 145–6) characterizes as "desirable chaos"? The answer can be found in several places. First is the strong post-war drive to rebuild Japan's decimated cities and to grow its economy at all costs. This drive quickly swept away much of the country's indigenous urbanism, largely completing the job begun by the bombing in World War Two and the regular fires and earthquakes that have historically ravaged so many Japanese cities (Beard n.d.). Second are the very strong property rights shaping a regulatory system that gives an open hand as long as basic land-use-based zoning and building code stipulations are met[3]. The Building Code, for example, determines permissible building heights against standard formulae relating to the type of road onto which a building fronts, the distance to adjacent properties, and north-side shadow-line stipulations. Developers quickly build to the maximum permissible volumes, leading to some very strange-shaped buildings (Figure 14.2, top) and to a new characteristic—some might argue, ubiquitous—urban form with higher buildings lining wider roads to take advantage of the higher height allowances. Beyond these, for the vast majority of buildings, if you comply then permission is automatic: no negotiation, no consultation, no fuss.

Third is an absence of public mechanisms to review design quality and to curb the worst excesses of discordant urbanism. Fourth, the architectural profession is generally complicit in this, eschewing traditional forms and materials, and instead pursuing a heightened sense of their right to express themselves as they see fit without regard to context. Fifth is the strong preference for detached buildings, avoiding the need for party walls, and unintentionally further emphasizing the individual building (and property rights) over the composition by requiring that a small gap of usually less than a meter be left between every building, irrespective of plot width and height; the result is some extremely strange tall thin detached buildings

Figure 14.1 Traditional and contemporary Japanese architecture compared. The former (top) is natural, harmonious, and organic (in material), the latter (bottom) hard, discordant, and inorganic

Source: Author, 2012.

Figure 14.2
In Japanese buildings,
typically form follows
regulation shadow-line
(top)and fire separation
(bottom)

Source: Author, 2012.

(Figure 14.2, bottom). Finally, there is the question of advertising regulations (or the general lack of them) and an advertising industry that flouts even the regulations that do exist (Ikebe 2005). While this final issue is being tightened up with a new national advertising law and registration system, here again private property rights guarantee the right to advertise which, when extended upwards across the multiple floors of a mixed-use building, can quickly cover even the most carefully designed building in garish neon signs.

Controlling Landscape

In Japan's largest cities, such as Tokyo and Osaka, where development pressures and built densities are at their most intense, the result of the desirable chaos is a uniquely Japanese townscape that makes even other south-east Asian townscapes look tame by comparison. For the outsider, the result is endlessly fascinating, if sometimes a little surreal, although at least a minority of insiders (among Japanese built-environment professionals) there is a hankering once again for a more ordered city and for greater efforts to define and manage coordinated local qualities of place.

This desire is reflected in the workings of the Landscape Law, which came into force in June 2004 and which makes it possible to designate Landscape Districts and Landscape Planning Areas. In these, for the first time on a country-wide basis, landscape ordinances can be drawn up to control the physical design of developments in both new and existing areas (built and natural; Ando n.d.). The measures represent a major move away from the anything-goes culture that has shaped Japanese cities since World War Two, although so far their use has been limited and they still represent the exception rather than the rule through much of Japan.

In Sapporo (Japan's fourth largest city), for example, only a relatively small area of the city center is covered by such a designation, where it was established to give greater control in an area around the main railway station, which has been undergoing large-scale change. There, as elsewhere, the system offers a form of more locally responsive zoning, controlling building height, bulk, aspects of façade design (although not style), and color. Like the national zoning system, this is an 'as-of-right' process, although with some negotiation between local authority and developers to ensure compliance. Unfortunately, instead of a new and sensitive approach to place, the process seems to have stripped away the small-scale diversity and innovation that accompanies the usual process of uncoordinated development in Japan, along with its hallmark visual and social dynamism. Instead, this is replaced by carefully designed but ultimately insular and soulless mega-development (Figure 14.3). In Sapporo (and other cities), discussions have been had about the development of a more rigorous design-review process around the provisions of the Landscape Law, but so far these initiatives have come to nothing as the discretion that is required flies firmly in the face of

Figure 14.3 Mega-development within the Sapporo landscape planning area
Source: Author, 2012.

the fixed regulatory systems that guide development across the country and guarantee property rights.

The Landscape Law sits on top of a longer-established system of area protection ('listing') for key townscapes of historic value. This protection is seen as particularly important in cities such as Kyoto, where a greater proportion of the historic built environment still remains. Such protection provides a further degree of control in the most historic areas, although still on a blunt as-of-right basis. Nationally enacted area listing powers, for example, give the right to excavate a basement under historic buildings, a practice that in cities such as Kyoto can easily destabilize neighboring historic timber structures[4]. Partly because of this, Kyoto favors designation through its own local area listing powers—although under these provisions, in order to compensate owners for the loss of potential basement space, a third storey can be added to the locally designated two-storey traditional building stock, again, as-of-right. Consequently, in order to preserve development rights, the system in effect sanctions major change to the city's historic townscape and architectural integrity. In doing so, it graphically illustrates a profound clash between the traditional city, contemporary development rights and pressures, and regulatory processes, with profound impacts on even the most sacredly held qualities of place

Individual vs Collective Rights and Aesthetics

In essence, the systems for shaping the physical/aesthetic form of cities in Japan reflect outcomes from a particular balance between the rights of the individual and that of the collective good. While townscapes in much of Europe (particularly those in historic settings) are the subject of much public debate, and (often) not inconsiderable state intervention, to try to ensure a level of aesthetic amenity and contextual integration, in Japan they emerge as a result of the imposition of simple, inflexible rules and the whims and creativity of private property owners and their designers. Property rights are considered sacrosanct, and development is largely left to the market.

Undeniably, this leads to some very perverse outcomes, for example the uncontrolled spread of private parking across the city, with every available nook and cranny turned into some of the smallest and some of the most high tech, but also physically disruptive, car parks. It also leads to some of the most dramatic and aesthetically alive townscapes that you will find anywhere in the world, with a vibrant social public realm to match (Figure 14.4). While some criticize these everyday Japanese urban landscapes as the

Figure 14.4 The life and vibrancy of Japanese cities. These are often more intense and visually stimulating than even other south-east Asian cities

Source: Author, 2012.

inevitable outcome of an extreme form of commodification (Waley 2006: 377), arguably, in their own way, these places that are so typical of the Japanese city can be cherished and enjoyed just like the carefully nurtured townscapes of the West. Their very 'ordinariness' for insiders to the Japanese scene is only matched by their very 'extraordinariness' for those unused to such exuberance. Such qualities are now being threatened by ambitious but ultimately unresponsive new design-governance processes and allied mega-development processes that threaten to strip away rather than preserve the essence of the Japanese city.

A Collective Neglect

Japanese culture offers a fascinating soup of tradition and modernity. While the Japanese embrace new technologies—perhaps more so than any other nation—at the same time they are determined to hang on to their traditions. On the face of it, retaining these traditions may be easier for a nation that is still relatively insular and culturally highly homogenous (just 1.5% of residents are not ethnically Japanese), although with regard to the built environment, this does not seem to be the case.

For the visitor the distinctive Japanese cuisine, impressive temples and shrines, beautiful gardens, culture of bowing, and the glimpses of more mysterious rituals such as tea ceremonies and the Geisha (who can still be seen in some surviving historic districts), are reminders of the very ancient and complex history of the nation. At the same time, more modern obsessions reflect Japan's extreme modernity, rubbing up against and occasionally colliding with tradition in the public spaces of the city. This collision of old and new is written into the built environment all around. The preoccupation of the state with safety, for example, is leading to the destruction through redevelopment of some surviving traditional (if aged and more than a little dilapidated) neighborhoods. These areas of the city—the *shitamachi*—consist of tightly knit, conjoined timber-frame houses arranged in narrow streets, often with local shops, small businesses, and local facilities of all sorts within the same locality (Ishida 1997). For Japan's public authorities, however, such places are 'dangerous,' because of the potential for fire and the difficulty faced by emergency services (fire and ambulances) to navigate their narrow, winding streets (Zarmati 1989).

The *shitamachi* also offer almost the perfect conditions for a healthy, sustainable community life: socially cohesive, mixed use, low car usage, lively, and proud (the last obvious in the well-tended plants and flowers outside many doors) (Sorensen 2009). They are 'places' in the full sense implied by Relph (1976)—centers of meaning constructed out of lived experience: "a secure point from which to look out on the world" accompanied by "a firm grasp on one's own position in the order of things, and a significant spiritual and psychological attachment to somewhere" (Relph 1976:

38). These positive characteristics might seem to more than make up for the remote 'safety' concerns; but the history and fear of fire in Japanese cities is a potent force to be reckoned with, and it dominates almost any other consideration in how Japanese cities are being re-shaped today (Figure 14.5).

Figure 14.5 Traditional *Shitamachi* streetscape (a) street
Source: Author, 2012.

Figure 14.5 (b) Street widening and redevelopment in a *Shitamachi* area

For outsiders who have not experienced the sorts of fire storms that consumed large areas of Japan's cities during World War Two or in the aftermath of major seismic activity, this is a context that is difficult to understand, but nevertheless must be respected. However, the fact that Japan's world-renowned building-technology sector is not called upon to better fire-proof these areas and thus avoid their demolition and redevelopment typifies a general lack of commitment to this uniquely Japanese urbanism.

Form Follows Tax

A further contemporary pressure on traditional neighborhoods is equally significant and well beyond the ability of those with built-environment responsibilities to control, namely fiscal policy that has direct and unintended consequences on the physical built environment. A distinct characteristic of Japanese society is the very static nature of its rapidly aging population, with many families living in the same house from cradle to grave. The populations of Japan's traditional neighborhoods exemplify this, but as homeowners age and pass on, punitive death duties (exacerbated by complex inheritance arrangements) become due. This results in descendants often unable to pay without first selling their inheritance, typically for redevelopment, which always occurs at a higher density.

To help in such circumstances, the new Landscape Law contains provisions to limit inheritance tax liabilities for properties in a designated Landscape District (Ando n.d.: 6). These work in two ways. First, by recognizing that because designation limits the potential for future land use and/or floor-area changes, they also limit the potential for betterment on the site, and consequently reduce the tax liability. Second, they provide tax relief in the case where land is transferred to the organization responsible for the management of the landscape area—the Landscape Formation Organization—for use in improving the area (although this 'improvement' may still imply demolition, for example to widen roads or create play areas—see Figure 14.5, bottom). In practice, these provisions have been rarely used, again demonstrating a lack of concern or will at the local level to engage with Japan's traditional neighborhoods.

Interestingly, the sorts of gentrification processes that have socially transformed, but physically preserved, so many historic areas in the UK and other Western countries do not seem to exist in Japan. Instead, the aspiration of younger less 'place-bound' Japanese with choice is typically to occupy an apartment in a modern block rather than to reuse and refurbish a traditional dwelling (Fielding 2004). For them, the place value of these older neighborhoods is outside their ken. While the sorts of blocks that they choose to occupy might be viewed as anonymous, reflecting Relph's (1976) characterization of placelessness in terms of standard landscapes hewn from the casual eradication of distinctive places, they are nevertheless the places where these populations wish to be, with meaning derived from their functionality (modern, connected, low maintenance, etc.), which clearly transcends their more limited physical appeal.

Large vs Local

Moving up a scale, one of the starkest divisions between old and new in Japan is that between the modern corporate/retail monoliths and the traditional shopping streets—*shoten-gai*—that historically developed at the center of numerous Japanese communities. Today, while Japanese shopping centers replete with the latest cloned brands (both national and international) thrive as the new temples for the young, many older shopping streets wither on the vine. In part this is because these traditional streets find it difficult to adapt to the new retail formats demanded by modern retailing. In addition, the severe climate of Japan simply makes the new air-conditioned centers more comfortable places to be for much of the year, even despite the roofing-in of many *shoten-gai*.

The sorts of inflexible demographic/housing practices described above also make modernization difficult. Thus, as the owners of shops age, instead of selling their businesses and moving on, they simply shut up shop, close the shutters downstairs, and retreat upstairs to live out their days. Today the phenomenon of Japan's 'shutter streets' represents a particularly difficult problem to crack (Figure 14.6), a problem that will only become more difficult as the effects of Japan's shrinking population becomes more pronounced[5], leading to a general lack of investment demand in cities, particularly in declining areas with fragmented and complex land-ownership structures.

Yet despite the marginal nature of some of Japan's local shopping streets, communities in the areas through which these traditional streets run remain as diverse and mixed as ever, combining living with business and small-scale industry (Mateo-Babiano and Ieda 2005). Like European high streets, they still have much to offer, but are being fast undermined by changing modern lifestyles and the relentless force of big retailing that removes so much spending power from local economies (Mori Memorial Foundation 2008).

A case in point is the Roppongi area of Tokyo, in which a traditional community and shopping street sits side by side with the sort of private corporate/retail/residential mega-development that has become ubiquitous in large Japanese cities. In this case, the Roppongi Hills development has created some of the most desirable and expensive real estate in the city, although any positive externalities seem locked within the very obvious and stark boundaries that mark the edges of this new (and very swanky)

Figure 14.6 A Japanese shutter street
Source: Author, 2012.

development. Here, Tokyo's largest developer painstakingly took 14 years to consolidate and then wipe clean an 11 hectare site,[6] removing in the process 400 smaller plots in multiple uses and occupancies (Bremner 2002). Completed in 2003, the development pre-dated the Landscape Law, and rather than benefitting from any protection, instead the area was (conveniently for the developer) designated a 'dangerous area' because of its narrow streets that made access for emergency vehicles challenging.

Even at Roppongi, however, and in numerous other developments like it, vestiges of the old city remain through the temples and shrines that pepper the older areas of Japanese cities and which cannot be conveniently swept away. In the face of massive redevelopments such as Roppongi Hills these survive because of the burial grounds over which they watch and where most Japanese citizens still end their days in closely packed family plots (Figure 14.7). As a consequence, a continued feature of Japanese townscapes (even the most modern) are formal gates in the street that lead to either a small temple or shrine and associated burial ground, many dating from the Edo period (1603–1886).

In an environment characterized for its propensity perpetually to destroy and rebuild (Waley 2006), these features demonstrate that some things are sacrosanct, locationally fixed, and place-dependent. However, not even these vestiges of the old city are entirely immune from development pressures, as many temple communities have long ago sold off their forecourts to be redeveloped for residential or commercial purposes

The Dangers of Homogenization

For their part the private mega-developments of Japan are typically highly designed, ultra-modern and come replete with large privatized public spaces (internal and external) that have been delivered by the developers in exchange for floor area bonuses that make their soaring towers even higher (Figure 14.8). The spaces vary greatly, and many are carefully designed, well-constructed, and well used, although in their 'corporate' ambience they closely resemble those that might also be encountered in Shanghai, Singapore, and Seoul, or even London or New York (Cybriwsky 1999).

That is not necessarily a criticism. Japan's cities are large and can encompass spaces—even globally ubiquitous ones—of diversity and difference, just like large cities elsewhere (Carmona and Wunderlich 2012). Indeed, research reviewing the 652 privately owned public spaces that exist in central Tokyo suggests that many of these are 'excellent' in quality, comfortably designed, and that local residents and workers benefit from their extremely high utility value (Mori Memorial Foundation 2011: 4). The concern persists, however, that in the near future such environments may be all these cities have to offer, particularly as Japan's youthful culture (despite its aging population) remains so wedded to the modern and, even if it were not, is often locked out from engaging in the traditional city because of the costs

Figure 14.7
Ropongi Hills public
(private) space (top) and one
of its neighboring temples
(bottom)

Source: Author, 2012.

Figure 14.8 Japan's 'bonus' public/private spaces
Source: Author, 2012.

associated with inheritance and the very inflexible housing market that leaves an elderly population clinging on to properties that might benefit from some youthful vigor to give them a new lease of life. In much of Japan a little targeted gentrification may be exactly what the doctor ordered!

Conclusion

Based on a snapshot review of Japanese urbanism in five cities, this chapter has argued that Japan's contemporary development processes have given rise to a form of development that strongly emphasizes property rights and individual vision rather than a notion of holistic place quality. This both distinguishes Japan's cities and creates tensions, which are reflected in their aesthetics and townscapes. While some see the resulting urban landscape as a placeless cacophony of conflicting image and experience that threatens the traditional forms and typologies of the Japanese city, others see the distinctive and vibrant cityscapes, where hyper-modern meets traditional, as a new distinct and characterful place in its own right. It has certainly given rise to some of the most distinctive and vibrant cityscapes in the world. At the same time, this very same private/individual emphasis, and the robust but inevitably blunt regulatory tools that it gives rise to, are threatening the sorts of traditional forms and typologies that represent the other side of the Japanese urban character and which seem to be so little valued, particularly by the young.

The culmination of all the pressures described here means that Japan's traditional urban areas are in the process of suffering a death by a thousand cuts. For an outsider, this would seem to represent a terrible loss, as for all their amazing energy, it is the split personality of Japanese cities, the traditional alongside and rubbing up against the outrageous and hyper-modern, that makes them so enticing. Arguably, the pause over the last fifteen years in Japan's relentless post-war economic growth that has been so hard for Japanese society at large to bear has also slowed down the relentless pace of physical change and has allowed the Landscape Law to be enacted. This may yet come to the rescue of those traditional parts of Japanese cities that help to make them so truly unique. Before it does, however, a more widespread change will have to occur in Japanese society bringing with it, first, an appreciation of the historic built fabric and the extraordinary ordinariness of the traditional Japanese city (Shelton 2012), and second, a determination among its citizenry (and therefore the state) to see these fast disappearing environments retained.

Recent innovations in Japanese design governance, although tentative, point to both a growing concern about these trends, and to some limited attempts to tackle the situation, although so far in a less than convincing manner. These efforts may need to be re-doubled if the dual character of Japanese cities—hyper-modern and yet also traditional—is to be retained and Japan's propensity to perpetually destroy and rebuild itself tamed. Of course, the outsider's perspective will always be skewed. While to Japanese communities their traditional and diverse modern townscapes may be simply ordinary, even placeless, to the outsider they are extraordinary and full of place quality. Conversely, while the outcomes from contemporary mega-development processes and crude regulatory practice are often seen as desirable in Japan, to the outsider they deliver none of the same richness and distinctive qualities that mark out the distinctive qualities of the post-war Japanese city. This illustrates the essential dilemma with such narratives, that place to one person is placeless to another.

Seen from this perspective, the place/placelessness divide is rarely as stark as the literature might have us believe, and we need to find ways to understand and appreciate the extraordinary ordinariness that we see all around, while accepting that such places may very well break many or all of the rules of place-making that underpin our modern understandings of place quality. They may not be good places but this does not mean they are placeless.

Notes

1   The chapter draws extensively from Carmona and Sakai (2014). Particular thanks are due to the Japan Society for the Promotion of Science for funding the research

on which this chapter is based, and to my host in Japan, Aya Sakai of Hokkaido University, whose insights were invaluable and to whom profound thanks are due.
2   Walks typically lasted from mid-morning to early evening and were conducted daily over a period of three weeks.
3   Land Use Control Regulation in Japan: www.gdrc.org/uem/observatory/land-regulation.html
4   Innovations in design governance in Tokyo inspired the national Landscape Law (Ando n.d: 1)
5   Today's population of 127 million is predicted to fall by 25% by 2060; see "Population Statistics of Japan 2012." *National Institute of Population and Social Security Research*, www.ipss.go.jp/p-info/e/psj2012/PSJ2012.asp
6   Compulsory purchase powers for commercial redevelopment projects do not exist in Japan and sites have to be assembled by developers themselves.

References

Ando, S. (n.d.) "New landscape laws that will reshape Japanese cities," United Nations Centre for Regional Development.
Beard, A. (n.d.) "Urban design in Japan," available at www.rudi.net/books/12240, accessed [June 2015].
Bremner, B. (2002) "Rethinking Tokyo Can Minoru Mori Make It More Livable?" *Business Week*, 4 November: 62.
Carmona, M. and A. Sakai (2014) "Designing the Japanese City: An Individual Aesthetic and a Collective Neglect," *Urban Design International* 19, 186–198.
Carmona, M. and F. Wunderlich (2012) *Capital Spaces: The Multiple Complex Spaces of a Global City*. London: Routledge.
Crang, M. (1998) *Cultural Geography*. London: Routledge.
Cybriwsky, R. (1999) "Changing Patterns of Urban Public Space: Observations and Assessments form the Tokyo and New York Metropolitan Areas," *Cities* 16, 223–231.
Debord, G. (1958) "Les Lèvres Nues #9," K. Knabb (trans.), available at www.cddc.vt.edu/sionline/si/theory.html, accessed June 2015.
Fielding, A. (2004) "Social Class Segregation in Japanese Cities: the Case of Kyoto," *Transactions of the Institute of British Geographers* 29, 64–84.
Ikebe, K. (2005) "Landscapes as cultural assets—The new Landscape Law tests the public's sensibilities and behavior," available at www.nli-research.co.jp/english/socioeconomics/2005/li050114.pdf, accessed [June 2015].
Ishida, H. (1997) "About shitamachi," available at www.shejapan.com/jtyeholder/jtye/young/shitamachi/e2_shitamachi.html, accessed [June 2015].
Mateo-Babiano, I. and H. Ieda (2005) "Street Space Renaissance: A Spatio-Historical Survey of Two Asian Cities," *Journal of the Eastern Asia Society for Transportation Studies* 6, 4317–4332.
Mori Memorial Foundation (2008) *City & Lifestyle Related Research: An Overview of Traditional Japanese Shopping Streets, "Shoten-gai,"* Tokyo: MMM.
—— (2011) *Making Tokyo's Open Spaces More Enjoyable—Rating the Appeal of 108 Privately Owned Public Spaces in Tokyo*, Tokyo: MMM.
Radovic, D. (2007) '"Casts, Roles and Scripts of Otherness,'" in C. Bull, D. Boontharm, C. Parin, D. Radovic and G. Tapie (Eds) *Cross-cultural Urban Design*. London: Routledge: 135–149.

Relph, E. (1976) *Place and Placelessness*, London: Pion.

Shelton, B. (2012) *Learning from the Japanese City: West Meets East in Urban Design*, Second Edition, London: E&FN Spon.

Sorensen, A. (2009) "Neighborhood Streets as Meaningful Spaces: Claiming Rights to Shared Spaces in Tokyo," *City & Society* 21, 207–229.

Waley, P. (2006) "Re-scripting the city: Tokyo from ugly duckling to cool cat," *Japan Forum* 18, 361–380.

Zarmati, S. (1989) "A city of towers and traditions—Streetscapes; Tokyo," *UNESCO Courier*, August: 1–3.

15 Extending Place

The Global South and Informal Urbanisms

Aseem Inam

Introduction

Theory emerges out of context. Theorization occurs in particular places, at specific moments in time, and with regard to certain intellectual movements. Thus, Edward Relph's *Place and Placelessness* (1976) was researched and written in Canada in the 1970s, helping to cultivate a humanist approach to place along with other geographers of the time such as Yu-Fi Tuan (1974). There have been similar movements towards a humanist approach in urbanism, as embodied in the work of Kevin Lynch, Jane Jacobs, William Whyte, and Spiro Kostof. What all these seminal works share is that even though they emerged out of specific contexts in space and time (e.g. Jacobs in New York), the tendency has been to universalize their ideas.

The purpose of this chapter is to extend and enrich ideas of place and placelessness. I do this in two ways. First, I shift the gaze out of the global north to the global south, where an astounding 84% of the world's population currently resides and where 97 of the world's 100 fastest growing cities are to be found (Inam 2013: 3–4). The global south generally refers to the regions of Africa, Asia, Central America, and Latin America, while the global north includes Australia and New Zealand, Europe, and North America (and countries from other parts of the world, such as Japan). In the context of this chapter, the global south refers not only to specific regions of the world, but also to dominant discourses regarding processes of development, however flawed these discourses might be (e.g. developing countries, emerging markets, western versus non-western). In this chapter, I think about place from a perspective that emerges out of the global south by investigating the particularities of informal urbanisms.

The second shift I articulate here is from detached observation to 'research as practice,' which is research-based engagement with qualities of place. Thus, places are not only observed and experienced, but are continually shaped through a wide range of direct and indirect interventions. Here, I am not particularly interested in conventional modes of practice, such as client–designer driven projects; instead, what I describe is a process by which collective inquiry (e.g. through empirical field work) leads to critical and democratic ways of shaping place. In this manner, I propose a more fine-grained approach that engages with actual on-the-ground empirics, and results in more contextualized understandings of place.

The rest of this chapter continues by looking at Relph's ideas and suggesting how they might be extended by examining the gaze through which we view place, including the dominant view from the global north that tends to be uncritically universalized. Next, a shift to the global south brings into view the prevalence of place-based informal urbanisms. The chapter then describes a project of comparative and empirical investigations in São Paulo and New York City as a collaboration between Parsons School of Design and University of São Paulo. In the concluding section, the comparative investigation reveals that informality and formality—like place and place-lessness—are in fact intertwined and that practice helps engage with the constantly changing nature of place.

Extending and Enriching Ideas of Place and Placelessness

One of Relph's original contributions to our understanding of place was the research method of phenomenology, which is the interpretive study of human experience (Relph 1976). The aim was to examine and clarify human situations, events, meanings, and experiences as they are known in every-day life but which lie typically unnoticed beneath the level of conscious awareness (Seamon and Sowers 2008). This raises the question of the gaze. Whose human experiences are Relph and others referring to? Are such human experiences truly universal? One way to address such questions is to look at places and experiences that may be different from those that emerge out of the global north. In my empirical study of the Viceroy's House (now known as Rashtrapati Bhavan) in Delhi, I examined how British colonial ideas of place show up in a different cultural context with a clear political agenda (Inam 2012). Thus, even supposed fusions of different traditions of design are actually weighted with hierarchies of cultural superiority and agendas of civilizing influences. What is particularly striking is how the largely English-speaking elite of Delhi are today uncritically championing places for historic preservation that in fact symbolized colonial oppression.

Since the publication of *Place and Placelessness*, Relph has revisited and built upon his ideas (1996). Thus, theories not only emerge out of specific contexts in time and place, but also evolve over time. For Relph, place and placelessness have become tangled together, in which places are now networked hybrids of distinctiveness and sameness, with placeless-ness involving detachment from the particularity of places. We understand distinctiveness and sameness in relational ways. That is the way in which these seeming dichotomies are useful—as a starting point for understanding a phenomenon that may actually be a spectrum or in fact interrelated. Further, place and placelessness are about distinct identity versus universal identity, in which place-making is the injection of identity.

In addition, Relph (1996) himself suggested that in hindsight a major weakness of *Place and Placelessness* was its lack of conceptual sophistication. This self-critique is not only a sign of intellectual rigor, but also an invitation to further extend and enrich his work. In this spirit, one can say that distinctiveness and sameness are in fact socially constructed, and often that such social constructions emerge intellectually from the global north. These are then formalized through institutionalized structures and mechanisms, such as global standards but also local public policies and urban practices. These kinds of theorizations about place also give rise to investigations of particularities and dissonances, which then challenge the effectiveness of current practices and lead to the formulation of alternative practices that engage with deeper power structures and relations.

In the context of place and, especially, placelessness, Relph has talked more recently about processes of re-embedding, which are formations of new social relationships and connections with places chosen for their distinctive attributes by like-minded groups. These places are occupied by people who are deeply engaged with them in a variety of ways, such as renovating buildings and becoming actively involved in local politics. Relph's vivid descriptions raise useful questions, including: Do the people who are able to *choose* to live in particular places (e.g. middle-income groups) have access to resources that others (e.g. the working poor) may not have? Although poverty may be more visible in the global south, several studies have continually shown how it is prevalent in the global north as well. Such conditions indicate that there are different types of relationships people have with places that are often dependent on issues of power and access to resources. Thus, examining a different gaze, such as one out of the global south, is an extremely useful exercise in further enriching our understanding of place.

Global South and Informal Urbanisms

There is increasing interest in finally acknowledging the significance of the global south, not only in terms of its sheer size of population and geographical area, but the fact that some of the world's continuously inhabited human settlements are actually found in Asia, Africa, Central America, and Latin America. Apart from deep historical and cultural traditions, the global south represents distinctive ways of viewing the world. Such acknowledgments have led to research such as revisiting notions of informality and examining the legacy of colonial urbanisms through empirical studies from urban Asia (Bunnell and Harris 2012; Inam 2012).

The term 'informal sector' was coined in 1971 by British anthropologist Keith Hart in a study of low-income activities among unskilled migrants from Northern Ghana to the capital city, Accra, who could not find wage employment (Chen 2012). Thus, informal urbanisms were 'discovered' in the global south. Conventional definitions describe informality in terms of economic activities that lie outside formal and legal systems of regulation, remuneration, and state control (Bunnell and Harris 2012). In this perspective, a wide range of activities and enterprises are collectively classified in opposition to the formal sector: street vendors, jitney drivers, day laborers, pedicab drivers, small artisans, and even criminal activities such as the drug trade, as well as the places, people, and housing associated with such activities.

In terms of urban practice, there are some common legal and financial codifications that are relatively clear and which govern places, the ways in which they are produced, and the activities that occur there. In the city, these include regulations such as zoning, financial mechanisms for funding development, and established procedures followed by the real estate development industry—all of which favor the production of certain types of places and associated activities over others. The most obvious forms of informality in the global south are informal settlements, more commonly and pejoratively known as 'slums.' These have been seen (and in many cases, are still perceived in the popular discourse) as places that are separate from the rest of the everyday city. At the same time, there is an increasing body of research that seeks to move beyond the dualism of formal versus informal, focusing on their interpenetration as well as on the very real ambiguity in understanding these two sectors (Roy 2011).

In fact, in my understanding, informal urbanisms are not marginalized forms of places and practices; rather they are central to understanding the logic of urbanism because they constitute debates about what is legal and illegal in the city, what is legitimate and illegitimate, and with what effects. I define informal urbanisms as the transactional conditions of ambiguity that exist between what is acceptable and what is unacceptable in cities.

In collaboration with Renato Cymbalista and researcher–practitioners at the Parsons School of Design and the University of São Paulo, I developed a project to investigate the nature of informal urbanisms via a unique method that integrated research, pedagogy, and practice. The project is a comparative investigation of the yet untapped potential of the remarkable efficiency, resourcefulness, and social dynamics of the informal city, whether it is the *favelas* of São Paulo or the street vendors of New York City. In this manner, the global south offers valuable insights into the surprising richness of informal urbanisms in the global north. The project also aims to understand the true complexity of the city beyond the formal aesthetics of conventional design or the quantitative data of policy analysis. We address the question: How is the ambiguous threshold between the formal (i.e. legally and financially sanctioned) and informal (i.e. extra-legal structures and unofficial modes of exchange) city created, expressed, and occupied in place?

São Paulo: Pier to Pier Lab

The first phase of this project was the Pier to Pier Lab, a collaborative workshop between Brazilian and American researcher–practitioners that built upon previous studies and municipal projects for the water reservoir of Guarapiranga in São Paulo (Inam et al. 2014). Faculty and students investigated the formal/informal qualities at the edges of the reservoir, which are a mix of middle- and upper-middle-class suburbs and *favelas*. Simultaneously, the group proposed a series of strategies that draw from the resourcefulness and innovations of informal urbanisms to improve the quality of life in the favelas at the water's edge, such as provision of social services, public spaces, or civic amenities.

The group of 14 researcher–practitioners prepared background research for two months, then came together in Guarapiranga for two intensive weeks to conduct field research, brainstorm ideas, and produce design solutions, with a two-month follow-up to fine-tune proposed strategies. We researched ways to bring communities together using the underutilized water reservoir, and to re-imagine the reservoir as more than water infrastructure by including its role as the ultimate public space for the surrounding communities. The research-based practice was conducted at three spatial scales of place: the São Paulo metropolitan region, the Guarapiranga basin, and specific sites around the reservoir.

In order to familiarize themselves with the metropolitan region, researcher–practitioners from New York conducted a series of investigations about the geography, politics, economy, and demographics of São Paulo, before arriving in Brazil. At this early stage of approaching the area of study, it was important to understand how Guarapiranga related to the greater metropolitan area, and sectors including transport, housing, and land use were analyzed. From its original role as a source of water supply to the possibilities of integrating the landscape, the reservoir indicates a great potential for intervention that would better connect to area residents.

In order to cultivate an informed understanding of the residents' and visitors' relationship to place at multiple scales, we conducted direct observations and extensive interviews: How did people travel to this place? How did they use the spaces? Were these places of congregation, isolation and/or conflict? How were these places perceived? The goal of the fieldwork was to discover the potential for emergent practices wherever they appeared, rather than to arrive with a set of preconceived problems and solutions.

One example is *Praia do Sol*, a public park located on the eastern shore of *Represa* (i.e. Reservoir) *de Guarapiranga*, which is quickly becoming one of its most popular recreational spaces. There is a serious issue of access to the park, as most interviewees travelled over 45 minutes to reach the space. Another example is *Parque Baragem*, a public park and beach on the north-eastern corner of *Represa de Guarapiranga*, which attracts swimmers, beachgoers, fishermen, and walkers. The place includes a community garden, a composting site, a playground, and a vast vegetated area. Our research found that the pier, the only public one in Guarapiranga, was not functional and that safe access to the waterfront was therefore limited. In fact, private residents, or private establishments like yacht clubs and restaurants, owned the majority of the piers. To reclaim the reservoir as public space, we concluded that more piers that are truly public must be created to democratize access.

Our proposals engaged with Guarapiranga at different scales, each inter-relating to the others. At the regional scale, the proposed movement systems improve existing infrastructure and create new transport possibilities (Figure 15.1). The central feature of the movement system is a new network of ferries that connect various piers around the reservoir, specially creating transverse routes across the water. Coupled with this new infrastructure system are pedestrian, bicycle, and bus infrastructure improvements in the neighbor-hoods surrounding pier locations. For the long term, the Lab designed connections to the São Paulo commuter train systems. The name of the Lab, 'Pier to Pier' not only refers to the interconnectivity facilitated by the water of the reservoir, but also is a play on the words 'peer to peer,' highlighting the non-hierarchical and collaborative nature of this practice.

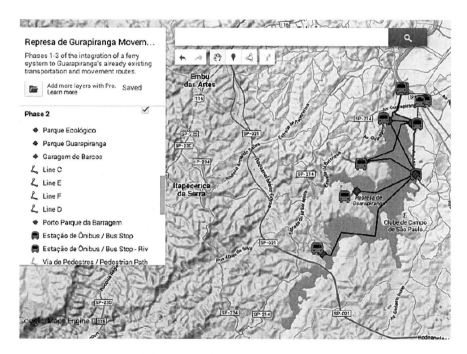

Figure 15.1 Diagram of the proposed movement systems that enhance existing public-transportation networks at the regional scale, with the *Guarapiranga* Reservoir in the middle

Source: Inam et al., 2014.

In addition to considering the physical qualities of place, the project sought to facilitate the provision of social services in and around the pier and floating square. The services were prioritized to meet the needs of local residents (e.g. health services), to radically improve the quality of life (e.g. economic opportunities for local vendors), and to bring diverse sets of people from different income groups together (e.g. public-boating and swimming-education programs).

The project also proposed additional piers that are designed to be generous public spaces that extend the public realm onto the water and link the land to the *praças flutuantes* (i.e. floating squares, described below). The piers are designed to function as expansions of the waterfront, safe docking locations for boats, and as public spaces in their own right, available for a mix of uses serving vendors, swimmers, fishermen, and pedestrians (Figure 15.2).

A particularly innovative proposal was the introduction of two *praças* designed to float on the surface of the water and rotate regularly in a network of piers. The innovation here is that instead of people from different neighborhoods having to seek out public spaces, the public spaces would literally come to them. While docked at each pier, each *praça* provides the neighborhood with much-needed services (e.g. informal library, computer room with internet connectivity, basic medical care, and legal assistance)

Figure 15.2 A rendering of the *Praça Flutuante*, left, Pavilion with social services and pier with public space in the middle, and the ferry in the foreground

Source: Inam et al., 2014.

and aims to create a seamless expansion of the waterfront's public space by expanding to its connecting pier. The design of this floating place is based on its dual function as public space and service provision.

This type of investigative approach towards informal urbanisms yielded two critical insights. The first is understanding the ambiguity that actually exists in between conventionally demarcated notions, such as formal versus informal, legal versus illegal, acceptable versus unacceptable, public versus private, and so forth. The second is in terms of emerging urban practices, by which we mean developing practices that emerge out of our interactions with each other, with the place, and with the communities. Ultimately, the Pier to Pier Lab revealed how place-based informal urbanisms are a central constitutive part of how the city is produced, something that empirical research in other parts of the global south has also demonstrated (McFarlane 2012).

A critical aspect of this research-based practice was the use of language as an urban practice for shaping places. All the researcher–practitioners from New York, including me, learnt basic Portuguese before arriving in Brazil. Furthermore, language was used to conduct research, to name strategies (e.g. *praça flutuantes*) and to communicate through the website, in which everything is communicated in Portuguese and English (Inam et al. 2014). This embodies the nature of mutual collaboration in investigating and shaping place, as opposed to more didactic ways of knowing and practicing that emerge out of the global north. This form of non-hierarchical horizontal collaboration and mutual learning between the global south and the global north was further articulated in our next project in New York.

New York: Agents of Public Space Lab

In January 2015, the same group of researcher–practitioners from Parsons and University of São Paulo gathered in New York for the Agents of Public Space Lab to work on place-based informal urbanisms in the Union Square area of Manhattan (Inam et al. 2015). The focus this time was on street vending, which is an integral part of the cities of the global south as well as the global north. As in Guarapiranga previously, the 'research as practice' approach resulted in a project that was open-ended, where goals and outcomes emerged throughout the workshop while we simultaneously researched the topic by engaging with street vendors.

In order to allow for more inclusivity within the complex realm of street vending and to explore further notions of language as urban practice, we introduced the term Agents of Public Space (APS) as a way of including those who may not identify formally as street vendors. The key term here is agents, in which those who engage with various aspects of the street vending system—including undocumented immigrants—in fact possess agency in their work and in the city. APS are citizens of place, best embodied in the economic and social transactions they make with the public. These transactions can take the form of physical and nonphysical exchanges with the public, which together make up the experience of place. Our understanding of APS in the Union Square area includes painters, theater performers, dancers, political protestors, costumed entertainers, chess players, artists, and general merchandise vendors, such as those selling gloves or umbrellas. The dominant type of APS are those who sell food (e.g. gyros and crepes, fruit, juices, and coffee). The actively public nature of the place that is Union Square would cease were it not for the catalytic presence of the APS, who contribute richly to its sights, smells, sounds, and complex networks of movements.

In addition to extensive background research, we engaged in intensive fieldwork to study other places with APS in New York City: Roosevelt Avenue in Jackson Heights, Queens; Fulton Street Mall in Brooklyn; Chinatown in downtown Manhattan; and the area near the Metropolitan Museum of Art and Central Park in the upper east side of Manhattan. In this manner, the comparative method was deployed within New York City as well, revealing similarities and differences among APS in different areas. For example, in the corridor along the avenue, there were groups of predominantly male food vendors selling halal near Diversity Plaza, and predominantly female vendors along Roosevelt Avenue selling Mexican and Ecuadorian dishes. These vendors have an alliance with local street-vending advocacy groups and the City Council, and there is a general feeling of support from the city and surrounding neighborhoods. In contrast, near the Metropolitan Museum and Central Park, there was a feeling of prejudice against most street vendors, as surrounding apartment tenants and security personnel expressed disdain. Some of this may be explained by issues of class (e.g. lower-income neighborhoods versus higher-income ones) and cultures (e.g. dominated by immigrants who are used to street vending while others may be more used to indoor public activities such as in museums and theaters).

A critical exercise that emerged from the process of 'research as practice' was the mapping of systems and networks. A map of power dynamics in the entire street-vending system elucidates the various informal and formal transactions that take place between APS and the city around them (Figure 15.3). While some aspects of APS work are reliant on informal transactions, such as negotiating with local businesses to use their bathrooms, their day-to-day existence is heavily regulated by various state, city, and private actors. For example, the city issues permits for food carts that require annual renewals and regular inspections. Additionally, the laws concerning where an APS may or may not work vary block by block, by time of day, and by what is being sold. The enforcers of these rules are themselves unclear on their exact definitions, thus creating a gray area of legality. APS therefore exist within complex systems in which their formality is being constantly negotiated.

We also found it important to consider the role of the city as a resource. For this analysis, we crafted a map of facilities used by vendors, buskers,

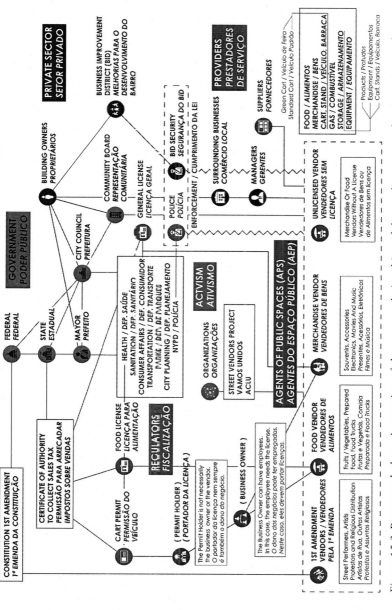

Figure 15.3 Power and place: A mapping of the power relationships of the vending system that emerge out of our analysis from the Union Square area. (Note that the diagram is in both English and Portuguese.)

Source: Inam et al., 2015.

and other types of APS across the wider New York City region. While storage and supply facilities are present across the entire city and parts of New Jersey, they are condensed within particular neighborhoods and access often comes along with ambiguous, unwritten rules. An example of this is differing storage rates, depending on whether the vendor also procures goods from the same business. By overlapping lived-experience and personal knowledge with the spatial distribution of these city resources, we began to uncover the structure of the wider system with which APSs must necessarily engage. The key implications for transformative practice, then, are to identify moments and opportunities in these larger systems and networks of economic, political, and social transactions for strategic intervention.

The strategic action framework that emerged was based on place and its relationship to temporal scales. For example, we proposed a series of pop-up classes hosted in Union Square to share knowledge, develop alternative narratives surrounding the informal urbanisms of the square, and design open-ended interactive scenarios for learning and capacity building. The classes would challenge the people to think about the significance of the daily informal encounters and transactions that continually reproduce the vibrant urban space encompassing Union Square. The curriculum begins with public-lecture style knowledge sharing within the space of the plaza and Union Square Greenmarket, addressing the long history of street vending globally and locally: How does the public view street vending? What is their perception of APS and their roles in the city? What is the value in holding a broader view and deeper understanding (other than seeing them as marginal)?

Another short-term proposal was to imagine 'A Day in Union Square without Street Vendors.' In an attempt to provoke public reflection, the idea was that grants could be provided to vendors to see what the public would say if they vanished for one day (e.g. at a peak time in the summer).

Short-term proposals were designed to work in tandem with more medium- and long-term strategies, including working with existing non-profit groups such as Vamos Unidos and the Street Vending Project, as well as coalitions like the Clean Streets Initiative. APS enhance the economic and social vitality of public space, thereby contributing to the constant flow of people who inhabit such spaces. For street vendors who are located within close proximity to a brick-and-mortar enterprise (e.g. store, cafe, restaurant), we suggested creating a policy that specifically allows for street vendors to use facilities such as bathrooms, or being able to take momentary breaks within heated interiors while it's freezing cold in the winter.

A longer-term proposal is the HUB, which would exist both in virtual reality and a physical place to serve the APS. As an abstract structure, the HUB creates an online guide for APS and encourages the development of a digital APS network throughout the city in three different forms: website portal, smartphone app, and printed material. A series of interactive maps provides public information about the location of licensed storage facilities

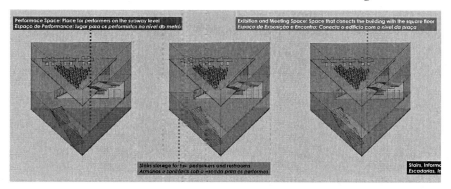

Figure 15.4 A partial diagram of the proposed HUB structure in Union Square, along with its multiple spaces and uses that serve as resources for the APS as well as the public at large

Source: Inam et al., 2015.

for carts, merchandise and equipment, and the location of food, equipment and merchandise suppliers, and commissaries. The Google Maps platform permits any vendor, APS, or even supplier (e.g. for buying wholesale material) and garage management (e.g. for storing vending carts) to add their location and contact information. Thus, anyone can find street vendors, supplies, and storage facilities, even as circumstances change over time.

The HUB is also designed as a physical place to symbolize the importance of APS to the city and everyday life, as well as a radical gathering point for the public (Figure 15.4). In the middle of the triangular plot next to Union Square would stand a three-level extruded triangle encased in transparent glass. Its prismatic structure, glowing at night, would become a natural gathering place and icon in the city. The lowest level connects to the subway station as an entry point for APS who utilize the station space for their activities. The main level is a public gathering point resembling a gallery space devoted to the history and significance of APS throughout the city. The openness of the main level accommodates large events, such as the existing annual street-vending awards in New York City, the Vendy Awards. The highest floor is dedicated to a variety of uses specifically for APS, ranging from business-development classes, organization meetings, and conflict resolution spaces.

In this manner, the APS Lab explored place-based informal urbanisms in the global north as they relate to street-vending systems. While it might take a somewhat different appearance, informality very much exists in the global north. As a negative example of this, research has shown that there is nowhere in the world that deals more with corrupt money than the City of London, which handles and invests trillions of dollars of cross-border profits from criminal activities and tax evasion every year (McFarlane 2012).

Taken together, the Pier to Pier Lab in São Paulo and the Agents of Public Space Lab in New York yielded several comparative insights and implications. The contribution of this approach is three-fold:

- examining the distinctive character of place-based informal urbanisms in each context through on-the-ground documentation and study,
- understanding the differences and similarities of this condition between the global south and the global north via comparative analysis, and through a dialectical process by which research and strategy are constantly feeding into each other, and
- proposing—in a highly collaborative and interactive manner—sets of place-based urban strategies and practices that harness the vast and largely untapped potential of informal urbanisms.

In São Paulo, our engagement with place was at multiple spatial scales, from the metropolitan region down to the design of the *praça frutuantes*, not only as floating public spaces but also as sites where much-needed services are provided to the surrounding communities. In New York, the engagement with place was more temporal, with the HUB symbolizing a virtual network of resources and a physical embodiment of the ways in which street vending is integral to the vibrant city.

Conclusion

This chapter extends and enriches Relph's notions of place and placelessness by reaching beyond the global north and examining the gaze out of the global south. The examination demonstrates the significance of informal urbanisms via the lens of the comparative method, not only as a mode of analysis but equally significantly as a form of practice. In this context, dichotomies such as place and placelessness are useful as categories of convenience, which serve as jumping-off points for further inquiry and complication that may capture the richness of cities, whether in the form of spectrum or further distinctions to represent more accurately the complexity of cities. These types of extensions and increased granularities contribute to a deeper grasp of the meanings and experiences of place. These in turn lead to the maintenance and restoration of existing places and the making of new places (Seamon and Sowers 2008) in ways that are much more sensitive to particular contexts and local aspirations. Such potentialities of practice emerged differently in São Paulo and New York. In the Guarapiranga area, the large body of water is not only a public place, but is also a resource for movement and interaction within the larger scale network of places. At Union Square, the system of place-based transactions presents an opportunity for strategic interventions such that the entire city becomes a resource for further economic and political empowerment.

The most significant aspects of place are experience and meaning. These aspects emerge most powerfully when they are practiced, when people do things in a place, and how what they do is at least partially responsible for the meaning a place might have (Cresswell 200). In addition, experience and meaning for individuals develop within larger societal structures, including the ways in which power is implicated in their construction, reproduction, and contestation. Thus, experiences can be influenced by people and institutions with the power to assign meanings, notably those who design and build the spaces, buildings, and infrastructures that constitute the material city (Harvey 1993, Inam 2013). At the same time, since the city is always in flux, places are never truly complete and are thereby open to contestation and transformation, which is the further promise of practice—that is, the constant and direct engagement with place.

There are other major implications of this 'research as practice' for extending and enriching Relph's ideas of place and placelessness. One is that places are both localized (e.g. living, working, and social interactions in specific locales) and what Agnew (2011) calls contexts that are more stretched over space (e.g. flows of people and material goods). As Massey (1999: 22) suggests, this is a notion of place where specificity such as local uniqueness and sense of place "derives not from mythical internal roots nor from a history of isolation—now to be disrupted by globalization—but precisely from the *absolute particularity of the mixture of influences found together there*" [emphasis added]. Another major implication is that places are the social settings or venues in which new ideas develop and to which they diffuse. Here the notion of the gaze becomes critical, for it is from within places that we view, understand, and engage with the world. The production of knowledge is always situated somewhere, and is one of the most critical forms of urban practice. Thus, place—whether in the global south or the global north—situates us and propels us in certain directions of theory and practice.

Similarly, formality and informality in the city are not dichotomous binaries (e.g. public spaces in downtown New York versus the *favelas* in São Paulo), nor does it mean that they constitute a spectrum of places in the city (e.g. chain stores such as Whole Foods, legitimate street vendors such as the Green Market, and undocumented immigrants selling food on the sidewalks of Union Square). Rather, they are inextricably related forms of practice that occupy and engage with place in distinct ways. Thus, informality and formality do not necessarily belong to different kinds of places; rather, the practices of informality reveal a geography that is fundamentally relational, thereby echoing a critical insight from Relph's notions of place and placelessness.

References

Agnew, J. (2011) "Space and Place," in J. Agnew and D. Livingstone (Eds.) *The SAGE Handbook of Geographical Knowledge*, London: Sage, 316–331.

Bunnell, T. and A. Harris (2012) "Re-Viewing Informality: Perspectives from Urban Asia," *International Development Planning Review* 34, 43–51.

Chen, M. (2012) *The Informal Economy: Definitions, Theories and Policies*, Cambridge MA.: Women in Informal Employment: Globalizing and Organizing.

Cresswell, T. (2004) *Place: A Short Introduction*, Oxford: Blackwell Publishing.

Harvey, D. (1993) "From Space to Place and Back Again," in J. Bird, B. Curtis, T. Putnam, G. Robertson and L. Tickner (Eds.) *Mapping the Futures: Local Cultures, Global Change*, London: Routledge, 3–29.

Inam, A. (2012) "Tensions Manifested: Reading the Viceroy's House in New Delhi," in V. Bharne (Ed.) The *Emerging Asian City: Concomitant Urbanities and Urbanisms*, Abingdon UK: Routledge, 99–109.

—— (2013) *Designing Urban Transformation*, London and New York: Routledge.

Inam, A., R. Cymbalista, J. Chicarelli, B. Dallaverde, R. Dalloul, J. Davis, M. DelSesto, P. Fernandes, B. Godoy, L. Leao, S. Minard, G. Novaes, A. Roesch and S. Wynne. (2014) *Pier to Pier Lab: An Interdisciplinary Workshop to Explore the Topic of Informal Urbanisms*, available at www.informalurbanisms.org, accessed June 6, 2015.

Inam, A., R. Cymbalista, D. Bender, T. Bostick, J. Chicarelli, B. Dallaverde, N. Elokdah, B. Godoy, S. Jadav, L. Leao, A. Lins, G. Novaes, W. Petrichyn, J. Vasandani and S. Wynne. (2015) *Agents of Public Space*, available at www.agentsofpublicspace.wordpress.com, accessed June 6, 2015.

Massey, D. (1999) *Power-Geometries and the Politics of Space-Time*, Hettner Lecture 1998, Heidelberg: University of Heidelberg Institute of Geography.

McFarlane, C. (2012) "Rethinking Informality: Politics, Crisis, and the City," *Planning Theory and Practice* 13, 89–108.

Relph, E. (1976) *Place and Placelessness*, London: Pion.

—— (1996) "Reflections on *Place and Placelessness*," *Environmental and Architectural Phenomenology Newsletter* 7, 14–16.

Roy, A. (2011) "Slumdog Cities: Rethinking Subaltern Urbanism," *International Journal of Urban and Regional Research* 35, 223–238.

Seamon, D. and J. Sowers (2008) "Place and Placelessness, Edward Relph," in P. Hubbard, R. Kitchen and G. Valentine (Eds.) *Key Texts in Human Geography*, London: Sage, 43–51.

Tuan, Y.-F. (1974) *Topophilia: A Study of Environmental Perception, Attitudes and Values*, Englewood Cliffs: Prentice-Hall.

16 Place as Multiplicity

Kim Dovey

Introduction

The concepts of place, place-making, and placelessness entered the discourses of the built environment professions from the 1970s, primarily informed by phenomenological philosophy. The language of 'place' has proven to be much more than fashion, because it resonates deeply with everyday concerns about the values and transformation of our cities and landscapes. Yet developers and politicians have long reduced such discourse to profitable slogans—slippery conceptions of place identity and urban character that fit easily into neoliberal ideology. Place and placelessness need to be understood as contested concepts that can be both empowering and dangerous in different contexts.

I begin this chapter with some personal reflections on changing understandings of place and placelessness. I then seek to unravel and problematize the concepts of place and placelessness in terms of everyday urban politics and urban political economy. I suggest an assemblage approach, wherein the experience of place is seen as an emergent phenomenon. Our concerns for the creation and protection of valued places need to penetrate to the multi-scale assemblage of interconnected parts and morphogenetic processes that produce it—place as multiplicity. I conclude with some comments on what I see as the two great place-making challenges of the era—car-dependency and informal settlements.

Encounter

My academic career began when I decided as a young architect that I was poorly educated for the tasks that I faced. These seemed to me more about practices and experiences of dwelling than the fixations on built form that so preoccupied the architecture profession—about relations between people and spaces rather than formal objects. I returned to university to undertake a research master's degree, and in those golden days when enrolment was free I also enrolled in a parallel philosophy degree. An interest in Heideggerian phenomenology soon led to Edward Relph's (1976) recently published *Place and Placelessness*. This really was a revelation, a wonderfully clear introduction to phenomenology and a seminal application to issues of built form and the city. In the early 1980s I undertook a PhD at Berkeley, where a number of people who seemed to be thinking in this way were working—Christopher Alexander, Clare Cooper Marcus, Donald Appleyard, and Lars Lerup. Alexander had recently published *A Pattern Language* and *The Timeless Way of Building* (1977; 1979), Cooper Marcus was writing on the "House as Symbol of Self" (1974), Appleyard on the concept of "home" (1979), and Lerup on "Building the Unfinished" (1977).

I discovered that none of them (except Lerup) had read phenomenology, and I suspect this is also true of other major figures of the North American scene such as Jane Jacobs (1961) on the "death and life" of cities and Kevin Lynch on concepts of image and place (Lynch 1969; 1972). A sensibility for place was embedded in such thinking rather than foregrounded as a discourse of the 'sense of place.' I have become ambivalent about the use of the word 'place,' which is a loaded and somewhat dangerous term, for reasons I will get to. Yet the discourse of 'place' remains because it is such an everyday term that is so widely used and seemingly understood by people in their everyday life, and is of such concern at an ontological level. This was a key Heideggerian insight—that there is no 'being' separate from our 'world'; our existence is always already 'being-in-the-world' (Heidegger 1962; 1971).

Returning to Melbourne in the mid-1980s, I co-organized a conference entitled 'Place and Place-making,' to which we invited Relph as a keynote speaker (Dovey et al. 1985). While this was early in the move toward place-based thinking, it was already seen as a contested discourse and Relph was part of a triangle of different approaches with the other keynote addresses by Leonie Sandercock (political economy) and Amos Rapoport (environment-behavior studies) (Sandercock 1975; Rapoport 1982). In those days, in order to get brochures printed, you had to send them off to a 'copy-setter' and when it came back it was misspelled 'lacemaking.' I did not notice at the time that this might be more than a typographical error. Lace is something you put together intricately with quite a lot of patience, you thread one thing through another to make connections and loops, and the result is relatively transparent—not altogether unlike place-making.

As I became involved in urban projects, the complexities inherent in both the discourses and practices of place and place-making multiplied. During the 1990s, I was hired by an urban design consultant to work as a sub-consultant to provide advice on a proposed development adjacent to the Sydney Opera House at the entrance to Circular Quay. Circular Quay is Sydney's centerpiece, framed by the Opera House and Botanical Gardens on one side and by the steep escarpment known as The Rocks as well as the Harbour Bridge on the other—a very dramatic sense of place indeed. The consultant wanted to pick my brain about place theory as applied to Circular Quay, and I soon realized that he wanted an argument as to how Circular Quay would be improved by being more fully enclosed by buildings like a European plaza. "Can't you do a Norberg-Schulz on it?" he asked.

Christian Norberg-Schulz was the foremost architectural phenomenologist of the time. His 1980 book *Genius Loci* argued for a concept of 'place' as an existential foothold that stabilizes who we are and where we are, where architecture is 'grounded' in a deep and unchanging 'spirit of place.' It was not necessary to believe in such a theory to figure out that my employer was in turn hired by developers who wanted to insert a new building between the Harbour and the Botanical Gardens, also blocking some views to the Opera House. My advice was not useful—the building was built, and famously christened by the art critic Robert Hughes (1998: 12) as "the Toaster, that dully brash, intrusive apartment block that now obscures the view of the Opera House from three directions."

There are some lessons in this about the ways that knowledge might be used and in whose interests the discourses of place might operate. Place is a nebulous and somewhat dangerous concept, which can be used to argue for more buildings or less of them, a bit like 'community,' 'home,' and 'character'—motherhood concepts that carry a positive charge that one cannot easily argue with. Place can be a legitimating discourse.

For many in the built environment fields, a critical approach to practices of power led to a retreat from the language of place, on the premise that if we stop using the word then its potency might be neutralized. Yet such linguistic politics did little but insulate critics from attack by other critics, a retreat from the everyday that left the city exposed to attack in the name of place-making. During the property boom of the early 1990s I worked with resident groups and local governments in Melbourne, where vital inner-city neighborhoods were often threatened with transformational change. In urban planning tribunals, developers with expensive lawyers and consultants would utilize the discourse of place to say how much they were going to contribute to the city with a 14-storey building in a two-storey neighborhood. There was particular interest in the theory of 'landmarks' and 'gateways.' The city, misquoting Lynch, needed more landmarks in the form of buildings that can rise to a greater height and bulk than their neighbors with a special status and protected views. Gateways were also very popular, because here the celebration of place required not one but two taller buildings to enhance the sense of entrance.

I was once faced with the argument by an urban design consultant in a legal tribunal that a tall building on the waterfront, overshadowing the beach, should be approved as part of a symbolic 'gateway' that would frame the view of the city from a yacht in the bay. This was perhaps the worst argument for place-making I have encountered, and while the standards of argument have improved over time, the planning decisions have not. In a recent satirical Australian television series on flagship projects called *Utopia* (2014), a developer wanted to build a 55-storey waterfront tower in order to give something back to the city, to contribute to the public realm. The planner asks: "Can we ask him to contribute a little bit less?" In the critical academic literature, we call this 'uneven' development, sometimes 'gentrification' or 'creative destruction'—part of a neoliberal political and economic agenda for deregulated urban development that has taken a powerful hold in most cities since the 1970s.

What is the scope for place-making in a political context of neoliberalism? I would suggest that the discourses of place and place-making are thoroughly interwoven with practices that can also be described as place destruction. A brief look at the advertising for any major urban development project shows it to be driven by desires for particular forms of place identity —shopping malls, residential enclaves, corporate towers. The 'Toaster' is surely a great place to live; it was not produced by desires to block views to Sydney Harbour, the Opera House, and the Botanical Gardens, but rather to capture and to privatize them. Deregulated, uneven development and creative destruction is a practice of place-making.

In most of my work I have been committed to the idea of trying to reframe what it is that 'place' means—away from any exclusively positive, closed, or backward-looking ideal and towards one that incorporates practices of power (Dovey 2005; 2008; 2010). I have been worried by the ease with which 'place' gets appropriated into discourses of privatization and political power. We need to be alert to the ways gated communities, shopping malls, and formularized global mega-projects construct an instant but privatized sense of place, as well as to the ways urban design in the public realm can work to legitimize tyranny and construct new forms of docile subjectivity. I would describe all of these as a form of anti-urban place-making, though not as 'placelessness.'

Placelessness

Places such as parking lots, fast-food restaurants, corporate towers, and shopping malls were originally described by Relph (1976) as placeless because they lack a rooted sense of identity and authenticity; they are bland and anonymous. If we view the concept of place as a positive sense of identification with valued places, then placelessness is the absence of such place identity. An alternative view, that the 'non-place' can be highly valued, derives originally from Melvin Webber (1964), who argued for a conception of the 'non-place urban realm' where everyone drives everywhere in a 'community without propinquity.' However, this vision of how social networks can be achieved at a larger scale without walkable neighborhoods simply increases the scale of place identification and, with the current focus on walkability, seems obsolete. Marc Augé (1996) defines the non-place in an even more positive manner as those parts of the urban and architectural environment without unique identity but where we nonetheless feel at home. Here non-places are often identified with travel environments such as airports. In an era of shrinking space and accelerating sense of time, levels of travel, and the circulation of images, we see the emergence of locations where we spend a lot of time and are quite comfortable but where we do not invest any sense of personal identity. Both Relph and Augé define the concept of place as sites identified with particular identities or groups; but while Relph's placelessness is portrayed as bland and dull, Augé's concept of the non-place has an openness that is less suffocating.

While conceptions of placelessness and non-place have a good deal of resonance with our experiences in everyday life, the opposition between place/placelessness and place/non-place is problematic. Only if we define place in terms of closure and rootedness does the idea of a non-place make sense. If we see place as an ontological condition of dwelling, then the opposite of place is not emptiness but absence; there is nowhere without a sense of place, and it is problematic to reserve the term 'place' for those places we wish to valorize. What is placeless to some people will not seem that way to others. Those parts of urban space that are least invested with identity often have the greatest capacity for appropriation—they are less invested in a stabilized sense of 'being' and therefore are more open to a sense of 'becoming.' In the jargon of Gilles Deleuze and Felix Guattari they are 'smooth' rather than 'striated' (Deleuze and Guattari 1987). Carparks are used by weekend markets, by skateboarders, and teenage lovers, and sometimes it is the very dereliction from the mainstream point of view that renders them available to others and for other practices and meanings. For Michel de Certeau (1984: 131), "places are articulated through a thousand uses"; there is no consensual view of what place might mean. The idea that only some of the city has a sense of place is loosely but problematically linked to problems of essentialism and authenticity—who is to decide the difference between place and placelessness, who authorizes authenticity?

Assemblage

There is an important distinction between 'place' and 'space.' When we say 'this is a great place,' or an 'awful place,' we mean something different from 'this is a great space'—space is more formal and less social than place. 'Place' is a socio-spatial concept, intimately connecting people with space. We need approaches that cut across this subject/object divide and phenomenology alone, with a focus on subjectivity, is inadequate to this task. I have argued elsewhere that the work of Deleuze and Guattari (1987; see also DeLanda 2006) offers the most sophisticated framework for a rethinking of place as a multi-scale assemblage that can link social theory and philosophy to architecture and geography on the one hand, and to the sciences and humanities on the other (Dovey 2010).

It is clear that place can mean many different things in different contexts and be used for different purposes. A key task is to avoid reductionism, particularly reductions to text and to essence. The reduction to text stems mainly from the discursive turn in social theory, where a focus on the discourse of place leads into a deconstruction of place as text. The sense of place in everyday life is reduced to a constructed discourse. While discourse analysis is a crucial research tool, the reduction to text strips place of its ontological potency—in the best and worst senses of that word. Potency is, of course, about power—the power of place in our lives, the power of place to sustain us, and also the power of places to frame our lives in ways that are against our interests (Dovey 2008).

The other key form of reductionism is essentialism, the idea of place becoming an original source, the authentic source of meaning, the exclusive one right way. The anti-essentialist argument is a powerful one, most effectively put in the work of Doreen Massey who vehemently opposes Heideggerian thinking on place as backward-looking, closed, and parochial (Massey 1993; see also Cresswell 2004). She argues instead for an open and global sense of place based in difference rather than singularity. Massey's critique is much more potent than those of Webber or Augé, because it does not oppose the experience or concept of place, only the reactionary versions marked by closed identities, myths of authenticity, and exclusionary boundaries. The progressive sense of place is defined by its relations with other places, by 'routes' rather than 'roots.' Massey does not turn away from the concept of home as a place of safety and yearning, but also portrays it as the place of dark secrets and the unhomely (Massey 2000). In later work, Massey explored some of the contradictions of place and the difficulty of any simple categorizations of open/closed and global/local. Her study of highly globalized and mobile workers in science parks near Cambridge (UK) found that a significant number of them lived in renovated cottages in local villages. These cottages were generally more open, and housed a greater multiplicity of people and practices places than the global workplaces (Massey 2005).

Massey does not explicitly cite Relph's work as a target in her original critique, but this was surely just academic politics. The tension between Relph's and Massey's work is a productive tension, and the deeper task is not simply overturning Heidegger but of moving beyond binary thinking such as open/closed and global/local. Heidegger's work is essentialist, but his insights about the spatial ontology of place need to be separated from the problematic essentialism. I suggest a move towards the idea of place as 'assemblage,' where place and placelessness are not binary opposites but are intertwined, where each becomes or folds into the other. In this conception, Heidegger's 'being-in-the-world' might be replaced with a more Deleuzian 'becoming-in-the-world'—a more dynamic and open sense of place as a multiplicitous assemblage (Dovey 2010).

Character

The concept of 'character' is a partial synonym for place, especially within urban politics where neighborhood 'character' is a form of place identity that needs to be defended against 'inappropriate' development. In a research project entitled *What is Urban Character?* (Dovey 2013), we found multiple and contradictory answers. Character is something that makes places different from others or authentic (as in "she's a real character"); character is also seen as a form of depth or reliability (as in a "character-building exercise"). Neighborhood character is seen as both social and spatial at the same time; it inextricably incorporates both neighbors and buildings.

In debates around neighborhood transformation, urban character is defended on two very different, even quite opposite, bases. First, urban character is described as consistency of both built forms and people; the place has a history and a legacy that is worth protecting against change. In some cases, this is experienced as a purified sense of place, backward looking and closed. Such a defense of character can be a cover for class- and race-based privilege, using the local planning scheme to keep out the wrong kinds of people under the cover of keeping out the wrong kinds of buildings; this is an essentialist notion of place (Dovey et al. 2009a).

The second basis for the defense of character is found in mixed inner-city locations, where character is defined in terms of difference and mix. Here character is found in the juxtaposition of different people, buildings, and activities where the mix is the thing that is threatened and is seen as worth preserving (Dovey et al. 2009b). This is place as multiplicity and the threat comes from the one right way.

In both cases, character is a form of place identity that is threatened with placelessness—with becoming like anywhere else—yet these are almost polar-opposite notions of what is threatened. The difference between them is exemplified by attitudes to graffiti; in the first case it represents a violation of place identity, and in the latter it is often a contribution to it as street art (Dovey et al. 2012). Both are senses of place; one is exclusionary, essentialist, and problematic while the other is not. One is a bounded and relatively static sense of place, the other is a space of flows—what Massey (1993) calls a progressive, open, and global sense of place. Both involve a defense of the differences between places; only the latter defends the differences within places. Yet while Massey portrays the open sense of place as one where 'routes' replace 'roots,' we found one where roots intertwined with routes.

In my home city of Melbourne, urban character has long had a position of great importance in planning schemes. This dates from the 1990s, when deregulatory neoliberal policies primarily took hold. Resident groups demanded that 'urban character' be protected, and the state responded by making 'respect for neighborhood character' the key criterion for all new development applications. In legal terms, this was the proverbial hole that you can drive a truck through—the discourse of character was used to deregulate the development process. This was linked to the replacement of prescriptive urban codes (height limits, etc.) with performance-based codes (respect for neighborhood character). The opposition between prescription and performance is another binary we need to move beyond since in many cases it is often prescriptive codes that perform best. In either case, the legal protection of place identity is a highly problematic enterprise—codes that stop change can paralyze valued places, and transformational change can be justified even when it destroys a well-loved place.

Multi-scale

Place is a wonderfully multi-scalar concept, extending from the armchair or desktop, to a room, building, street, neighborhood, city, nation, and planet. There are a lot of resonances between these scales that are rarely explored in the literature. The essentialist conception of place often translates into practices of border control. At the scale of the household, border control is practically universal—we lock the door for security. At the scale of the neighborhood, border control is a highly contested notion—gated communities are anti-urban and the defense of urban character can be a form of border control or soft gating. The walled city is largely obsolete, except where it operates like a city state—whether to keep people out or to imprison them (e.g. Gaza). The gated community at the national scale is the way in which the defense of place is deployed to maintain the gap between rich and poor nations—to stop the flow of migrants and refugees.

One of the challenges with regard to scale is to overcome what I see as the hegemony of scale—the presumption that the important influences are those that cascade downwards hierarchically from above, like planning policies and politics. In this conception the global trumps the local, and the abstract encompasses the everyday; geography encompasses planning, which encompasses urban design, which then encompasses architecture and everyday life. Places are a mix of top-down and bottom-up processes. While there are powerful tree-like hierarchies, there are also powerful rhizomic networks. Cities emerge from buildings, streets, and neighborhoods, as much from informal adaptations as from formal plans and founding fathers. The primary value of a city is found at the smaller scales, in its streets, the ways in which we encounter others in the street, the ways in which buildings frame space and mediate its flows through pedestrian networks and constellations of attractions. If the streets work, then by and large other things work. Yet small-scale analysis is not enough—understanding place requires multi-scalar analysis, because the interconnections between scales are crucial.

Discussion and Conclusions

Developing from the discussion above, I want to outline three challenges for rethinking conceptions of place and placelessness in the 21st century; the first is theoretical and the other two are very practical. The first I have already mentioned, and involves seeing place as multiplicity rather than singularity, moving beyond simple binaries such as place and placelessness, beyond any reduction of place to text or essence.

Places are both/and phenomena rather than either/or; involving both roots and wings. In my mind, this is not so far from Relph's original work where a multiplicity of place experiences was outlined, including various types of insideness (existential, vicarious, empathetic) and outsideness (existential, objective) (Relph 1976). A part of the challenge here is to see the interconnections between different conceptions, the intertwinings, alliances, and synergies; place as a "between" condition and a set of relationships.

One of the connections I would like to see more of is between the sciences and humanities. There is a lot of research in the sciences that has great relevance for place—the key parts relate to complex adaptive systems thinking, complexity theory, resilience thinking, and theories of emergence (Batty 2013). From such a viewpoint, place can be seen as an emergent phenomenon rather than an original source. A part of the challenge here lies in getting better at understanding urban morphologies—what I call the urban 'DMA' of density, mix, and access (Dovey and Woodcock 2014). This is the material basis of how cities concentrate activities in close proximity, how they mix different people, practices and built forms together, and how the access networks enable flows between them. I have become particularly interested in urban mapping as a form of spatial knowledge in this regard; knowledge about place cannot be restricted to words, numbers, and pictures but needs to extend to maps and diagrams as well as the interrelations between them. Ultimately, places cannot be captured only in images, words, or numbers but also require an understanding of a morphogenetic process of change.

The science of cities, however, will never be more than another form of reduction if it cannot connect to the humanities and particularly philosophy and social theory. My preferred framework here lies in the forms of assemblage thinking derived from the work of Deleuze and Guattari and particularly the book *A Thousand Plateaus* (Deleuze and Guattari 1987). While there is little scope here to outline such a model, it forms the basis for an understanding of place as multiplicity, as assemblage, as plateau. Gregory Bateson (2000 [1972]) was the great anthropologist who theorized the notion of a plateau as a cybernetic system that escalates to a certain level, and then certain cultural controls become self-organized. A plateau is a level between levels that is held in place by different tensions, sharing an etymology with place (L: *platea*). Place is neither pre-existing nor made by designers, but something that emerges from a multiplicity of forces.

The two practical challenges are those that we face at the global scale, threats to the place we all share. The first of these is global poverty and the growth of slums and informal settlements. We talk a lot about this being the age of urbanization, with a majority of the global population living in cities due to massive rural to urban migration over the last 50 years. Do we imagine that they live in new towns or in the suburbs on the outer rims of cities? Most of the new urbanites are housed in the informal settlements and slums of developing cities of the global south—over a billion people and growing. This is where the action has been happening in architecture, urban design, and urban planning but the built environment professions have been largely irrelevant to it. The scale of informal settlements, and the degree to which they are now integrated with the cities they are housed in and the livelihoods of the poor, means that we need to accept that these informal settlements are here to stay. They cannot be erased, but neither can we accept such unjust inequalities of wealth. We need to distinguish the slum conditions of overcrowding and poor sanitation from the informality that is best seen as a resource for managing poverty (Dovey 2012). While there are always problems—lack of open space, poor construction, lack of opportunity, closed to outsiders—these communities can embody a powerful sense of place that is potentially quite livable.

This leads in turn to the other major challenge, climate change. Informal settlements resonate to some degree with emerging models for the low-carbon city—car-free, walkable, mixed, compact, and low-energy, with good access to jobs and shopping. The larger challenge here involves dramatic reductions in carbon emissions in the rich cities of the global north, particularly the car-based cultures of North America and Australia who lead the global league tables of carbon emissions per capita. Setting emission targets is a small challenge compared to redesigning our cities to meet them. A large part of this challenge lies in designing cities where it is faster and easier to get around by public transport than by car. This is a challenge of designing and managing transformational change through transit-oriented development; yet there are high levels of resistance to even the most minor forms of change. The fear is that livability and amenity will be damaged by increased densities and urban intensification; the reality is that the opportunities, if we get the design right, far outweigh the negatives and part of the challenge is to develop visions, scenarios, and pilot projects that demonstrate the possibilities (Dovey and Woodcock 2014). It is hard to overstate how much is at stake here; the danger of climate change, and some believe we are already past the turning point, is that we will render the planet relatively uninhabitable for human life. Much of the damage continues to be done under the name of place-making.

The problems I have canvassed in this chapter cannot be addressed with singular approaches. We can articulate the deeper meanings of place and the processes through which they emerge, but we also need to understand how such places are produced by interconnected networks. We can point out the place-destructive force of global capitalism through a penetrating political economic critique but also empowering local practices of self-organization and resistance. We can deconstruct the deeper meanings of place and the complicities with power, but we also need a critical focus on the materialities of everyday life and local adaptation. Place is a multiplicitous, multi-scalar assemblage and it requires multiple responses.

References

Alexander, C., S. Ishikawa and M. Silverstein (1977) *A Pattern Language*, New York: Oxford University Press.

Alexander, C. (1979) *The Timeless Way of Building*, New York: Oxford University Press.

Appleyard, D. (1979) "Home," *Architectural Association Quarterly* 2, 4–20.

Augé, M. (1996) *Non-Places*, London: Verso.

Bateson, G. (2000 [1972]). *Steps to an Ecology of Mind*, Chicago: University of Chicago Press.

Batty, M. (2013). *The New Science of Cities*, Cambridge, MA.: MIT Press.

Cooper, C. (1974) "The House as a Symbol of Self," in J. Lang, C. Burnette, W. Moleski and D. Vachon (Eds.) *Designing for Human Behavior*, Stroudsberg: Dowden, Hutchinson and Ross, 130–146.

Cresswell, T. (2004) *Place: A Short Introduction*, Oxford: Blackwell.

de Certeau, M. (1984) *The Practice of Everyday Life*, Berkeley: University of California Press.

DeLanda, M. (2006) *A New Philosophy of Society*, New York: Continuum.

Deleuze, G. and F. Guattari (1987) *A Thousand Plateaus*, London: Athlone.

Dovey, K. (2005) *Fluid City: Transforming Melbourne's Urban Waterfront*, London: Routledge and Sydney: UNSW Press.

—— (2008) *Framing Places: Mediating Power in Built Form*, 2nd edition, London: Routledge.

—— (2010) *Becoming Places: Urbanism/Architecture/Identity/Power*, London: Routledge.

—— (2012) "Informal Settlement and Complex Adaptive Assemblage," *International Development Planning Review* 34, 371–390.

—— (2013) "Planning and Place Identity," in G. Young and D. Steveonson (Eds.) *The Ashgate Research Companion to Planning and Culture*, London: Ashgate, 257–271.

Dovey, K., P. Downton and G. Missingham (1985) *Place and Place-making. PAPER 85*, Melbourne: RMIT.

Dovey, K., S. Wollan and I. Woodcock (2012) "Placing Graffiti," *Journal of Urban Design* 17, 21–41.

Dovey, K. and I. Woodcock (2014) *Intensifying Melbourne: Transit-Oriented Urban Design for Resilient Urban Futures*, Melbourne: The University of Melbourne.

Dovey, K., I. Woodcock and S. Wood (2009a) "Understanding Neighborhood Character," *Australian Planner* 46, pp.32–39.

—— (2009b) "A Test of Character," *Urban Studies* 46, 2595–2615.

Heidegger, M. (1962) *Being and Time*, New York: Harper & Row.

—— (1971) *Poetry, Language, Thought*, New York: Harper & Row.

Hughes, R. (1998) "Fighting for a Clearer Vision," *The National Trust Quarterly*, July, 8–13.

Jacobs, J. (1961) *The Death and Life of Great American Cities*, Harmondsworth: Penguin.

Lerup, L. (1977) *Building the Unfinished: Architecture and Human Action*, Beverly Hills: Sage.

Lynch, K. (1969) *The Image of the City*, Cambridge: MIT Press.

—— (1972) *What Time is this Place?*, Cambridge: MIT Press.

Massey, D. (1993) "Power-geometry and a Progressive Sense of Place," in J. Bird, B. Curtis, T. Putnam and L. Tickner (Eds.) *Mapping the Futures*, London: Routledge, 59–69.

—— (2000) "Space-time and the Politics of Location," in A. Read (Ed.) *Architecturally Speaking*, London: Routledge, 49–61.

—— (2005) *For Space*, London: Sage.

Norberg-Schulz, C. (1980) *Genius Loci: Towards a Phenomenology of Architecture*, New York: Rizzoli.

Rapoport, A. (1982) *The Meaning of the Built Environment*, Beverly Hills: Sage.

Relph, E. (1976) *Place and Placelessness*, London: Pion.

Sandercock, L. (1975) *Cites for Sale*, Melbourne: Melbourne University Press.

Utopia (2014) Directed by R. Stich, Australia: Australian Broadcasting Corporation/ Working Dog Productions.

Webber, M. (1964) "The Urban Place and the Non-Place Urban Realm," in M.M. Webber, J.W. Dyckman, D.L. Foley, A.Z. Guttenberg, W.L.C. Wheaton and C. Bauer Wurster (Eds.) *Explorations into Urban Structure*, Philadelphia: Pennsylvania University Press, 79–153.

Afterword

Edward Relph

Time flies, place is grounded and endures. The chapters in this book have made me aware of just how long I have been thinking and writing about place and placelessness. I have been delighted to learn that there is still currency to ideas I formulated in the 1970s, a time when the standardizing forces of modernist design, cookie-cutter urban developments, and mass-produced goods of multinationals were close to their zenith. The world then seemed to me a much simpler place than now it does, and in spite of some equivocations in *Place and Placelessness* about the occasional drudgery of place and shades of insideness, the gist of my argument was obvious—place was good, placelessness was not, and most things modern were eroding good old places. The authors who have contributed to *Place and Placelessness Revisited* make it abundantly clear that while my original ideas may still provide useful insights, things are no longer that straightforward.

After the publication of *Place and Placelessness* in 1976, one of my colleagues wryly asked me whether the title of my next book would be *More Place and Placelessness*. I took the point, and for the next fifteen years most of my attention was devoted to investigating why modern urban landscapes look the ways they do. In fact, until about 1990 the idea of place remained a topic of intermittent interest for a few people scattered across several disciplines. During those fifteen or so years there were, however, the beginnings of significant technological and social changes that have had fundamental, ongoing impacts on places and the ways they are experienced. These changes include, in no particular order, electronic connectivity, heritage preservation, urban design, mass migrations from the global south, multiculturalism, postmodernism in design and philosophy, ecological planning, the relative ease and affordability of long-distance travel, economic and cultural globalization, the idea of sustainability, and megacity growth, none of which were much in evidence in 1976. It was only when their combined impacts on place experiences became obvious, in the early 1990s, that place came to the foreground in geography and other academic disciplines, the design professions began to turn their attention to place-making, and place began to acquire its current complexity and multiplicity.

There has subsequently been a veritable torrent of writing about place. It has been theorized, philosophized, and contested in dozens of books and hundreds of articles in the humanities and social sciences, it has been branded and marketed by corporations, and it has been promoted by local municipalities and regulated through the policies of government agencies. Placelessness, however, has been mostly ignored. I know of only a handful of papers and two books that focus on anti-place processes. The symposium in 2014 at the University of New South Wales, Australia, which was the origin of this book, was the first I am aware of that explicitly gave critical attention to placelessness.

I find this unbalanced treatment surprising, because I am convinced that place cannot be fully understood without consideration of its antithesis. That said, I realize that my original definition of placelessness, as nondescript uniformity, is now effectively obsolete and, as several of the contributors to *Place and Placelessness Revisited* point out, the blunt opposition to place that was associated with it has endured neither in theory nor in experience. Various chapters in this book show, for instance, that airports, which I described forty years ago as archetypes of functional neutrality, have been transformed into more or less distinctive portals to the regions where they are located; that local place-making initiatives in Detroit draw upon global, corporate, and otherwise placeless initiatives; that regulations to promote place distinctiveness can promote a sort of cloning or strip away life in public spaces; that the anonymous, placeless ordinariness of modern developments in Japanese cities is in fact attractive to many of their citizens. In short, place has intruded into placelessness, placelessness has assimilated elements of place, and what was once a dualistic opposition has evolved into a symbiotic, diverse, and tangled relationship.

Interpretations of place, placelessness, place-making, and insideness now stretch far beyond the ones I suggested four decades ago. Most of these interpretations have been, or can be, contested theoretically, while actual places—the ones we live or work in or travel to visit—are filled with contradictions and the confusions attendant on increased connectivity and mobility, unprecedented ethnic juxtapositions, the manipulation of identities to attract investment, and numerous other changes and strategies. A particular place may offer a secure sense of belonging, or be exclusionary, or both at once; a placeless landscape can be seen as an expression of the geography of anywhere that reflects a view from nowhere, or as an expression of efficiency and standardization that makes travel convenient; worldwide mobility can be compatible with, rather than a threat to, insideness; place-making can be responsive to local meanings or manipulated for corporate ends.

What I gather from the remarkable range of discussions in this book is that places are particular, familiar, meaningful fragments of the world, yet little about them can be taken for granted. There are no obvious restrictions to the scale or character of places, and their particularity is everywhere now permeated by processes and products that originate elsewhere or nowhere in particular. A place at any scale is a world fragment that is a specific focus of meanings and activities, yet is both open to the world and an opening to the world. This openness was not obvious when lives were mostly rooted, and place-making was mostly a local activity. In this context I suggested in *Place and Placelessness* that meaningful places have to be made through the efforts and experiences of those who live and work in them. This conclusion needs to be revised to correspond to contemporary global mobility and displacement that result either from choice, as in the global north, or are forced by war and deprivation, as in parts of the global south. The challenge is to bring thinking, politics, and place-making practices into line with new realities of disembedding and re-embedding.

I continue to think that people should take, and be able to take, significant responsibility for the places where they live and work, but this responsibility needs to be supported by both informal and formal political processes that can facilitate re-embedding and inclusion for those who come from elsewhere. At the same time, I believe it will become increasingly important to develop principles for place-making that address not only the quality of public spaces but also provide direction for how different places might adapt to the variable and superimposed effects of the mostly placeless challenges that will confront most of humanity for the foreseeable future, such as burgeoning megacities, demographic shifts, economic fluctuations, social inequalities, and the ramifications of climate change. Reacting to these challenges one by one will involve fragmented strategies from different government agencies and corporations not much concerned with the particularities of places. I think it is better to think proactively from place outwards rather than placelessly downwards. The multiplicity of place means this will not be easy, but the contributions to *Place and Placelessness Revisited* suggest that some of the groundwork has already been laid.

Index

Note: Illustration page numbers are in **bold**; titles are in *italics*